Faster Horses,
Younger Women,
Older Whiskey

A Pictorial Archive
of the
Routt County Fair
1914-1995

By Sureva Towler and Jim Stanko

*This book was complied under grants from the
Colorado Endowment for the Humanities
Routt County Board of County Commissioners
City of Steamboat Springs
The Steamboat Pilot
Steamboat Ski & Resort Corporation
Miriam and Harold Steinberg Foundation*

*The Steamboat Pilot, Wednesday,
September 10, 1919 – (Lawrence
"Tuffy") Wren was given second
money in the bucking contest at the
Hayden Fair. He narrowly escaped
serious injury when the horse, which
he later rode, turned a complete
somersault... putting his head on the
ground and going right over with Wren
underneath... Wren says that he was
one of the hardest bucking horses he
was ever on...even rougher than
General Pershing."*

*"Faster Horses, Younger Women, Older Whiskey" is the title of a song by Tom T. Hall,
and is used by permission of Hallnote Music, Franklin, Tennessee.
The cover photos are from the collection of Margaret Squire Hogue.*

*All photographs in this book have been generously donated by
The Steamboat Pilot unless otherwise credited.*

*Book Design: Susan Schneller
Printer: Northwest Graphics, Steamboat Springs, Colorado
Library of Congress Catalog Card Number: 96-061164
ISBN: 0-9652327-0-0*

*Copyright © 1996, White River Publishing Company,
Box 770768, Steamboat Springs, Colorado 80477, (970) 879-2500.*

Introduction

This book is about women who still can peaches. The ones who know how to churn butter, keep the check book, feed the hired men, and raise children and chickens. The ones who still grow zucchini in the back yard and flowers in the front.

This book is about men who still refer to them as "The Old Lady." The ones who sweat while repairing combines, branding cattle, clearing ditches, stacking hay. The ones who lose fingers in machinery, drink water out of a tin cup, trap beaver and shoot coyotes.

These are the sons and daughters of our homesteaders. They are still working in the mines in order to support the ranch or send "the boy" to vet school. Their grandfathers were raised in the 1890s and their grandchildren are being raised in the 1990s. Somewhere in between, the outhouse was hauled away, the plow horse was replaced by a John Deere and the oldest son majored in agribusiness. Their families came into the country before the railroad and before the land was divided into 35-acre tracts. Before the country became populated by bartenders, maids, developers, architects and property managers. Before people who dedicate their lives to others were labeled "co-dependent" and Perrier replaced creek water.

They came from a time when children did chores, arrowheads could be found on the back 40, and ice was cut from the river. Their stories prove that our forefathers were not ghosts. They wear their pioneer heritage with pride and do not whine about change. They do not rag on "the quality of life" in Routt County and they do not attend public meetings to "vision" the future. The history of the Routt County Fair is their story; their gift to us. It is the story of hard times, good times and survival. It is the story of a very special place: a 37-acre tract in Hayden, Colorado where the Routt County Fair has been held for 82 years. It is the story of very special people: the residents of the Yampa Valley who have gathered there since 1914 to share laughter and lies.

This book was written for everyone who has ever been to a Routt County Fair in order to prompt smiles and memories of good times past, and for everyone who has never been in order to encourage them to participate in molding the future. Although only 3% of Americans are agricultural producers, all are consumers and that makes us all part of the land.

The Routt County Fair is where the agricultural and nonagricultural communities meet, equal parts carnival, encampment, family reunion, homecoming day, fish fry and block party. Historians have described the fair as a place of order, ritual and tradition. Like Thanksgiving or Christmas, you remember the total experience, not the year.

Agricultural fairs began in the 19th Century. They were designed by agricultural societies formed following the Civil War in order to repair a tattered economy. They were the direct result of picnics and barbecues which brought agricultural and church groups together to socialize, talk politics or promote religion. Most were organized by private organizations and picked up by local governments during lean war or depression years.

America's first cattle exhibit was held in Port Washington, New York in 1645. The first state fair was held at Flint, Michigan in the late fall of 1849, immediately prompting area Townships to organize "to promote agriculture, horticulture and mechanical arts" in Genessee County, Michigan. The first county fair was held in Berkshire County, New York in 1811, and canning products did not become available until 1925.

This is the first history of a county fair in Colorado. It was written to commemorate the past and celebrate the future. It shows us where we came from at a time when we are not certain about where we are going.

Sureva Towler and Jim Stanko
Steamboat Springs, Colorado
July 1996

2

The Lay Of The Land
And Other Demographics

Routt County is 75 miles long, and 42 miles wide with an area of approximately 2,231 square miles. Although located in the Northwestern corner of the state, it is an extension of the Western Colorado Great Plateau Region whose eastern borders run along the Continental Divide on the Park and Gore Ranges. Elevations drop from a soaring 12,000 feet in the Mt. Zirkel Wilderness area to less than 6,200 on western boundaries.

Fifty-nine per cent of the county land is owned by federal agencies. More than 576,397 acres are in agriculture and over 450 square miles sit on 8,485 million tons of bituminous coal.

The County is crossed by the Yampa River which has its source high in the Flattops at Stillwater Reservoir. The river flows in a northerly direction from the Flattops, through the northern end of Egeria Park to just above Oak Creek, then into Pleasant Valley and out into the Mesa east of Steamboat Springs. At Steamboat Springs the Yampa River makes an almost perfect 90 degree bend and flows west to the Moffat County Line. Major creeks feeding the river are: Five Pine Mesa, Chimney Creek, Morrison Creek, Oak Creek, Morgan Creek, Wolf Creek and Trout Creek. Its main tributaries are the Bear and Elk Rivers.

Routt County's climate is severe: long winters, heavy snowfall and short cool growing seasons. Growing season ranges from approximately 55 days, along the base of mountain ranges, to 75 days in the western and southern ends of the county. The annual average temperature is 39.3 degrees, although, during July and August, daytime temperatures can reach highs in the 90s and, in December and January, lows have plummeted to nearly 60 below. The average rainfall is 23.5 inches and the average snowfall 167.8 inches. In some winters, mountain ranges have experienced over 300 inches of snow.

Routt County was formed from Grand County in 1877 and named for John L. Routt, the first elected Governor of Colorado. The original area included Moffat County until February, 1911 when the present boundaries were established. The area has always been noted for outstanding coal, cattle, grain, and sheep. Some gold, silver, copper, zinc and petroleum have also been mined. Winter sports and summer recreation have also played a major role in the development of the county.

The first settlements were made by gold prospectors in the Hahns Peak area in the late 1860s, and were followed by large cattle outfits in the Browns Park region and small settlements at Hayden, Steamboat Springs and Yampa. The railroad spawned the coal industry, producing mining towns like Bear River, Coalview, Haybro, McGregor, Mt.Harris and Oak Creek. Other small communities such as Milner, Phippsburg, Sidney and Toponas were created as railroad shipping points. Several small agricultural communities developed around rural post offices, grange halls or country schools, including Brookston, Clark, Dunkley, Elkhead, Eddy, Mystic, Pagoda, Poole, Trull, and Willow Creek.

Steamboat Springs became the county seat in 1912, after acrimonious disputes with Hayden, where it was originally (1877-78), and Hahns Peak (1879-1912). Oak Creek failed in a bid to take the county seat in 1912 and ten years later Steamboat Springs built one of the most elegant courthouses in the state. Today Steamboat Springs is the largest of four incorporated towns and six unincorporated "frontier" communities with populations under 400.

The county's population has always fluctuated. It soared from 3,661 at the turn of the century (1900) to 10,525 (1940) when the coal industry peaked, to more than 13,000 at the end of the war (1945). When industries and the railroad converted from coal to petroleum after the war, population rapidly declined. The Census reported 8,940 residents in 1950 and only 5,900 people in 1960. A rejuvenated coal industry and efforts to create a world-class ski resort turned things around in the mid 1960s and the population reached 6,592 in 1970.

Since 1980 population growth has remained consistently at just over 1%. The 1993 population (15,553) is composed of 3,528 households and 2,120 housing units. It is estimated 52% of these residents live in rural areas and 48% in incorporated towns. Their median age is 32; 39% of them were born in Colorado. Ninety-two percent have graduated from high school and 35% have four-year or higher college degrees.

Routt County provides over 10,000 jobs and the unemployment rate is around 5%, below the state average. Primary components of the economy are construction and miscellaneous occupations (38%), restaurant/hotel businesses (19%), mining (8%) and agriculture (1%). Although a small percent of the total, agriculture currently generates more than $9 million and, according to recent surveys, the farming and ranching communities play a major role in "quality of life" issues by preserving open space areas and attracting visitors and new residents. It is interesting to note that the 1993 Census shows 434 farms/ranches in Routt County averaging 1,316 acres compared to 829 averaging 1,350 acres fifty years ago in 1940.

POPULATION TRENDS

	County	Steamboat Springs	Hayden	Oak Creek	Yampa	# Farms/ Ranches
1890	2,369					
1900	3,661					
1910	7,561	1,227	314	222	332	1,113
1920	8,948	1,249	455	967	200	926
1930	9,352	1,198	554	1,211	310	928
1940	10,525	1,613	640	1,769	426	829
1950	8,940	1,913	767	1,488	421	532
1960	5,900	1,843	764	666	312	403
1970	6,592	2,340	763	492	286	337
1980	13,404	5,098	1,720	929	472	344
1990	14,080	6,695	1,444	673	317	425
1994*	16,096	7,981	1,520	740	347	NA
2000*	19,565					

*Estimate

Source: US Department of Commerce, Bureau of the Census (population); Colorado Department of Agriculture, Resource Analysis Section linear interpolation (farms/ranches)

4

Routt County
Land of
Opportunity

From the 1940 Premium Book and Classification List

Routt County, with its many rich, undeveloped natural resources, offers a veritable land of opportunity for those in search of a place in which to establish homes where they can gain the necessities of life, and comfortable luxuries, in return for a reasonable amount of honest toil. In this section there have been no extreme drouths, there is no imminent danger from floods, tornadoes, cyclones, earthquakes — and other sectional terrors are unknown. Here we find a happy, contented, neighborly people that make the section one of the most desirable on earth.

Income in Routt County is derived chiefly from livestock raising, coal mining, diversified farming and other allied lines. Head lettuce production, poultry raising, dairying, raising of purebred cattle, crude oil production, potato farming, the growing of pure registered seed, such as rye, wheat, oats, barley and alfalfa, is practiced on a liberal scale.

Routt County offers unlimited attractions for those in every walk of life—and for nearly every conceivable desire. Learn more about Routt County by contacting those who make their home here. You'll find they are all anxious to point out the fine qualities of their home communities.

5

Railroad Day

Most regions are fortunate to have one historic event to celebrate. Routt County has three, and they all happened in 1914: Two Smith College

girls, Charlotte Perry and Portia Mansfield, opened the nation's first school of dance in Strawberry Park in June. Carl Howelsen, a Norwegian stone mason, organized the first winter carnival west of the Mississippi in December. The first Routt County Fair was held in September.

Nineteen fourteen was a good year for Routt County. Telephone wires were strung along the Bear River. The highway over Rabbit Ears Pass was opened. A

First train into Hayden (Photo: Hayden Heritage Center)

gold mill opened at the Royal Flush Mine at Hahns Peak. The Sarvis Timber Company opened a new camp and mill. Colorado-Utah Coal Company began erecting "splendid" new houses at Mt. Harris, seven miles east of Hayden. Strawberry growers produced 20,000 crates, the largest crop in history.

Hayden installed water and sewer systems. Oak Creek formed a Booster Club. Steamboat Springs organized a volunteer fire department, built a 15-bed hospital and closed the pool halls on Sunday. This was the first "boom" in hardscrabble country, destined to repeat boom-bust cycles.

First came the Utes, a fairly sluggish lot, who loitered in the hot springs, shot game from the flap in the teepee, and spent more time fishing than crafting the things we associate with Native American culture. Then came the missionaries who left only footprints. Then came scouts, guides and mountain men – Jim Baker, Jim Bridger, Kit Carson – enroute to Fort

(Photo: Hayden Heritage Center)

Railroad Day October 21, 1913 (Photo: Colorado Historical Society)

Davy Crockett, a stop-over called "Fort Misery" up in Brown's Park.

They were followed by the map makers: John C. Freemont, Thomas Jefferson Farnham, and Ferdinand V. Hayden. Farnham is billed as Routt County's first tourist and, in the first book to describe Northwest Colorado, reports meeting

four Canadian trappers in 1839. It has long been said that one of these trappers observed that the chug of a little geyser down by the river "sounds like a steamboat, by gar." Steamboat Springs clung to the name, which was used by prospectors and surveyors criss-crossing the country, although the first home-steaders did not arrive until 1875.

The area remained isolated until freight and mail wagons began hauling from the railroad at Wolcott into Steamboat Springs, across Twentymile Park into Yampa, and over Ute Pass into Hayden. What separated then from now was the arrival of the railroad. It came into

Wolcott in 1880 but the century turned while David Moffat spent $10 million building a railroad from Denver toward Salt Lake in order to open access to Routt County's rich coal fields. The first freight

trains reached Yampa in August 1908, Steamboat Springs in December, 1908 and Hayden in December, 1912, but never passed Craig where they arrived in November, 1913. Each town raised money to build its own depot.

The Routt County Republican, which boasted that it kept "the reader posted on most important current topics" was convinced that Hayden was destined to become "the industrial center of Northwestern Colorado." The 250 teams building track in June were proof, it reported, that "We are not on a jerkwater line." Speculation about a $22 million line between Hayden and Casper made front page news: Hayden was sitting in the center of the largest field of high grade bituminous coal in the country, just south of the biggest anthracite coal field west of Pennsylvania at California Park, and west of the gold and copper mining districts at Hahns Peak.

The arrival of the Denver & Salt Lake promised to usher in a new world. The railroad was offering prizes for the best car loads of steers ($100) and hogs ($75) and the two-day Railroad Day Celebration was to be "the biggest celebration ever witnessed in the Hayden Valley." The first passenger train pulled into Hayden at 11:30 am on Friday, October 24, 1913, seven years after the town was incorporated.

More than $1,200 was donated for the festivities which took place in two white tents placed in the vacant lots adjoining *The Republican* office. Head Chef Dick Caraway barbecued two beef donated by the Cary, Adair, Solandt, and Summer families, a 500-pound elk from the J. B. Dawson family and four sheep from John Ottenberg.

Laying rail through the Hayden Valley in 1912. (Photo: Hayden Heritage Center)

Said *The Steamboat Pilot*: "Many old-timers stood around or sat in their buggies or autos while tears of joy rolled down their faces...1,200 plates of the good things of the valley were given out (each day) with the 'keys of liberty' to the Town of Hayden...Jim Norvell and Sam Walker stood on top of the caboose, right behind the engine, as the train pulled into Hayden, waving their hats and shouting...It was a perfect October day, not a cloud in the sky and the pleasures of the program were enjoyed by all...It was like a family reunion..."

The trip took one and a half hours from Steamboat Springs and cost $1.20 for the round trip. There were speakers, foot races for boys and an automobile race. Steamboat Springs beat Hayden (24-4) in basketball; neither Hayden nor Craig scored in the first football game ever played in the valley.

Bobby Robinson claims that the only reason the Routt County Fair was located in Hayden was because Si Dawson liked to race horses. At the Railroad Day races, Dawson took home a first in saddle horse, second in the pony race, and third in the free-for-all.

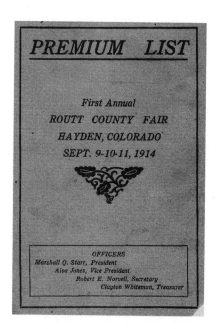

Routt County Racing Association
Board of Directors (1914)

Marshall Starr, president
Alva Jones, vice president
Clayton Whiteman, treasurer
R.E. Norvell, secretary
Sam Adair
George Anderson
Stanley Brock
Ferry Carpenter
Si Dawson
D.L. Sellers
B.T. Shelton

Routt County Fair Association
Board of Directors (1996)

Robin Lighthizer, chair
Arny Holly, vice chair
Delbert Kemry, treasurer
Linda Long, secretary
Doug Button
Byron Dean
Scott Flower
Maury Bunn
Debbie Williams

Parade Themes

The Fair Parade began in 1946, organized by the Hayden Women's Civic Club which supervised it for 36 years. It has always focused on children's floats, horses and collector vehicles. It winds from the west end of town near the school to the east end, led by a mounted Color Guard from Benjamin J. Hofstetter American Legion Post #89. Since 1982 the Hayden Lions Club has organized the parade and provided prizes. Until the Hayden Lions Club began selecting the annual theme, the Routt County Fair was simply billed as "The Best Show in the West."

1968 Fun for Everyone
1977 What Next Routt Country?
1978 Progress in Routt County
1979 Kids from 1-90
1980 Hurrah! For the Red, White and Blue
1981 Working Together—Growing Together
1982 Hey, Look Me Over!
1983 America's Pride: The Family
1984 Pioneer Pride
1985 Pride in the Past—Footsteps in the Future
1986 Yampa Valley—Wagons to Jets
1987 Yesterday's Actions, Today's Planning,
     Tomorrow's Successes
1988 Where the Old West Is Still Young
1989 75th Anniversary of the Routt County Fair
1990 Where the World Meets the West
1991 Proud To Be An American
1992 Mount Harris Revisited
1993 Harmony With Nature
1994 80 Years of Routt County Pride!
1995 Love A Fair
1996 A Family Affair

Routt County Fair Officers

PRESIDENTS

1914	Marshall Q. Starr	1960-1964	
1915	R.E. Norvell	1965-1971	Kenneth Whiteman
1916	J. C. Temple	1972-1979	Gordon Booco
1917-1923		1980-1982	Joe Rossi
1925-1930	C. T. Roberds	1983-1984	Leonard Flanders
1930-1932		1985-1986	Diane Hillewaert
1932-1934	none	1987-1988	Norton Jacobs
1935-1941	Earl Erwin	1988-1989	Bill Gay
1942-1945	none	1990-1991	Chuck Perry
1946-1948	Kenneth Carroll	1992-1994	Jocko Camilletti
1949	Harry Temple	1995-	Robin Lighthizer
1950-1959	George Simonton		

Routt County Fair Officers

COUNTY AGENT

1928-30	Percy Ingram
1930-1936	Floyd D. Moon
1937-1941	E. N. Barr
1942-1946	Ray Sprengle
1947-1950	Guy Robbins
1951-1953	William R. Culbertson
1954-1959	Buck Taylor
1960-1964	Robert F. Hamill
1964-1965	Charles Miller
1966-1967	Robert F. Hamill
1968-1969	Billy R. Coffey
1970-1987	Sam Haslem
1988-1989	Cherrilyn Wallace
1990-	C.J. Mucklow

HOME AGENT

1930	Frances Jones (Young)
1930-1932	Josephine Chambers (Linger)
1933-1936	Esther Elliott
1937-1938	Helen Prout
1939	Mildred Timm (Paxton)
1939-1940	Georgia Thomas (Franklin)
1940-1944	Jean Knowles (Deurloo)
1944-1945	Dorothy Carlson
1946-1948	Ruth Need
1948-1950	Alice Storey
1950-1952	Jean Chandler
1952-1954	Ester Eicher
1955-1957	Lorene Pzinski (Linke)
1957-1958	Barbara Freeze (Jolly)
1958-1960	Peggy Hendricks
1960-1963	Verna Mae McNenny (Greenfield)
1963-1964	Anne E. Heermann (Gillespie)
1964-1965	Mary Dyer (Schalnus)
1966-1971	Theresa Ross
1972-1984	Shirley Portouw
1985-1989	Cherilynn Wallace
1990-1992	Sheila Gains
1993	none
1994-1995	Elaine Sturges

SPORTING EVENTS DIRECTOR

1914	
1915	David Sellers
1916	R.E. Norvell
1917-1918	J.J. Toole
1919	J.C. Temple
1920-1922	
1923	W.W. Holder
1914	Charley Tipton
1925	
1926	Ben Anderson
1927	
1928	Stanley Larson
1929	L.E. Fitzgerald
1930	L.E. Fitzgerald and Thomas Iles
1931-1934	
1935-1959	George Cook, board member
1960	Darwin Lockhart
1961	George Simonton
1962-1963	Leon Green
1964-1965	Larry Whiteman

RODEO MANAGER

1966-1971	Larry Whiteman
1972	Pat Mantle
1973	Carl Murphy
1974-1983	John Hayes
1984-1990	Gary Fagg
1991-1995	Larry Mosher
1996-	Ray Mazzola

RACE MANAGER

1966-1969	Nick Deluca
1970-1971	Lee and Sally Williamson
1972	Jim Camilletti
1973-1975	John Hayes
1976	Pat Robson
1977-1978	Delbert Chockley
1979-1982	Mike Dorr
1983-1984	Doug and Carolin Monger
1985-1987	Ed Duncan
1988-	Kathy Duncan

Grand Marshals

Connie Moore suggested having a Parade Marshal when she was chairman in 1968. Marshals are selected by the Routt County Commissioners upon recommendation of the Routt County Fair Association Board.

1968   Blain "Pop" Wixson
1969   Max Williams
1970   Bill Foster
1971   Ferry Carpenter
1972   Winnie Carroll
1973   Sandy Sandercook
1974   Sumner Hockett
1975   Truman Leslie
1976   Ed and Laura Moore
1977   Pioneer Families in the Centennial Year: Calla Appel (Steamboat Springs), Ivan and Birdie Decker (Toponas), Erma Fisk (Hayden) Nancy Gilleland (Elk River), Sam and Angelina Iacovetto (Phippsburg), Elmer and Ilda Margerum (Yampa), Ida Monteith (Mt.Harris), Mabel Myers (Oak Creek), Opal Page (Steamboat Springs), Sigrid Smith (Milner), Edna Trullinger (Clark) and Josephine Yoast (Dunkley)
1978   John Bird, Gib Lazor and Ray Yoast
1979   Mike Benedict, George Sauer and Bruce Yoast
1980   Lewis and Fanny Phillips and Marguerite "Mac" and R.N. "Bobby" Robinson Sr.
1981   Evelyn Monger, Violet Kuskie and Jack and Ayliffe Zehner
1982   Billy Milner, Julia Pizor and Robert Swinehart Sr.
1983   Lucienne Stetson
1984   Mike Benedict, Chester Dunckley and Vernon Summer
1985   Quentin Semotan
1986   Dan and Doris Knott
1987   Berenice Whiteman
1988   John Utterback, D.V.M.
1989   Mavis Peavy, Evelyn Semotan and Delphine Dawson Wilson
1990   Bob and Elaine Gay, Jim and Avis Funk, and Joe and Virginia Rossi
1991   Bill and Sally Meek, Leonard and Rose Flanders, and Frances and Hazel Wheeler
1992   Carl and Rita Herold, Bill, Kenny and Carol Rhodes, and Helen Sherrod
1993   Perly and Bonnie Green, Bob and Ann McKune and Glen and Betty Robson
1994   Past Fair Board members still living: Linda Archuleta, Glen Barber, Gordon Booco, Vince Carnahan, Ed Duncan, Bob Duzik, Leonard Flanders, Bill Gay, Jerry Green, Dottie Greget, Otto Gumprecht Jr., Diane Hillewaert, John Hayes, Carl Herold, Aaron Huffstettler, Norton Jacobs, Eric Johnson, KayKayser, DanKnott, DougMeacham, Les Mergelman, Wayne Morton, Renae May, Chuck Perry, Roy Pitney, Joe Rossi, Russ Steele,Frank Stetson, Keith Studer, LarryWhiteman, GaryWilliams
1995   CentennialRanchers: Mabel, Jerry and Judy Green, Arny and Diane (Hitchens) Holly,andVernonSummer
1996   Jim and Joanne Stank

Queens

Selection of a Fair Queen and her Attendants became a continuing part of the Routt County Fair in 1953 and has been limited to 4-H and FFA members since 1971. Criteria used for selection are skills in horsemanship and personal attributes.

Prior to 1953 there was a contest for the title of Miss Routt County, who reigned at the Fair. E. F. Bissel organized the contest which selected town champions in Steamboat Springs, Hayden, Oak Creek and Yampa before identifying an overall winner. The first newspaper account of a Miss Routt County is in 1927 when Ayliff Jones (Zehner) won it. As the following list indicates, records prior to 1971 are incomplete.

Darcy Camilletti in 1978, five years before she became Queen.

1946 Joanna Stevenson, Hayden
1947 Laura Peavy, Steamboat Springs
1953 Pat Wymore, Craig
1960 Barbara Lee, Hayden
1962 Charlene Marshall, Hayden
1971 Debbie Wheeler, Steamboat Springs
1972 Jacque Wheeler, Steamboat Springs
1973 Valeen Jacobs, Steamboat Springs
1974 Vicki Morton, Hayden
1975 Deanna Kuntz, Steamboat Springs
1976 Jackie Lazor, Steamboat Springs
1977 Christy Hawk, Steamboat Springs
1978 Dorinda Valdeck, Steamboat Springs
1979 Traci Hayes, Hayden
1980 Queeda Chew, Clark
1981 Jody Kayser, Toponas
1982 LaRae Camilletti, Milner
1983 Darcy Camilletti, Milner
1984 Samantha Shupp, Steamboat Springs
1985 Tina Keller, Steamboat Springs
1986 Raylene Vetter, Yampa
1987 Cindy Kline, Hayden
1988 Tina Williams, Hayden
1989 Molly Forsyth, Hayden
1990 Tina Williams, Hayden
1991 Robin Duncan, Steamboat Springs
1992 Shawneen Guire, Steamboat Springs
1993 Sheri McNeal, Hayden
1994 Keri Wilson, Steamboat Springs
1995 Kristina Kuntz, Steamboat Springs
1996 Sheri McNeal, Hayden

Joanna Stevenson on Pepper at the Hayden Fairgrounds. She was crazy about Pepper ...

The 1946 Fair Queen Remembers

From Joanna Stevenson (Sampson)

I rode Pepper in the parade. Pepper was a young horse Henry Hindman broke for me, a nervous high-stepping horse. But he was fairly calm as we started leading the parade. Then an airplane behind us turned around, its propellers blasting us with a tornado-like wind full of paper, leaves and dirt. It was a hang-on-and-hope ride from there on!

Hayden horseman Jack Driefuse, livery barn owner and ex-jockey, was the Parade Marshal and rode beside me on a paint horse. The streets were lined with folks who had come from miles around to celebrate the Fair. One of my duties was to lead race horses on to the track and past the grandstands. There were so many fast horses in Routt County it was easy to see why race horse owners in other parts of the country said, "If you have a good horse and want to see it get beat, take it to the Routt County Fair."

At the 1946 rodeo, everything went well until the last race of the day. Two horse owners got into a dispute about the start of the race and began a fist fight that immediately turned into a brawl. People poured out of the grandstands to join the fracas. The judges kept playing "The Star Spangled Banner" in hopes the combatants would come to attention and stand in patriotic silence. It didn't work. A jockey, who had ridden the last race and was headed for the barn on his hot horse, rode into the angry mob. Just as the presence of a horse in such close quarters was beginning to slow down action, the jockey suddenly leaped off into the crowd. The battle roared on and it was only later we learned the jockey had jumped in to take a gun away from a drunk Deputy Sheriff from Oak Creek. The hostilities ended when the fighters got so tired they couldn't slug it out anymore. There were a lot of black eyes, bloodied knuckles and swollen noses at the Fair Dance the year I was Rodeo Queen.

The Hamburger Stand

They made 'em four to the pound except for the year when production was boosted to five to the pound. Effie Bailey remembers a lot of complaints because "they looked like chips." The best hamburgers in the West have always been served at the Routt County Fair.

So say the ladies of Benjamin Hofstetter Post No. 89 in Hayden who have helped the American Legion run the legendary Hamburger Stand at the Fairgrounds for some 50 years. The Hamburger Stand is a ritual, for many years nurtured by longtime members Leonard and Rose Flanders who came early and stayed late.

In the early days, the Legion Auxiliary made the patties in the back of Earl Erwin's Hayden Merc from good ol' homegrown beef. No one can remember how many pounds, how many burgers or how much they cost. It was just "a lot of them." Today the quarter pound burgers come pre-patted, but they are seasoned with sentiment and served with gusto by Legion and Auxiliary members.

Proceeds from sales have been contributed to national and state health organizations and charities, the Hayden Community Scholarship Fund, Food Bank, Girls and Boys State, Hayden Heritage Center and programs to help handicapped veterans. Years ago the American Legion used the money to pay for lights on the Hayden football field; and for many years the Auxiliary sponsored and paid all expenses for the annual Hayden Community Fund Drive.

The ladies, who meet the third Thursday of the month from September through May, delight in the fact that you can smell their hamburgers all over town during Fair. Pat Holderness and Myrtle Rhodes recall the first hamburger stand which was built in 1936 by Glen Frentress, Ray Goree, Paul Hein, Jack Holderness and Harry Kaiser. It was on wheels and rolled from the Fairgrounds to Cuber's Hall at Walnut and Washington Streets for the Legion's two Fair-night dances.

"But now we're modern: icebox, cabinets, sink and stove with a fan over it. Having electricity is a real luxury but we still pack water to the stand from the hydrant," says Avis Funk. The new stand was built around 1968 and often has been loaned to other organizations. Avis remembers when a horse got loose back of the grandstand and ran into Myrtle Frentress. "I can still hear her leg pop," she says. "Working together is what it's all about. We dread it and enjoy it." According to Helen Medvesk, "It's hard to believe you can have that much fun when you drag home tired with grease in your hair and all over your clothes." Ruby Wright says her most vivid memory is selling $200 worth of pop in the pouring rain and Rosemary Flanders recalls filling an order for 40 carry-out hamburgers.

The American Legion was organized August 1, 1920 and memorializes Benjamin J. Hofstetter, a member of a pioneer Hayden family and the "Lost Battalion" who was killed fighting in France on October 7, 1918. The Legion Auxiliary was chartered in March 1930 and the only surviving charter member is 94-year-old Flo Hein who lives with the family of her son-in-law, Jay Hockett, in Colorado Springs.

History of the Routt County Fair

Hayden was the perfect place for a county fair. Although located at the Western end of Routt County, it was the center of Northwest Colorado which included vast areas of Routt County and the newly formed Moffat County. The success of Railroad Days, coupled with the town's enthusiasm for hosting an annual celebration, led to the birth of the Routt County Fair in September 1914.

State Senator John Cary of Hayden encouraged using a fair to promote the agricultural products of the region and proposed that land south of town, site of some ball fields and a crude race track, become a permanent fair and racing track. The group which hosted Railroad Days, meeting informally in the back of a local store, organized the Routt County Fair and Racing Association in November 1913. Supervised by temporary officers and directors, the Association began selling $1 stock certificates in order to raise $25,000.

The Association was incorporated in August 1914 and, at a public meeting in the High School Assembly Room, stockholders elected a board of directors: B. T. Shelton, F. R. Carpenter, D. L. Sellers, S. A. Adair, S. M. Dawson, George Anderson and Stanley Brock. This group then appointed Marshall Starr, president; Alva Jones, vice president; Clayton Whiteman, treasurer; and R. E. Norvell, secretary and general manager.

The Routt County Commissioners contributed $500 for advertising and premiums on grains, vegetables and livestock, suggesting the money be used to send a collection of the best to the State Fair to promote Northwest Colorado. When the Commissioners refused to pay premiums to exhibitors from Moffat County, the Routt County Fair Association agreed to pick up the tab.

The spirit surrounding preparation for the Fair pervaded both counties during August and September. Volunteers worked tirelessly to grade the race track, a sloping oval surrounded by a plank fence. They built a wire fence around the grounds, a ticket office at the main gate and temporary grandstands, and installed a water line. The location became "permanent" when the Association purchased 40 acres at $50 per acre from Wilson Cary who took half the payment in stock.

15

THE FIRST FAIR: September 9-11, 1914

According to *The Steamboat Pilot*, "Providence was good to Hayden and to the promoters of the first Routt County Fair for everything turned out even better than had been anticipated, and the weather was perfect." Because there were no buildings on the grounds, good weather was essential and everyone was delighted that it did not start snowing until the day after the Fair closed, continuing intermittently during the following week.

Huge tents, rented in Denver, housed exhibits and most of the activities were outdoor events. Although the focus was on agricultural exhibits and education, the Fair Association took pains to assure ample entertainment. Special days were dedicated to each town in the hope they would declare a holiday and promote attendance.

The railroad ran one-day Fair trips with special trains and reduced rates. Parking areas were reserved for automobiles, and newspaper ads urged drivers with extra seats to bring a friend or neighbor. Promotion paid off; despite the sparse populations of Routt and Moffat County, attendance exceeded expectations. It peaked on Thursday, Steamboat Springs Day, attracting more than 2,000 people; 500 rode the train to Hayden. Friday was also busy with large delegations from Yampa, Oak Creek and Craig.

The principal attraction: "aeroplane ascensions" by W.B. Cooke of Ashland, California. They were the first witnessed in the valley and preceded by slighting remarks from "disbelievers" anticipating a fake. But on Thursday evening Cooke amazed the crowd with an excellent flight; a shorter flight on Friday morning thrilled spectators but not the Fair Association. Because he failed to make the agreed number of flights, they paid him $500 of the $650 contract fee.

There were other crowd-pleasers. Captain A.H. Hardy of the Peters Cartridge Company demonstrated "fancy shooting" from the ground and from a moving

Hazel Stratton, born in eastern Kansas in 1899, was 10 years old when her family came over the pass with a wagon, buggy and Jersey milk cow named Old Daisy. Hazel drove 20 head of "fine saddle horses" into the country where her father began working for the Dawson Ranch in 1909. An eight mile roundtrip to school in Hayden honed her skills as a horsewoman. She is shown here on Badger, her prize winning gaited horse in 1916. Below: Anna Smith McDowell took first prize in Ladies Riding on Sam Diamond at the first Fair in 1914. (Photos: Hayden Heritage Center)

automobile. Routt County defeated Moffat County in a tug-of-war, and Hayden took the small end of a 10 to 7 baseball game with Craig. Although bucking events were reportedly tame, the horse races were run on a fast track and the relay races were described as "close as anyone could desire." Nine people entered the potato race. *The Steamboat Pilot* claimed the slow auto race was more exciting than the fast race and applauded Raymond Yoast for winning the hearts of the judges in the Most Perfect Baby Contest. There were special features at the moving picture show and Adelbert Mills filled the dance hall with

music. A four-round boxing match between Fred L. Beck of Steamboat Springs and Percy Peacock of Williams Fork drew many men folk. Said *The Steamboat Pilot*: "Taking into consideration Beck's lack of training and unpreparedness for the match, he put up a remarkable scrap."

Newspaper reports said the exhibits were "gratifying and showed to some extent what agriculture can do in this county...Excellent exhibits of horses and cattle were shown. A few chickens were on display, but no sheep or hogs." Sam Adair won three of the five Shorthorn classes while cattle from the Carpenter and White herds took first and second places in all Hereford classes. Coke Roberds dominated grade cattle classes and had the best registered steer. The horse division, divided into grade and registered horses, primarily attracted draft horses.

Overall Champions, in every breed, received a special prize awarded by the State of Colorado Livestock Inspection Commission and were: Best Stallion, Sam Lighthizer; Best Mare, J. W. Cary; Best Pair of Draft Horses, William Cawlfield; and Best Buggy Horse in Harness, J. C. Temple.

(Photos: Denver Public Library)

Top honors in embroidery and fancy work, again "better than expected," were won by Mrs. D. L. Sellers. The domestic science department, "good in quality but sparse in exhibits," presented "Best Awards" to Mabel Havens for yeast rising bread, Mrs. R. E. Norvell for angel food cake and Dora Temple for best cake baked by a girl.

Grains and vegetables were "best of the exhibits." Ezekiel and Byron Shelton, whose vegetable display at Railroad Day helped foster the idea of a Fair, arranged another "outstanding display" and C. A. Ranney showed a "champion collection of grasses." They were sent to Denver to be displayed at the Chamber of Commerce, "To speak the praises of Routt County to thousands of sightseers."

The Association earned enough to cover premiums, purses and rent for the tent. The board was so pleased with the first Fair that, at their very next meeting, they allocated $1,500 from the sale of stocks to build a permanent grandstand and Exhibit Hall. The money was turned over to B. T. Shelton who secured the services of Uncle Joe Bruce as construction foreman. Volunteers working on the project took half of their pay in Fair Association Stock.

THE TRADITION IS ESTABLISHED: 1915

By the time the 1915 County Fair opened, the grounds boasted a 1,000-seat grandstand, an improved race track, a 150 x 70 foot livestock shed, a large corral, and a 32 x 60 foot Exhibit Hall, housing Fair offices and surrounded on three sides by a balcony for agricultural displays. Immediately prior to opening, it was decided to build another small building for rest rooms and the Pioneer Association. The decision to dedicate the first morning and evening to Northwest Colorado's pioneers set the theme of the Fair for the next 15 years. Governor George Carleson opened the ceremonies making the Fair a regional event, social as well as economic.

Festivities celebrated the end of harvest, friendly competition, community pride and entertainment. The focus of future Fairs, which continued to be three-day events held during the first (or at times the second) week in September until 1930 was clear: raising improved livestock, encouraging agricultural production, and promoting education and the exchange of information.

The Fair Association operated on income from the sale of stock certificates, admission fees and occasional funding from the County Commissioners. The basic format stayed the same: livestock shows and exhibits, sporting events and a variety of entertainment. The railroad ran special trains and fares from each of the towns along the line, and added a special car to pick up and deliver exhibits before and after the Fair.

IN THE 1920s

Livestock classes continued to expand and horse classes remained divided between purebred and grade horses. In addition to purebred Shorthorn and Hereford classes, classes for one and two year old steers and a pen of yearling feeder steers were added. Dairy cattle, first shown in 1915, were judged by breed, most often Ayrshires, Guernseys, Holsteins, Jerseys and Milking Shorthorns. Swine were also judged by breeds, primarily Berkshire, Poland China, Duroc and Hampshires.

In an attempt to promote hog classes, Jack White and the Agricultural Agent for Western Colorado started a contest for boys under 18. The distinction of being the county's most scientific pig feeder carried prizes of $50 and $25 and required keeping the best records on pig feeding between July 1 and the first day of Fair. The prizes sparked interest from 14 boys in Hayden and 6 from Steamboat Springs.

Sheep classes began in 1925 for Rambouillet, Cotswold, Lincoln, Hampshire and Shropshire. Surprisingly, Suffolk, the most common breed shown today, were first introduced as a special exhibit in 1929. Poultry remained popular, with classes for chickens, turkeys, ducks and geese.

The livestock arena attracted special interest in 1929 when, in addition to these classes, a new 4-H Division introduced classes in dairy calves, beef calves and swine. A bum lamb and baby skunk, decorated in ribbons and bows, appeared in a class for boys and girls under 17.

Grains, grasses and vegetables raised on irrigated or non- irrigated land remained the primary focus, although a class for "Monstrosities," the largest single vegetables, immediately became a favorite. Needle and fancy work dominated sewing exhibits, while canned and dairy products outdistanced domestic science and cooking in popularity. An Education Department, added in 1915, prompted displays and a day off to examine them from schools throughout the county.

Other new departments opened for 4-H sewing and foods, amateur photography, art and flowers. Bronc riding and horse racing continued to dominate sports with the occasional addition of tugs-of-war for adults and foot races for youngsters.

(Hayden Heritage Center)

IN THE 1930s

The first real change came in 1930 and 1931 when the Routt County Fair officially consolidated with the Moffat County Fair. Moffat County, which hired an Extension Agent in 1917 and held a county fair in Maybell between 1918 and 1922, joined forces in sponsoring the Northwestern Colorado Fair.

The Association board of directors was expanded to include four members from Craig and three from Hayden. Coke Roberds of Hayden was named president and I. P. Beckett of Craig secretary-treasurer. County Agents T. J. Snyder of Moffat County and Floyd Moon of Routt County joined Routt County's Home Demonstration Agent, Francis Jones, on the board. To assure cooperation, each department had co-superintendents, one from each county.

Although the concept of a Northwestern Colorado Fair was the goal of the Fair's founders, the accomplishment was short-lived. Despite enthusiastic support, a special Craig Day and excellent exhibits from the "low country," Moffat County remained aloof and the timing was bad. The Depression hit and, with tightening budgets, neither county was willing to commit funds for a 1932 Fair. It was impossible to sell stock certificates and 1931 gate receipts did not cover expenses. The Association was forced to cancel the Fair in 1932, 1933 and 1934.

On March 13, 1934, in an attempt to save the event, the Association deeded the Fairgrounds to Routt County for $2 on condition that the land would revert to the original owners if a Fair or rodeo was not held for two years. When the economy improved in early 1935, the Routt County Commissioners contributed $500 to restart the Fair and appointed five new directors: A. E. Erwin of Hayden, R. I. Gwillim of Oak Creek, J. C. Wilson of Yampa, A. A.Curtis and George Cook of Steamboat Springs, County Agent Floyd Moon and Home Demonstration Agent Ester Elliott. The Routt County Board of County Commissioners has appointed the Fair board since this time.

With additional support from 40 local businesses, the Fair opened as a two-day event on September 17, 1935, awarding only blue and red ribbons. There were no admission or exhibitor fees, no cash premiums and exhibitors were allowed to use their space to sell or promote products. Although departments and classes mirrored those in 1931, heirloom and hobby exhibits were introduced.

The Fair was again incorporated in 1936, this time as the Routt County Fair and Rodeo Association, the name it carries into the present. The new board of directors, one person from each section of the county, was comprised of Andy Black of Oak Creek, George Cook of Steamboat Springs and A. E. Erwin of Hayden, County Agent Edson W. Barr and Home Demonstration Agent Helen Prout. Although County and Home Demonstration Agents changed, these regional representatives gave continuity to the board until 1942.

The Fair continued to be a two-day event during the second week of September until 1941. Departments and classes remained consistent, stressing purebred livestock, but dropping breeds from dairy and swine classes and eliminating all rabbit classes. The canning department was restructured as "Pantry Stores" and included baking classes.

Racing became so popular that in 1936 starting gates were used for the first time, and by the 1940s, Fair races were drawing horses from as far away as California and Alabama. Bucking chutes were moved to provide better views from the grandstands, a judges tower was built, and calf roping and cow riding was initiated. WPA funds permitted major improvements to the grounds in 1938. These included additions to the grandstands, increasing seating to nearly 3,000; a new barn with box stalls for race horses; and a 38 x 72 foot livestock barn for purebred cattle, the pride of the Fairgrounds.

IN THE 1940s

A successful purebred livestock sale in 1940 again made the Fair the highlight of fall activities in Routt County.

Old-timers in the stands complained that there was too much emphasis on rodeo and not enough on agricultural exhibits, but as Extension Agent Bill Culbertson, now retired in Ft. Collins, observes "There's never been a Fair that everyone was happy." The decade marked the end of the railroad's involvement with the Fair; attempting to recover from the Depression and in various stages of receivership, special trains were replaced by automobiles and trucks.

In order to generate interest, the 1941 rodeo purse for the Best All-Around Performer, based upon points collected at rodeos throughout Northwest Colorado, was hiked to $300 and the event began being promoted as "The Best Outdoor Show in the West." However, with the exception of the 4-H Division, the Fair Board again found itself without premium money because a series of 1940 forest fires had drained the County's General Fund. Purebred breeders volunteered to exhibit livestock for ribbons and, although the 1941 Fair generated optimism, December 7, 1941 abruptly ended all plans. Involvement in the war effort made a Fair impossible and it was cancelled from 1942 through 1945; however, in order to meet the obligations of the deed, rodeo and racing events were held on the Fairgrounds in 1944 and 1945.

When the war ended in September, 1945, too late to consider a Fair, county residents were anxious to reinstate tradition and the County Commissioners appointed a new board: Kenneth Carroll of Hayden, Andy Black of Oak Creek, George Cook of Steamboat Springs and County Agent Ray Sprengle. Support

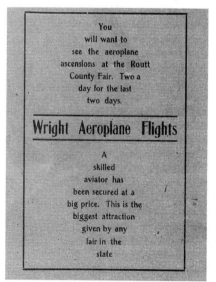

Back of 1914 Fair Book

from the Commissioners was supplemented by entry fees of $1 per head for cattle and horses, and admission fees of $1 for adults and 50 cents for students.

Eternally optimistic, *The Steamboat Pilot* that month crooned: "The revived Routt County Fair, long noted for the high quality of its livestock and agricultural exhibits and its rip-roaring entertainment, will be held next Tuesday and Wednesday at Hayden with promise of being bigger and better than ever before." But just as the Fair was about to open, the State Board of Health and the Colorado Emergency Polio Committee banned any public gathering of children under 18; the Fair was postponed for a week until heavy frosts were believed to minimize danger.

Classes remained consistent except for dairy and swine which were open only where entries were sufficient. Most exhibits were from purebred breeders, demonstrating why Routt County enjoys a national reputation for fine livestock. Because it had been several years since products had been exhibited, agricultural and home economic entries attracted a great deal of attention. By 1946 the Fair included a parade down Hayden's main street, dances each night and a boxing match with a card of local fighters. George Cook continued to expand the rodeo to include bareback bronc riding, head and heel roping and boys' calf roping.

(Photo: Hayden Heritage Center)

IN THE 1950s

Suddenly, in 1951, the County Commissioners cancelled the Fair because, according to both county newspapers, it represented too much expense and too little interest. There were two fatal blows. First, a Junior Livestock Show, started in Steamboat Springs in 1949, featured a sale which gave 4-H and FFA members the opportunity to raise funds for school or future investment in livestock. Unfortunately the show was in August, three weeks prior to Fair, so most 4-H project animals had been sold even before the Fair started. In addition, proposed changes in the Farm Bill triggered dissension among livestock producers over whether to accept farm subsidies.

County Commissioners J. Frank Stetson and William S. Green were instrumental in reviving the institution in 1952. During the year off, they revitalized the board with two appointments – George Simonton of Hayden and Ben Reary of Oak Creek – leaving George Cook to direct the rodeo and races.

The new directors wasted no time in making major changes. They moved the Fair to the third week in August, placing it ahead of the Steamboat Junior Livestock Show and eliminating conflict with schools and athletic programs. They expanded it into a three-day event, Thursday through Saturday. They canceled the Adult Livestock Show and instituted a strong Junior Livestock Show, supervised by two highly respected men: Howard Elliott, agricultural loan officer at the Routt County National Bank, and Mack Jones, Steamboat Springs' FFA advisor. The race program was bolstered with the purchase of a set of mobile starting gates in conjunction with the Moffat County Fair Board.

An attempt to reinstate the Adult Livestock Show as an exhibition in 1953 attracted little support and was dropped in 1954 when several new events were added: the American Quarter Horse Show, a Junior Rodeo and a Tractor Driving Contest. A new Quonset building was added to the grounds to house the livestock show and Kenneth Whiteman became Livestock Superintendent, a position he held until 1965. Results of these changes were not overwhelming so in 1956 the Fair reverted to a two-day event.

In 1957 the Fair returned to the second week in September in response to claims that many breeds of flowers and vegetables were not mature enough in August. Two years later, in 1959, the Junior Livestock Division was revitalized when Si and Darwin Lockhart organized a Junior Livestock Sale at the Fair. Showmanship classes were started, a Wool Show for adult and junior exhibitors was added and a Catch-it-Calf Contest introduced. This move eliminated the need for a Junior Livestock Show in Steamboat Springs and the Routt County Fair became the focus of 4-H and FFA programming and activities as it is today.

IN THE 1960s

The early 1960s were unsettled by George Cook's retirement as rodeo and race director, a position he had held since 1935; turn over in County and Home Demonstration Agents; and the death of two board members. Momentum from construction of the livestock shed and imaginative plans for facility improvements were tabled until the County Commissioners began laying groundwork for a management system, enacted between 1965 and 1975, which is credited with the continuing success of Rout County's Fair.

In 1965 the Fair board was expanded to six members, appointed by the Commissioners from each of their districts: Kenneth Whiteman and Leonard Flanders of Hayden, Bill Sherrod and Bob Gay of Steamboat Springs, and Dan Knott and Glenn Barber of Oak Creek formed the new team. Extension Agents, the Fair Manager and Rodeo and Race Directors became ex-officio members. New bylaws broadened the board's regulatory powers and financial responsibilities, and the Commissioners gave them $5,000 to operate the Fair and $10,000 for capital improvements.

Despite controversy, the 1965 Fair was moved back to the last week in August as a three-day event, ending only two days before Oak Creek Labor Day celebrations. Under the direction of Larry Whiteman, the rodeo began making headlines with the addition of bull riding, steer wrestling, a cutting horse event and barrel racing for the ladies. The race program was condensed to only six contests. But an Appaloosa Show, organized by Wayne and Olive Morton, became a major draw between 1967 and 1981.

Improvements to the grounds, just in time for the 1965 Fair, included a new L-shaped livestock barn, enclosed on three sides, on the northwest end of the livestock area. The east section of the grandstand was rebuilt, an announcer's tower erected, the garage on the east end of the Fairgrounds extended 20-feet, and a concrete floor poured for a new Exhibit Hall. The old Exhibit Hall was torn down to create a parking area and, during the next two years, water lines and concrete wash racks for livestock were installed.

IN THE 1970s

The Fair board continued to concentrate on improving facilities. A new metal barn, built in 1974 to function as a horse barn during the first days of the Fair, was equipped with portable bleachers so it could serve as a sale barn. It was named the Lockhart Auction Barn in honor of Si, Darwin and Cookie Lockhart whose efforts had earned the Junior Livestock Sale a reputation as "the best in Northwest Colorado."

In 1978 the Exhibit Hall was the Quonset building on a lot across the street from the main gate, and the rodeo arena was lined with poles and lights donated by Energy Fuels. The next round of improvements did not come until 1983 and 1986 when water lines were completed, and old horse stalls were replaced with roofed metal stalls adjacent to the Lockhart Barn. Restrooms were installed between the livestock barn and grandstands, landscaped with a donation from Colorado Yampa Coal Company and named Bobby Robinson Park.

IN RECENT MEMORY

The biggest improvements to the grounds have been fortuitous: The Quonset building collapsed in the winter of 1983 and the county moved its road shop off the grounds in the spring of 1984 allowing the Fair board to convert the shop into an Exhibit Hall, complete with office, kitchen, restrooms, office area, and sound system. The building, boasting a seating capacity in excess of 300, immediately became a center for community, 4-H and Fair activities.

A State Department of Local Affairs Energy Impact Grant permitted purchase and construction of new metal grandstands, replacing the old wooden seats which still included a section from the 1916 stands. The old stands were last used during the 1992 Fair, and the 1993 rodeo opened with new stands and a barbecue area, changing both the physical appearance of the fairgrounds and the character of the exhibits.

The Quarter Horse Show and the Appaloosa Show were discontinued in the early 1980s and an Open Horse Show launched in 1989. An Open Beef Show was reinstituted by Bill Gay, Delbert Kemry and Extension Agent C.J.Mucklow. Changing focus also impacted 4-H livestock classes. In the 1970s the emphasis was on market steers and lambs. By the 1980s steers were upstaged by lambs; more than 150 were entered in one Fair. Numbers of horses, hogs and rabbits increased steadily.

SHIFTING FAIR DATES

The date on which the Fair is held has always generated controversy. In 1967 it was changed, to the last four days in the first week of September. In 1970 it switched to five days, September 2-7. In 1971 it became an eight-day event, the last four days of August and first four in September.

Frustrated by failed attempts to accommodate school activities, the Oak Creek Labor Day Celebration, State Fair and growing seasons, the Fair board in 1972 finally agreed to a four-day fair on the first Thursday, Friday, Saturday and Sunday after Labor Day. These dates held for the next 20 years until 1992, when concern about absenteeism, homework and athletic programming in the three county school districts prompted yet another move to Wednesday, Thursday, Friday, Saturday and Sunday of the third week of August.

FAIR SUPERINTENDENTS

Volunteers have always been and will always be the heart and soul of the Fair. They build and paint, clean barns, cut grass and weeds and move rocks. Foremost among this energetic and enthusiastic group are Department Superintendents who devote countless hours to moving panels, tables and display stands; cataloguing, displaying and tracking exhibits and livestock.

Fair Superintendents are a unique breed because they not only prepare the exhibits for judging, but also assure that every exhibit and animal is directed to the appropriate class, listen to the public explain how this or that should be done and complain about how it was not done their way. It is remarkable that Fair Superintendents enjoy such long tenure, averaging ten years in a department. It is less of a surprise that most are former 4-H or FFA members or long-time exhibitors. Their dedication, smiles and cheerful attitudes embody the spirit of the Fair.

CROPS SUPERINTENDENTS AWARD

For the past 10 years Crops Superintendents have recognized the recipient of the most blue ribbons in produce with a plaque. These "Best of the Best" awards honor the outstanding adult produce exhibitor.

1986	Ernie Graham
1987	Ernie Graham
1988	Ruth Gray
1989	Beth Sundberg
1990	Linda Long
1991	Linda Long
1992	Angelo Iacovetto
1993	Mary Wixson
1994	Darrell Hockett
1995	Greg Richards

Angelo Iacovetto, Reserve Grand Champion in the Open Class (garlic) in 1992, the same year he was elected Outstanding Adult Produce Exhibitor. (Photo: Linda Long/ Susie Crowner)

SPECIAL EVENTS

While rodeo and racing have been the mainstay, the Fair has never lacked for special events. Every variety of foot race, baseball game and tug-of-war was featured between 1914 and 1919. By 1929 the Most Perfect Baby Contest required three physicians to examine infants for "vitality and physical perfection." Highlight of the 1915 Fair was a poker game, promoted by a Brooklyn saloon owner who was rewarded with a few days in the County Jail.

The Fair's racing tradition began with footraces between 1914 and 1920: a 50-yard race for boys and girls, a 100-yard race for men, and a variety of races for fat men, slim men, people in sacks or carrying eggs, or three-legged teams.

An obsession with speed led to automobile and motorcycle races held at the first Fair and occasionally until 1921. The Craig Auto Company won a "slow" one-eighth mile race and Clifford McClelland took the "fast" five mile race in 1914. Roy Houston of Steamboat Springs won the first motorcycle competition in 1915.

In 1921 Will Starr edged out Marshall Peavy's Packard at the finish line. Anything involving motorized vehicles drew crowds and, when auto races at early Fairs proved the track more suitable for horses, automobiles began racing to and from Craig.

(Photo: Hayden Heritage Center)

Special entertainment often preceded or was incorporated in rodeo performances. The 1918 crowd was amazed to see Maud Tarrt ride broncs and steers, considered man's sport. Her first performance prompted chatter in the stands because she was thrown by both horse and steer, but she redeemed herself with successful rides the following two days. Jack Henderson also previewed future rodeo events by riding steers and demonstrating the art of steer wrestling.

Other special celebrations have included craft shows and tribal dancing by Ute Indians in 1918 and 1924; the Lakewood Westernaires' Precision Drill Team in 1983; Draft Horse Contests for halter and pulling classes, a favorite at early Fairs, was reinstated as a local draft horse pulling contest in 1981 and held sporadically until 1985 when the purse was increased and a calcutta added. The contest drew as many as 16 teams on Friday nights, moved to Sunday when a draft horse hitch event was added in 1989, but was dropped in favor of a variety of Sunday morning events in 1992.

Between 1989 and 1994, live Country-Western band performances brightened Friday nights. They followed in the tradition of town bands from Mt. Harris, Steamboat Springs, Craig and Steamboat Springs' American Legion Drum Corps. Other local favorites were directed by Joe Cuber (mid-1920s), Vernon Blevins (1952), Emmett Currans (1954) and regional favorites who entertain at the 4-H pre-sale barbecue.

1917's Blue Ribbon Story: A 24-year old, promised anonymity by a reporter, confessed that she and her boyfriend had such a wonderful time at the Fair that they borrowed a car, drove out in the country and roused a Justice of the Peace in order to get married.

JOHN MARSHALL loves root beer but he instigated wine judging at Colorado Fairs, first in Routt County in 1975 and, after Shirley Portouw hosted a wine tasting for County Agents throughout the state, at the State Fair in 1981. By the time the State Fair opened with 50 exhibitors, Routt County had 70. Today microbrews represent 33% of the local market and "baby boomers" are drinking less but more expensive wines and liquors.

Although the state permits judges to serve only two years, in order that they remain fresh, John lasted eight. He works very hard at ignoring exhibitors' names and scores in order not to prejudice his judging. "The looks, swirl and smell tell me everything I need to know. I drink very little, only to break a tie or make the final call, or as an excuse to eat more of the Grand Champion homemade bread." Superintendents at the Routt County Fair, where he presided over wine tasting until two years ago, cut the middle out of the bottom of "the best breads in the world" so he could clear his palate.

John grew up on a dairy farm in northern Wisconsin and started making wine while attending the University of Wisconsin in the late 1960s. He began working at the Bottleneck in 1973 and three years later bought it with his college classmate, Terry Hefty. Terry and he began making wine in college, from oak leaves and grass. Most of their beer blew up in the cellar but he still has a 1968 bottle of "not very good" wild grape, saved for a very special occasion.

According to John you can make wine from anything: berries, fruits, veggies, any food product, any red or white grapes. Champion winemakers must treat the product properly: pick the product at just the right time in order to maximize flavors and minimize spoilage. The process must be precise, sanitary, carefully controlled. "Doris Knott's wines," he says, "are very well made. Some of the best wines come out of Hayden because their growing season is longer and the fruit is more mature."

Demonstrations by Roger Culbreath's Border Collies, the Yampa Valley Carriage Association, the Team Penning Association and 4-H Vaulting Club have gained recent popularity. Hands-on events for children, introduced in 1992, bring hundreds of tykes too young for 4-H into the arena to Catch-A-Calf, Bunny or Greased Pig. Program expansions in 1994 included Mutton Bustin, an eight second sheep ride for small people; a Calf Scramble and Calf Riding for youngsters under 14; a Battle of the Bulls for jackpot bull riding; and a Ranch Woman's Contest. The following year the Blind Man Tractor Drive prompted laughs from blindfolded husbands attempting to navigate an obstacle course guided by oral instructions from their wives.

Three Routt County Fairs have included carnivals: 1916 featured a carousel, 1929 had a merry-go-round and ferris wheel, and in 1952 the Mid-West Carnival provided rides and games of skill and chance. Another novel event, held first in 1929 and again in 1940, was the Mine Safety Contest which tested the rescue and first aid skills of teams from local mines. The P-K Mine (Pinnacle-Kemmer) beat teams from the Moffat, Pinnacle, Haybro, Mt.Harris, Wadge and Bear River mines in 1929.

Trick riders and ropers who have enlivened the Fair include: Johnny Vance with Lola Burdette riding a trick horse (1930); Audrey Cozard-Williams, a former county resident, on her trained stallion Honorable Patches (1936);

George Hand and Anna Lee Mills (late 1930s); Don and Gene McLaughlin, seven- and nine-year old fancy ropers; and Connie and Tad Griffith (1980). Connie set the crowd abuzz when she crawled under her horse's belly and back up into the saddle while he was circling the arena at a run.

Elin Carns, 1987

Anna and Allen Lighthizer, 1989

WHO RUNS THE SHOW

THE ROUTT COUNTY FAIR ASSOCIATION INC. is an independent nonprofit organization incorporated on April 14, 1969 in order to:

Sponsor and conduct educational and recreational activities which promote agricultural and livestock exhibits, horse and cattle shows, fairs, rodeos, races and related activities which will enhance their appeal.

The Board of Directors consists of seven members, two from each commissioner district and one at large, appointed to staggered three-year terms by the Routt County Board of County Commissioners, and limited to nine-years of service. In 1995 the board was expanded to nine members with the addition of three at-large members.

The county owns the fairgrounds and annually appropriates funds to the Routt County Fair Association which conducts the fair and supervises all use  and maintenance of facilities for the county, which receives fair-related revenues. On November 18, 1993 the Internal Revenue Service granted the Routt County Fair Association, formerly exempt under the county's 509(a)(1), foundation status as a 501(c)(3) under an advance ruling which begins June 11, 1993 and ends December 31, 1997.

Routt County continues to serve as fiscal agent, and since 1984 all county income from state lottery funds is earmarked for grounds improvements. In 1995 the Fair board operated on a $61,000 budget generated by the county (76%), ticket sales (16%) and fees (8%).

The Routt County Fair Association is exclusively responsible for: (1) The Fair and rodeo, nine days culminating the third weekend in August; (2) Fair livestock and open exhibits; (3) maintaining Fair grounds and facilities; (4) non-fair use of the facilities which are rented to campers, hunters, churches and other private parties. Their job is to provide facilities for livestock exhibits and general exhibits; establish rules and regulations to conduct the Fair and govern its dates and length; supervise and maintain Fair staff, grounds and facilities; and oversee other uses of the grounds including the Exhibit Hall, arena, livestock barns and the baseball diamond.

The Routt County Fair Association is currently examining the feasibility of building a closed livestock pavilion. Their goal: to make the Fairgrounds a year-round facility where people, stock and machines can gather or compete; where Routt County residents can enjoy special events during a three-wire winter; where the grounds can be utilized 52 weeks a year regardless of weather. They are exploring the location, cost and type of building which will make this possible.

THE COLORADO STATE UNIVERSITY EXTENSION OFFICE was created in 1917 as an educational outreach service of State Land Grant Universities in order to:

Provide information and education to individuals, youth, families, agriculture enterprises and communities in the fields of agriculture, natural resources, economics and consumer sciences.

Cooperative Extension reflects the organization's "cooperative" relationship between the county, state and federal Department of Agriculture. At the courthouse it is affectionately known as "The Extension Office" and staffed by three state-funded positions: an Agricultural Agent (formerly County Agent), Consumer & Family Education Agent (formerly Home Demonstration Agent) and a 4-H/Youth Agent. Agents are ex-officio members of the Routt County Fair Association board of directors and have always played a major role in organizing 4-H programs and supervising the management and administration of the Fair. This took on increasing importance when adult livestock classes were dropped and those shows restricted to 4-H and FFA members.

THE 4-H COUNCIL/4-H CLUBS and FUTURE FARMERS OF AMERICA (FFA) are an integral component of the Routt County Fair, as the chapter on the history of 4-H in Routt County indicates.

OTHER FRIENDS AND NEIGHBORS

The Hayden Valley Roping Club devotes countless hours to building and maintaining pens and alleyways. The club was instrumental in installing lights, welding, painting and working the arena area.

The County Road Crew grades roads, runs backhoes and water trucks, sprays weeds hauls manure, and moves shade tarps and bleachers.

The Sheriff's Posse controls traffic, parking and security. Former Posse member Henry Dorr is well remembered for the many long nights he checked steers, returned lambs to pens and kept the all-night barbecue crew awake with fascinating stories.

The Hayden Lions Club sells tickets at the gate and grandstands, picks the theme and masterminds the parade.

Hayden High School Future Business Leaders Program students assist in paying premiums and compiling event results.

The American Legion hosts dances and the legendary Hamburger Stand, the only source of sustenance on the grounds from 1936 until 1992. The relationship began in 1919 when they held a special banquet for Routt County soldiers returning from the war. The banquet was attended by the Governor who "gave a rousing speech" and teams of veterans competed in a tug-of-war in which Sgt.Vannie Kitchens' outfit took the honors. The first event sponsored by the American Legion was a dance in the 1920s which has become an annual event.

(Photos: Hayden Heritage Center)

Hayden Rebekah Lodge #75, since the mid-1950s, has served a fried chicken dinner—complete with potato salad, sliced fresh tomatoes, homemade pie and beverage—after the Saturday Parade. Originally $2.50, 40 years later it costs only $5.25. Through the years these ladies have also provided meals for Fair judges, superintendents, clerks and other volunteers.

Hayden Chapter #99 of the Order of the Eastern Star prepared and served dinners at the Masonic Hall from 1971 to 1989. Those meals have been served at the Fairgrounds since the kitchen was installed in the Exhibit Hall, prepared first by Faye Meeks and then by Xi Delta Chi Sorority since 1992.

TURNING FRONTIER INTO HOMELAND

Honoring the county's pioneers and their accomplishments is an integral part of the Fair. Most early Fairs began with a Hayden Pioneer Day, first held in 1915. In 1916, these pioneers lined up in front of the grandstands for a classic picture, reproduced on the inside cover of this book.

The Pioneer Society turned the Fairgrounds into one of the area's first museums in 1923. The log building which housed the original county courthouse on the Walker Ranch at Hayden (1877-1878) was restored on the grounds, and the first threshing machine ever used in the valley was pulled in by Marion Yoast. They stood on the grounds as reminders of a pioneer heritage until the 1960s when the thresher was moved to the Hayden Heritage Center, and pieces of the old courthouse were painstaking labeled, disassembled and stored behind a local business until local preservationists could locate a new site for the building. When the business was remodeled, cleanup crews failed to realize the historic significance of the logs and they were burned.

Through the years the Fair has developed special activities to honor county pioneers among them: Color-coded badges indicating the number of years in residence (1929); antique displays in the old courthouse, (1940s); a Centennial Year Salute (1977); antique equipment display (1990); Pioneer Day Tribute at the 75th Anniversary Rodeo (1989); and a Salute to Century Ranches (1995).

Following is a list of Routt County pioneers who registered to prove up on land prior to the first Census in 1890. These are the first homesteaders. Proving up on the land required improving property during a six month occupancy for five consecutive years. Most of these families were instrumental in creating and supervising early Routt County Fairs, as purchasers of initial $1 stock certificates, as volunteers or as contestants and exhibitors. It is also interesting to note how many sites throughout the county still bear their names.

B.T. Shelton left (Photo: Hayden Heritage Center)

1860	Benjamin Long and wife
1870	Richard Clements
1870	James H. Crawford and family
1879	J.W. Whipple, D.W. Whipple and Samuel A. Reid
1880	E.A. Brooks and family
1881	C.R. Fiske, W.W. Adair and wife, E. Shelton and wife
1882	John W. Adair, W.N. Rose, J.M. Whetstone and wife, B. T. Shelton and wife, Horace Duquette and wife, J.L. Norvell
1883	A. McLachlan, William Shelton, Fred Akhurst and family, George Vail, Donald Taylor, David Taylor, Mary B.Crawford, F.E. Milner, W.E. Crowner, F.B. Ranney and wife, Jean Sturdevant, H.B. Peck and family, James Wadge and wife.
1884	Mrs. Cora Hull, Preston King and family, W.T. Laramore and wife, Mrs. J.F. McKinnis, Horace Hull, Henry Schaffnit, G.M. Haughey, Albert Squire and family
1885	Mrs. Douglas Lee and daughter, George Lee, Edward Myers and wife
1886	Alex Walker, W.M. Patton, W.S. McKinley, Mrs. E.S. McKinley, H.A. Monson, T.W. Monson and wife, Frank Arnold, C.W. Denny
1887	L.M.Long and wife, George E.H. Franz and wife, J.G. MacLaughlin, John Koll and wife, Dr. L.D.Campbell, J. Hitchens and wife, W.J. Cook
1886	Benjamin Shuster, J.E. Miles and wife, Elizabeth Schnauber, C.H. Leckenby and wife, John Geil, John A.Campbell, F.A. Metcalf, John Dunckley, C.F. Egry and wife, Mrs. Nora Templeton, Mrs. Sadie Shaw, Alva T. Monson, D.M.Chapman, F.W. Parkinson
1889	W.H.Tucker and wife, Marion Yoast, W.T. Teagarden, M.J.Rhodes, W.L. Yoast, Elizabeth A.Bartz, Josie Bartz, Myrtle A. Adams, J.C. Adams, Mrs. D.W. Whipple, W.H. Bashor and family, Ben Collins, W.H. Baer
1890	W.G. Jones, J.N. McWilliams, C.N. Mason, A.J. Leckenby and wife, Mrs. Mary W. Humphrey, Miss Belle Humphrey

B.T. Shelton at home in Hayden circa 1947 (Photo: Bob Temple)

ANNA SHELTON'S JELLY ROLL

From Anna Ralston Shelton, 1889 bride of B.T. Shelton, who contributed the "hefty" potatoes for the Railroad Day celebration. Mrs. Shelton, raised on a homestead on Round Bottom below Craig, died in 1956 at the age of 90.

5 eggs
2 teaspoons baking powder
1 teaspoon lemon extract
2/3cup sugar
1 cup flour

Separate eggs and beat yolks. Add sugar to yolks and beat again. Add flour, baking powder and lemon extract. Add stiffly beaten egg whites last. Bake at 375 degrees in large shallow, buttered pan for about 20-25 minutes or until done. Have cloth sprinkled with powdered sugar ready, and turn cake out upon it. Spread with any jelly and roll, using cloth. Leave wrapped until ready to eat.

31

TO HAYDEN FOR THE FAIR
By Frances M. Wheeler, 1994

Pigs a squealin', lambs a bleatin'
Steers a gruntin' with their cud.
Folks all busy cleanin' stalls
If it rained, a sloppin' mud.
The farmers and the gardeners
Bring the best of all their crops.
Cooks with canned and bakery goods,
Crews building display props.

Buckin' stock a millin'
Race horses chomp their bits,
A band is playing loudly
With all their latest hits.
People decorating floats,
Some sideshows cry their wares,
Judges walk around importantly
Ignoring anxious stares.

It has not changed a whole lot
In all these eighty years;
4-H has brought the youngsters,
Sale of pets sometimes brings tears.

They don't have as many races,
Most of the music's canned,
There are no country schools
To put up booths so grand.

The announcer has a sound truck,
Excitement fills the air
As friends a neighbors gather
At Hayden for the Fair.

From the 1994 80th Anniversary Book
published by the Hayden Heritage Center.

First Ladies of the Routt County Fair

Rachel Ann Keller, age 3, says she loves the "Counting Fair" because you can count the sheep, and cows and pigs. The ladies described here – Elaine Gay, Doris Knott, Bonnie Lighthizer, Linda Long, Helen Sherrod, Elinor Williams and Mary Dean Annand Wixson – count ribbons. They pride themselves in setting, achieving and maintaining standards of excellence and they have bouquets of rosettes and ribbons to attest to the skills they learned from their grandmothers and are sharing with grandchildren.

Bill and Elaine Gay

ELAINE GAY lives across the river from the Pleasant Valley ranch her husband's Swiss parents homesteaded in 1898. Bob Gay (1915-1994) died working the land that was his life, a folk hero continuing to feed with sled and team, opposing the development of Lake Catamount and radiating laughter and generosity. The sign on their porch door reflects that spirit: "Hurry back. May you always ride a good horse and eat good beef."

Elaine, who attended schools at Sidney and Mesa, shares her memories of 52-years of marriage and life on the Green Creek Ranch in "Cowpokes, Cowpies & Otherwise: Recipes of the Old West," a 1990 cookbook, and "How Pleasant Is the Valley," a history of area she published in 1996.

The cookbook is a smiling account of the foibles of hired men who have helped on their 2,000-acre spread. She says she never met one who wasn't hungry. Elaine is amused by romantic stories about cooking on coal stoves before electricity, and literary comparisons of stressed, modern mothers to their supposedly carefree, rocking-chair-bound grandmothers.

Because the Gays, their three children and hired men were frequently fencing loose hay well into September, her participation in the Fair was limited although her daughter, Roberta, became a Home Demonstration Agent. Two Fair entries remain vivid memories: one was fudge that was eaten before the judges appeared; the other was the following family favorite Grand Champion pie.

ELAINE GAY'S BANANA CREAM PIE

1/2 cup sugar	1 1/2 teaspoons vanilla
3 tablespoons flour	2 medium bananas, sliced
l tablespoon cornstarch	3 egg whites, at room temperature
1/4 teaspoon salt	1/4 teaspoon cream of tartar
2 cups milk	6 tablespoons sugar
3 egg yolks, slightly beaten	Baked pie shell
2 tablespoons butter or margarine	

Mix sugar, flour, cornstarch and salt. Fold this mixture into scalded milk in a double boiler. Stir while cooking over medium heat, until mixture begins to thicken. Beat some of hot mixture into beaten yolks and add remainder, stirring rapidly to prevent lumping. Return to low heat; cook another three minutes, stirring constantly (do not boil). Remove from heat; stir in butter and vanilla until butter is melted. This can also be done in a microwave. Fold in bananas, or slice bananas into the bottom of pie rather than folding them into the filling.

In a small bowl with mixer at high speed, beat egg whites and cream of tartar until foamy. Gradually add sugar, one tablespoon at a time, beating well after each addition until sugar is completely dissolved and whites are stiff but not dry. Preheat oven to 350. Pour filling into baked pie shell. Spread with meringue, sealing it well to the crust. Bake for 10 to 12 minutes until golden. Serves 8.

D ORIS KNOTT says she "really got into the Fair" when the wine competition began in 1975. She loves making and serving wines and she's good at it.

Doris and Dan Knott, 1986 Routt County Fair Marshals, became involved with the Fair back in 1928 when the Moffat Road brought in heifers and tied them to a fence and the kids drew numbers for their animals. Dan was one of the first 4-H members in Yampa.

Doris and Dan Knott, 1990

Dan says he "learned how to go broke with livestock at an early age." He paid $125 for his first heifer in October 1928, and by spring could have bought five for that price. According to Dan it took five years to pay for the heifer and it's been like that ever since. "The Fair teaches kids to win and lose, a darned good lesson because you can't be on top all of the time."

Now 77, Dan was one of the first members of the Fair Board, appointed by Frank Stetson in the days when the Fair had no sheds, corrals, water, or fence around the race track; the horse barns were barely standing; the grandstands were dilapidated; and no one understood how the Exhibit Hall could lean so far without falling over. "In those days a lot of elbows were bent pretty regular and someone was always bucking a horse down the sidewalk, but no one got too serious because you'd just have a fight on your hands."

"We sometimes had to tell the Commissioners how it was gonna' be," he smiles, "We told them to put the Fair on themselves if they were only giving us a $5,000 budget. We told County Attorney Bob Gleason he'd be putting it on alone if he failed to get the Routt County Fair Association Incorporated. Time, patience and perseverance are solvers of all things, it just seems to take more of 'em these days," he observes.

Dan is the only living founding member of the Routt County Woolgrowers Pool (a group he served from the 1950s until 1995) still in the sheep business, and the sole original member of the Routt County Woolgrowers Association (launched in 1965) who still raises sheep. He has run sheep and cows together for 50 years. "The college boys said it couldn't be done so I just send 'em out

back to see how it is done, he beams. "Ewes move faster than cattle and are picky eaters. They eat the best and the cows follow right along and clean up after them. So there is no waste."

The Knotts run 400 ewes and 100 head of cows. They have lived in Routt County 65 years and began feeding with a Thiakol this winter. Dan was schooled in Yampa and Phippsburg; Doris in Steamboat Springs. They raised two children on their Trout Creek Ranch, 12 miles southwest of Oak Creek, where they have lived since 1932. Both are veterans of 4-H livestock and homemaker projects: Arloa Carnahan who lives down the road and Bernard who manages the homeplace while wife Debbie teaches school in Yampa.

Doris became a 4-H leader in cooking and sewing in 1957, and still frets whether the four girls and three boys in her sewing club hold a grudge because she "made them rip when it wasn't perfect." In 1995 Doris took 32 blue ribbons in candy, pickles, bread, cookies, dried fruit and wine. "You can't do that if you aren't aiming for perfect," she grins, "I like a little friendly competition with the best of 'em."

34

DORIS KNOTT'S PECAN BRITTLE
"The best of everything I make"

2 cups pecans	1/2 teaspoon salt
1 cup white corn syrup	2 tablespoons butter
2 cups granulated sugar	2 teaspoons vanilla
1/2 cup water	1 1/2 teaspoon soda

Cook syrup, sugar, water and salt in a cast iron skillet, stirring constantly, adding pecans when it begins to boil. When mixture comes to a hard crack stage in cold water and turns amber in color, remove from stove and add butter, vanilla and soda. Cool on a cookie sheet. Raw Spanish peanuts can be substituted for pecans.

Bootlegging On Trout Creek

Routt County Fair was the first to hold a wine competition. It was launched at the 1975 Fair, picked up by Moffat County four or five years later and introduced at the Colorado State Fair in 1981.

Doris Knott relished early competition with Don Lorenz and Bob Gleason. She claims she "runs a wine factory," making as much as 40 gallons a summer: clover, dandelion, beet, kiwi, persimmon, even pea pod. Dan, her husband of 57 years, says the long and the short of it is, "Grandma is a bootlegger."

John Marshall judged the first competition at the State Fair and Doris, who doesn't drink wine, brought home the Best of Show ribbon. At that time it was illegal to transport any kind of alcoholic beverage, so it was no surprise when state law enforcement officers called the Extension Office to find out how Doris' wine got from Hayden to the State Fair. Shirley Portouw said she didn't have the faintest idea, it must have walked, and hung up on them.

According to Doris, getting a ribbon from Marshall is a real honor because he doesn't like sweet wines and the only way she could win was on "clarity." She got a kick out of watching him use the Grand Champion bread to clear his palate and still smiles about the days when the Hayden ladies would polish off the uncorked bottles.

Wine tasting out at the ranch has been the cause of several cars ending up in the borrow pit but no fatalities. Once, when a local packrat began stealing cakes of kitchen soap, the Knotts baited a trap with berry mash. Doris says there's a lesson for everyone in the fact that the rat could not be caught until the night he got drunk on chokecherry pulp.

DORIS KNOTT'S GRAND CHAMPION BERRY WINE

According to Doris this recipe is "outstanding" for chokecherry, raspberry and cherry wine and best made with wild berries which are more tart than "tame" berries." She picks and freezes wild berries one cup at a time until enough are accumulated. For boysenberry wine she adds three cut up lemons.

1 gallon berries	3 gallons boiling water
10 pounds cane sugar	1/2 yeast cake, dissolved in water

Cool the yeast water to room temperature and pour over berries in a crock. Let set 25 days, stirring every day. On the 26th day strain the berries and toss the pulp mash. Let set 10 days and run through a milk or coffee filter one or more times to assure clarity. Bottle but do not screw the lids on too tight as it still could be working. As soon as it finishes working tighten the lids.

BONNIE LIGHTHIZER says her kids knew they were going to eat casseroles and do the dishes when Fair came because she was there all the time. She spent 25 years at the grounds, supervising crafts or wine tasting, until demands for teaching textile painting and meeting orders for craft shows began to usurp her time.

Last year her 11-year old granddaughter Anna, who has been showing since she was eight, took a Grand Championship for peanut butter cookies. She is the fourth generation to grow up in Hayden.

Anna's great-grandmother, Pearl, was one of the first ladies in the valley to make whole wheat bread; and her great-grandfather, Samuel Lighthizer, ran the Hiway Bar and trained horses, among them the renowned racehorse Red Bird. Their boys, Dorsey and Leonard, raised registered Quarter Horses. Bonnie married Dorsey's son, Edwin, and their son Robin is president of the Routt County Fair Association.

Bonnie Lighthizer

Four of Bonnie's nine grandchildren live in Hayden and are active in the Fair. Her specialty, and source of dozens of Championship ribbons, is crafts: hand painted quilts and clothing, tablecloths and tea towels, cross-stitch, stuffed bears, and stick horses "to save my own brooms from riding away."

Bonnie misses the luncheons the Rebekahs held in honor of the Superintendents. She misses the "sampler" Doris Knott would bring to share tastes of all her wine entries with the ladies setting up the exhibits.

She still cans a lot of peaches and thinks a lot about the days when 50 cent and $1 premiums paid for next year's garden and some families took home $40. When home economics was taught in schools. When women did not work outside the home and preserved, salted and dried foods in order to feed their families. When people ate canned meat and the Exhibit Hall leaked.

"There's only one certainty about the Fair," she smiles, "It will rain. It can be a drought year and it may be a clear day, but it will rain on the Fair."

"Today's teenagers think the three food groups are take out, order in and frozen. I met a youngster recently who said she used Pillsbury and Duncan Hines but, she asked, what brand is Scratch?"

LINDA LONG gives real meaning to the word "roots." The Routt County Fair is an integral part of life for Linda and Dusty Long, as it was for their grandparents and is for their grandchildren. "We represent five generations of Grand Champion and blue ribbon winners," Linda smiles, "Each and every ribbon holds a special memory of family, hard work and accomplishment. It's part of our ranching heritage and we want to pass that heritage on to a sixth generation."

Linda has received Champion and Grand Champion ribbons in clothing, canning, crafts, baked products, flowers, needlework, embroidery, crocheting and quilting, vegetables and crops. The only field where she has not taken a ribbon is art.

Linda and Dusty Long

Linda is a professional homemaker and volunteer. She has been a 4-H Leader in clothing, crocheting, foods, forestry, snowmobiling, leathercraft and many special projects for 15 years; a Boy Scout Leader and a Routt County Fair Superintendent for 24 years; and a County Fair judge trained in clothing, canning, baked goods, needlecraft, quilting, vegetables, flowers and crafts for 16 years. She is currently serving her second term on the Routt County Fair Association Board.

Linda's great-grandfather, Logan Marshall, homesteaded outside of Yampa on September 17, 1894. Her grandfather, Lawrence "Doc" Marshall was the second of five sons, a bronc buster and self-trained vet. The loves of his life were a good horse, a good hunting camp, a good fishing hole and his family. He homesteaded on Sunnyside, later trading the place for the Finger Rock Ranch south of Yampa which he owned in part until his death in 1984.

Doc and his brothers ran a livery in Yampa, using the horses for outfitting, stage and mail routes, construction of the road over Gore Pass and guiding author Zane Grey on adventures described in "Mysterious Rider." Linda's grandmother, Eva Evans Marshall, was a fine horsewoman, seamstress and cook who left four children when she died young. Linda's mother, Marguerite, was the third of the four children raised by Doc's second wife, Lucy.

Lucy was an outstanding cook, canner and tailor who could do anything with a needle and thread. She shared those skills with Marguerite who married Glenn Glaze of Egeria Park. Glenn was one of the first riders for the Colorado Cattlemen's Association in Egeria Park in the 1930s. A life-long rancher, his love of carpentry was displayed in the home he built for Marguerite and their three children.

Dusty's grandparents were Lydia and Joseph Long, who homesteaded in Twentymile Park in 1911. Joe served as Routt County Commissioner from 1933-1944. Dusty's father John, the eighth of eleven children, was born and raised on the homestead. He married Edith "Toots" Nelson who was also from a ranching family in Twentymile Park. Toots, now 78, still lives on the Trout Creek ranch they bought in 1934.

Linda and Dusty met at the "Crossroads Dance" when they were 15. The Community Hall at the crossing of County Roads 27 and 29 was perched on the flats of the Trout Creek Ranch owned by Dusty's parents. The Miles Family Band came over from Morrison Creek, where they homesteaded in the 1890s, to play for the dance. Harriet Miles played the piano. Twenty-four years later Harriet's granddaughter, Kammy, married Dusty and Linda's son David.

David "Dusty" Long has been employed a the Edna Mine since 1972 when Linda and he moved to the family-owned Trout Creek Ranch. For the past eight years he has served as Mine Superintendent. The Longs raised two sons, David and Donald, and a small herd of registered Limousin cattle on the old home place, now known as the Lazy J Quarter Circle Ranch. David and Kammy share in the ranching operation with their children, Glenda, Joseph and Courtney who this year starts her first 4-H project. Donald, a carpenter, lives in New Mexico with his two children, Dustin and Kelly.

LINDA LONG'S RAISED POTATO DOUGHNUTS

2 cups milk, scalded
1 cup sugar
1/2 cup shortening
1 1/2 teaspoon salt
1 cup (not packed) mashed potatoes
1 1/2 package or 1 1/2 tablespoons dry yeast

1/4 cup warm water
1/2 teaspoon lemon extract
8 cups unsifted all-purpose flour
3 eggs, slightly beaten
1/2 teaspoon cinnamon

Combine milk, shortening, sugar and salt. Mix until shortening is almost melted. Add potatoes. Mix well. Dissolve yeast in the warm water. Stir yeast into milk mixture. Add eggs, lemon extract and cinnamon. Gradually add flour, working it in with hands. Dough will be sticky.

Place dough in covered greased bowl and let rise until double. Punch down dough and knead slightly. Pat or roll out dough on floured surface about 1/3 inch thick. Cut dough with cutter. Place rings on floured towel and cover with another towel. Let rise until double. Cook in deep fat fryer, about 375 degrees, turning each doughnut as it gets golden brown. Dip in cinnamon, sugar or glaze. For glaze: Beat until smooth 2 1/2 cups powdered sugar, 1/2 cup water, 2 tablespoons melted butter and 2 teaspoons vanilla.

Helen Sherrod's front yard
(Photo: Steamboat Springs Beautification Committee)

Helen Sherrod
Recipient of the Most Rosettes and Ribbons, 1947-1995
Fair Participant, 47 years
4-H Clothing Leader, 45 years
Fair Judge, 24 years
Make It Yourself With Wool Leader, 25 years
Colorado State Grange Sewing Leader, 5 years
Colorado Homemaker of the Year, 1964
Grand Marshal July 4th Parade, 1983
Grand Marshal Routt County Fair, 1992

1983

HELEN SHERROD may be the oldest person entering the Fair and she certainly has won a lion's share of Fair ribbons. In 1995 she brought home 37, "a little above average," including Overall Grand Championships (clothing) Grand Champion and Reserve Grand Champion (breads), six Champions, six Reserve Champions and fifteen blues.

As usual she exhibited in crafts, canning, vegetables, garments, flowers, cookies and breads, jams. "I never count and I usually return the ribbons to the Extension Office for recycling," says the county's most accomplished seamstress and upholsterer.

Helen seldom uses recipes, and takes the cookbook down maybe six times a year. She shares cooking tips with the authority of someone who was raised on a wheat farm in McDonald, Kansas, has canned for 65 years, and is used to serving three hot meals a day to six children and ranch hands. She cooked on a coal stove until 1957, the same year she got her first washing machine. She doesn't care what they say about cholesterol. She uses butter because it tastes better. She has always prided herself in being a professional homemaker and insisted on using only the very best ingredients.

Helen is the eldest of nine children in a family where "Papa could fix, Mama did everything and we all had chores." She met her husband of 48 years at a dance in McDonald and says that, because his girlfriend played the piano, she danced with Bill all night. They were married three years later, surviving in the windswept Depression. Helen remembers covering Doug's crib with wet sheets in order to protect him from the dust.

The Sherrod children, all active in 4-H, include Sandra Pflieger of Houston, a professional artist, and Jacquelyn Grimaldi, owner of travel agencies in Washington, D.C. The boys are Doug, a retired Navy Lt.Commander pilot; Duane, a plastic surgeon who lives surrounded by horses, sheep and small animals in the suburbs of Joplin; Don who, with wife Judy, runs the homeplace seven miles northwest of town on the Lower Elk; and Delbert who is the foreman of Forest Warren's spread on the Upper Elk and, with his wife Lynne, operates a parcel of the Sherrod Ranch.

After being widowed in 1982, Helen moved to a sun-filled home perched on four lots at Third and Pine Streets in Steamboat Springs, where she still sews, makes lye soap, gardens, cans and is surrounded by souvenirs of the days when she put by 15 bushels of fruit a year.

Helen began making clothes for her sisters at the age of 15; last year at 83, she designed a regal purple velvet riding habit for a granddaughter who shows horses in Missouri. In the years between she "made good seamstresses" out of members of her Rip-and-Stitch-It 4-H Club, who consistently took honors at state.

Her "sewing girls" often spent weekends and summers at the ranch constructing garments, suits and coats. Or she traveled to Hayden and Oak Creek to give adult tailoring classes similar to those she conducted in town. Helen beams with pride describing former students who include a teacher, fabric buyer, 4-H leaders and several who sent their husbands through college by taking in sewing. She remembers when 120 local girls studied sewing and modeling after the War and feels we're lucky to have 20 in the county today. One of them is a 17-year-old Dawn Underwood who recently took a Grand Champion and a blue in modeling and a fourth in construction at State.

HELEN SHERROD'S BUTTERSCOTCH ROLLS

"They are not going to taste exactly like mine," she says. "Because I use a handful of this and a smattering of that. I've been in the kitchen making the exact same thing with another cook and our batches just don't taste alike. But these are quite yummy no matter who makes 'em."

Rub the bottom of a loaf pan with butter. Sprinkle it with white and brown sugar, drizzle white Karo syrup and 3-4 tablespoons of whipping cream over the top, and cover with pecans. Make sweet dough. Roll it out and rub with butter. Sprinkle with sugar and cinnamon. Roll, cut into 1/2" wedges and place on the prepared pan. Bake at 350 for 35-40 minutes.

BREAD SPONGE
Cook two peeled medium potatoes with one quart water until mushy. Mash, cool and add flour until it makes a sponge. Let set 3-4 hours or overnight.

Elinor Williams
(Photo: Jill Montieth)

E'LINOR WILLIAMS never takes home fewer than a dozen ribbons and is thinking about making them into a quilt. She's been showing at the Fair since 1960, although she came into the country from the Southside of Chicago with her mother in 1953 at the age of 16. Today she has 17 grandchildren.

She lives in a log cabin at the end of a lane adjacent to the Carpenter Ranch, which her husband Mel managed for 38 years before it was purchased in 1995 by The Nature Conservancy. A gift from Rosamond Carpenter started Elinor's collection of button hooks. She still uses a 1961 Maytag Wringer, tends a 1,250 square-foot garden, and goes to Steamboat Springs only to buy stoneware mixing bowls at Art In the Park.

Although Mel's roots reach deep into history, he began collecting blue ribbons only after the Open Beef Division was launched in the 1980s. His mother's great-grandfather, Al Durham, homesteaded the land on Milk Creek where the Meeker Massacre took place in 1879 and, fortunately, his mother's great-grandfather was freighting between Meeker and Rawlins at the time of the attack. Mel grew up running a 35-head dairy herd and plans to retire running a 45-head cow/calf operation.

Elinor bakes bread for seven families. She always bakes on Thursday in a modest kitchen filled with classical music. She makes 60 one-pound loaves a month, weighing them to assure consistency. She starts at 6:30 in the morning, takes the loaves out of the oven at 1 and delivers them promptly at 3. She never makes more than six loaves at a time, white and lite rye and dinner rolls. The lady who ordered the whole wheat died.

"Anyone can buy a bread machine. That's not homemade bread," says Elinor who began using a mixer when her four children gave her one for Christmas several years ago. That's when she began using yeast instead of a starter, cutting production from twelve to six hours.

Elinor admits to a lot of disasters, lumps in the rye flour and "lousy cinnamon rolls" since she began baking as a 17- year-old bride 40 years ago. She attributes her rosettes to two "secrets:" a 1966 recipe from *Old Time News* which requires making a "foamy sponge" from flour, water and yeast; and using just a touch of brown sugar in the rye bread and Wixson's honey in the whole wheat.

ELINOR WILLIAMS' WHITE BREAD
(Two Loaves)

2 1/4 cups water	1/3 cup sugar
1 package dry yeast	2 cups white or unbleached flour

Mix well. Let rise for one hour and knead in:

2 tablespoons sugar	2 tablespoons salad oil
2 teaspoons salt	4 cups flour

Let rise 1 1/2 hours or until double in bulk. Punch down. Divide into two even size loaves and place in "Baker's Secret" pans. Let rise 1 hour or until double in bulk. Bake at 350 for 35 minutes.

Elinor sews, crochets, braids rugs or gardens while her bread is rising, and more than a dozen Grand Championships bear testimony to her skill in crafts and canning. Eleven years ago she was the Fair's Overall Grand Champion for a rag rug that brightens her living room.

"There's a difference between crafts and craftsmanship," says Elinor, who laments how little "real home arts" we see. "Real craftsmen do not use hot glue guns. Real homemakers can educate and provide for their families by relying upon God and the land." The Williams children did not participate in 4-H programs because their parents believe that Christian children should be taught at home, not by Extension Agents paid by state and county government funds. Living without a TV set also gave them more time to spend with their children.

Painting by Elinor (Photo: Jill Montieth)

Elinor and Mel Williams

Mary Dean Annand Wixson
(Photo: Jill Montieth)

MARY DEAN ANNAND WIXSON checked in crops for the Fair from 1952-1966. This year her grandchildren, Joel 12 and Heather 14, took rosettes in leatherwork. Her father-in-law Blaine (1884-1970) served as Superintendent of Crops for a dozen years before being elected first Grand Marshal of the Fair.

Like so many Hayden residents, Blaine worked for ranchers in summer and for the mines at Mt.Harris in winter. Mary married his son Harold, a game warden for 23 years, and still tends the chickens and bees Blaine raised in retirement. The alfalfa and clover honey, which boasts a Grand Champion ribbon, sells as Medicare Acres Honey.

Mary began exhibiting at the Fair in 1934 when she was in seventh grade. She holds Grand Championships in crocheting and knitting, a special ribbon in 1937 for judging canning, and a plaque for the most blue ribbons in vegetables in 1993.

Mary has never lived more than three miles from where she was born on an 80 acre tract east of Hayden, fronting a small remaining strip of old US 40, now County Road #69. Her father, George "Scotty" Annand (1880-1963) took care of the Shorthorns on the Cary Ranch before becoming a herdsman for Herefords at the Carpenter Ranch for 29 years. He loved good cattle and frequently showed at the Fair and Denver Stock Shows.

Mary was five when premiums were prizes from local merchants and her father won a coat with a fur collar for her. She remembers the late 20s when so many racehorses came to town for two days of novelty matches that they were put up in every barn in town. She remembers when the oversized vegetables were called "monstrosities" and Bill Epps received a ribbon for a giant zuke and a pumpkin which was carried into the Exhibit Hall by two men.

"You can grow a lot on a little patch if you pay attention," she says. "It's worth it because home canned just tastes better than bought. The reward was dressing up and taking it to Fair."

42

Citizens Of Consequence

Dedicating the Fair premium and classification book to a prominent citizen was the idea of Nick DeLuca, former Sheriff and Editor of the Hayden Valley Press. Through the years Fair books have memorialized 14 prominent citizens. As early records are fond of pointing out, these are "citizens of consequence who have won comfortable esteem from hard conditions by industry, sobriety and frugality." Their brief biographies in these pages merely suggest the scope of the contributions the following men have made to Northwest Colorado, Routt County and the Fair.

1993	Pat Mantle (1929-1992)
1992	Bill Green (1897-1979)
1991	John Charles (J.C.) Temple (1867-1950)
1989	Frank Squire (1890-1959)
1988	Si Dawson (1880-1917)
1987	Ferry Carpenter (1886-1980)
1986	Coke Roberds (1870-1960)
1983	Frank Stetson (1908-1983)
1982	Bill Sherrod (1911-1982)
1976	Henry Hindman (1902-1975)
	Kenneth Whiteman (1908-1975)
	Max Williams (1907-1976)
1975	Darwin Lockhart (1934-1975)

FARRINGTON (Ferry) REED CARPENTER

Ferry Carpenter came to Routt County with an undergraduate degree from Princeton and a law degree from Harvard. No one in Northwest Colorado seemed to care much about his credentials, least of all Ferry who had learned to love ranching as a teenager.

The son of a wealthy Chicago shoe manufacturer, Ferry was sent in ill health at age 13 to the Dawson Ranch in New Mexico. Working summers throughout his schooling, Ferry came to embrace the ranching lifestyle with a passion that never wavered. His impressive academic credentials and extensive knowledge of the law, Western range and water rights, coupled with experience and talent earned him respect as "Renaissance Man of the West."

Ferry followed the Dawsons to Routt County, filing a homestead claim in 1909 on 160 acres of government land near Hayden. After receiving his law degree at his father's insistence, he settled into the territory as a small town lawyer, cattle breeder, district attorney, government grazing official, stockyard salesman, representative to the state legislature, and community volunteer and fundraiser for numerous worthy causes.

Ferry and his school friend Jack White, who homesteaded nearby, began an innovative cattle breeding operation that made his registered Hereford herd the largest on Colorado's Western Slope and famous throughout the West. In 1919 Ferry married a local school teacher, Eunice Pleasant, who was an active partner in ranching operations until her death in 1954. The couple had three children. His second wife, Rosamond Perry, died in 1974.

Mel Williams, who began running the Carpenter Ranch in 1954, recalls his friend and employer fondly in a recent newspaper interview: "He was an eternal optimist and a great storyteller; he whistled all the time although he couldn't carry a tune." Williams remained at the Carpenter Ranch until its recent purchase from the family by The Nature Conservancy, which intends to continue long-established ranching practices and to develop innovative educational programs.

In December, 1980 Ferry Carpenter died at 94 while working on his memoirs. His autobiography, "Confessions of a Maverick," was published by the State Historical Society of Colorado in 1984. In the forward Marshall Sprague says: "The state of Colorado has had its fair share of strange and wonderful people but none of them matched Farrington Reed Carpenter in the length and depth of his Colorado experience...Through his long and turbulent career, Ferry's idea of heaven on earth was northwestern Colorado...(where) he gathered ideas which he used to expose the follies of life...Ferry made it a rule never to do anything the way he was expected to do it. And having done it in his own novel way, he was impatient to get along with something new."

SIRIA (Si) DAWSON

A life of adventure and accomplishment is the legacy of Si Dawson, a native New Mexican rancher who settled in the Yampa Valley at the turn of the century and became the founding breeder of the American Quarter Horse. Si's

life was closely intertwined with that of his good friend and horse business partner, Coke Roberds, going back to high school days together in Trinidad, Colorado.

Si was born near Cimarron, New Mexico on a huge family ranch. His daughter, Delphine Dawson Wilson says he was "born a horseman." His great-grandfather was Henry Clay. His father, John (J.B.) Barkley Dawson was a trail scout for Charles Goodnight and the first scout to trail a herd from Texas to Colorado: through Oklahoma and up the Arkansas River into Pueblo and Denver on what became known as "The Dawson Trail."

At the age of 12 Si lost his left hand in a roping accident, though it never stopped him from playing the violin or becoming an expert horseman. He married Lucy Ann McKean in New Mexico in 1896. Two years

(Photo: Delphine Dawson Wilson) later, during the Alaskan Gold Rush, he and his brothers took horses and sheep to the Yukon in a wild and eventually successful business adventure.

After the men returned from Alaska, Si's father bought a large ranch four miles east of Hayden and the family moved to Northwest Colorado. Si's daughter Delphine Dawson Wilson, now residing in California, was born on this ranch in 1903. In 1915 the Dawson ranches were sold to the Victor American Fuel Company and coal mines opened nearby, advanced by the coming of the railroad. While running cattle to and from Hahns Peak, Si would camp out in the deserted mine cabins.

When the Dawson ranches in the Yampa Valley were sold, Si moved to Albuquerque to work as a cattle appraiser for the Stockman's Guarantee and Loan Company. He later went down to Brazil to manage the Fazenda Morungava, a ranch owned by the Brazil Land and Cattle Company, reportedly "larger than the state of Connecticut." It was here that he died unexpectedly, at

44

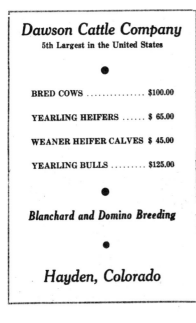
the age of 49, from a ruptured appendix.

Si Dawson was an outstanding cattleman and horseman and is credited with being a founder of the American Quarter Horse. His Champion Sire, Peter McCue, is related to nearly all registered Quarter Horses today. Si is honored in the American Quarter Horse Hall of Fame in Amarillo. According to family diaries, he sent his hired man with two mules, Jake and Judy, to Hayden to build the race track which was dedicated to him in the 1930s. For several years a silver cup was dedicated to the winner of the Si Dawson Race.

1935 Fair Book

WILLIAM S. (Bill) GREEN

Bill Green was born on the family homestead in the Williams Fork Valley on August 18, 1897 to Leon H. and Mary Green. They had come from Sterling, Colorado to file on land in 1895. Bill was raised on the ranch by his father and knew the rough life required to survive without the conveniences of the city. He learned the duties required to care for the land and operate a ranch so that it could provide for the family. He raised cattle, registered Quarter Horses, hogs, sheep, grain and hay.

Bill was educated in the schools on Williams Fork and in Illinois where he stayed with his Aunt Kit. His main love, however, was the ranch in Routt County. After his marriage to Elizabeth "Babe" Dorey they raised two sons, Leon and Raymond, and a daughter, Virginia.

Bill Green on Slippers, 1934 (Photo: Jerry Green)

As a young man Bill belonged to the Woodsmen of the World Lodge and participated in community plays at the Willow Creek Hall. He served as county road boss on the Williams Fork in the 20s and 30s, maintaining roads with an eight-horsepowered road grader. In later years he was a member of the Routt County Cattlemen's Association, the American Quarter Horse Association, the Democratic Party and the Hayden Valley Roping Club where he was a charter member. He was elected to four terms (1949-1956; 1961-1968) as a Routt County Commissioner.

Bill was always involved in the Routt County Fair. He competed in the rodeo in calf roping, team tying and stake races. He and his sons, who raced horses at various fairs, furnished stock for cow riding in 1940 and 1941. On more than one occasion Bill and Babe swept or whitewashed the entire grandstand prior to the Fair. He remained an active contributor to the Fair and ranch until his death in 1979.

HENRY HINDMAN

Henry Hindman, who was born in 1902 and raised on the family homestead on Grassy Creek near Twentymile Road, enjoyed working with horses all his life. He was well known for his abilities with horses and broke many of them for Coke Roberds. Throughout the years he was a big supporter of the Fair and race track in Hayden and volunteered many hours to maintaining the facilities there until his death in 1975.

Henry Hindman with Joker just before a race at the Fairgrounds sometime in the 1940s. (Photo: Joanna Sampson)

One of six children of Del and Cora Hindman, Henry began ranch work when he was only eight years old. As a teenager Henry worked for many family ranches in Dunkley Park. He attended school in Hayden and married his high school sweetheart, Helen Kuen in 1926.

During the early 1920s Henry worked for H.L. Jones at the Dawson Ranch near Hayden, and in 1925 began working for the Routt County Road and Bridge Department using a team of horses bought from Elmer Yoast. After the Depression, Henry returned to ranching and worked for Ralph Pitchforth for 12 years and at the Mt.Harris Coal Mine for three. He then returned to working on the county roads until his retirement in 1967.

Si (left) and Darwin Lockhart. (Photo: Jane Lockhart)

DARWIN LOCKHART

Darwin Lockhart was the son in Lockhart & Son. He was born on a dryland farm south of Ft. Collins and began speaking and auctioning about the same time. By the age of five he was advertising sales on the radio. For years their sale bills promoted "Your Sale Next."

In 1939 the family moved to Steamboat Springs where Si continued to build his auction business and Darwin graduated from high school in 1953. After graduating from the Reisch American School of Auctioneering in Mason City, Iowa, Darwin became a realtor and partner in the business, and married Wanda Jane Edmundson, a hellion from Baggs, Wyoming who clerked sales while raising four children.

46

Darwin rode the rodeo circuit in saddle bronc, announced rodeos and won cutter races throughout Colorado, Utah and Wyoming. He announced Junior Livestock Shows in 1949 and 1957, and began auctioning the Junior Livestock Sale at the Routt County Fair in 1959.

Conducting sales was a labor of love for Si, Darwin, his sister Cookie, who still runs Lockhart Auction and Realty in Steamboat Springs, and his son Bart, the only three-time winner of the Gelende World Championship. In 1974 the ring in the new Livestock Barn was named The Lockhart Arena, and in 1983 the Junior Livestock Sale Barn was renamed the Lockhart Building. Si's wife, Lois, died the day of the sale in 1975, the year the Fair Book was dedicated to Darwin.

Si Lockhart (1901-1989) loved selling the Grand Champion hog. He began auctioning in 1932 when, as he put it, "Roosevelt put the feedbag on me" and he started outfitting WPA loan recipients with harnesses, horses and cows so that they could operate on land they obtained through government loans. Si sometimes ran two sales a day when families, who could rent the land for three years, opted out of agriculture and dispersed. Si was a Western history buff and a superb story teller, and the thank-you letters he received from 4-H kids were his most cherished possessions.

PAT MANTLE

Pat Mantle was "a damn good cowboy." Everyone said so. The Northwest Colorado native was born on the family ranch in Hell's Canyon, now part of Dinosaur National Monument, in 1929 and died 62 years later while visiting friends in California. He was buried in the Browns Park Cemetery near his childhood home. Pat grew up with horses—the only mode of transportation on the remote family ranchlands—and became well known as a young roper and rider on the rodeo circuit.

(Photo: Rod Hanna)

As a teenager Pat helped drive 100 head of cattle from the ranch to Craig to be shipped to market on the Moffat Line. In later years his annual drives— pushing a herd of 1,000 saddle horses from their summer range near Craig to winter range in Browns Park—were much photographed and well attended by eager volunteers.

After graduating from high school in Craig Pat served in the Army, then returned to Routt County to marry Sue Woolley of Meeker in 1957. Two years later he began Sombrero Stables with his brother-in-law Rex Walker, first in Estes Park and later in Grand Lake, Boulder and Steamboat Springs. He also operated a hunting camp on the Williams Fork.

Pat wore his years of experience with a wiry, natural grace; his weathered good looks were much sought after by advertisers and filmmakers seeking to document the "cowboy image." But for Mantle, the cowboy life was his reality. His death was mourned by friends, family and many who saw him as part of the genuine West.

COKE ROBERDS

Born in Texas in 1890, Coke Roberds grew up on a horse and cattle ranch near Trinidad, Colorado. It was here that he met Si Dawson who became a lifelong friend and business partner. In 1898 Coke was working a ranch in Texas when he married a young woman named Beulah. The newlyweds moved to Western Oklahoma where he bought several Steel Dust mares with many attributes of an early Quarter Horse prized by Chicasaw Indians, and a thoroughbred racing stallion named Primero.

The dusty Oklahoma air continued to aggravate his asthma and, when his doctor in 1908 recommended moving to a high, dry climate, Coke began to look around the Yampa Valley. He bought a ranch near his friend Si Dawson, who also raised Quarter Horses and Thoroughbreds. In 1915, Dawson bought the legendary, aging Quarter Horse stallion Peter McCue and brought him to Hayden, and both men began breeding their mares. Soon thereafter Dawson left the Yampa Valley to work in Albuquerque and ranch in Brazil. When he died in 1919, his widow gave Peter McCue to Roberds.

Coke owned another Quarter Horse foundation stallion, Old Fred, discovered pulling a freight wagon in Northwest Colorado. "You could breed Old Fred to a draft mare and get the best work horse you ever hitched, and you could breed him to a race mare and get yourself a race horse," Coke said

(Photo: American Quarterhorse Association)

in a newspaper interview. Most of the Quarter Horse-type Palominos in the West today are descendants of Old Fred. Of this truly great sire, Coke observed, "A man can raise a good horse but only God can create a truly great one."

After Beulah died in the 1940s, Coke married a widow, Isa Smith, and lived in Hayden for many years until her death when he went to stay with his niece in Denver. He died in 1960 at the age of 90. Coke Roberds is honored in the American Quarter Horse Association Hall of Fame in Amarillo, at the Rodeo Hall of Champions in Colorado Springs, and at the Hayden Heritage Center as a founder of the American Quarter horse breed.

WILLARD (Bill) FRANK SHERROD

Bill Sherrod, the youngest and only boy in a family of six, was raised on a farm in Goodland, Kansas. He was born on June 22, 1911 and blessed with a ruddy smile, quick humor and a legendary ability to predict the severity of a Routt County winter by "reading" skunk cabbage leaves. The story that Bill could predict the depth of snowfall in an upcoming winter by the height of the summer skunk cabbage was born at the VFW Bar. When it was picked up and broadcast by the national press, he received orders for skunk cabbage seed from all over the country.

"You could hear his laugh everywhere in town," recalls his widow, Helen Sherrod. The Sherrod household was headquarters for her homemaking and Bill's livestock 4-H Clubs. According to Helen, "He had a way with children. He could get them working with no fuss. They

(Photo: Helen Sherrod)

respected him and loved sitting around our family dinner table and laughing about how the day went."

Bill completed his formal education at high school in Topeka, where he and

Helen moved when they were newlyweds. Bill worked $5-a-day jobs as a milkman, grocery and filling station clerk and she did alterations. Then they spent a year in Goodland where Bill ran a wheat farm for $1.50-a-day, and another year in Topeka where they lived in back of a cleaners. Bill ran the steam pressers, a trade he learned when he was 14 and his widowed mother moved the children 14 miles into town so they could attend school. Helen washed, pressed and ironed white shirts for ten cents each. Shortly after they returned to McDonald to herd sheep for Helen's folks, the neighboring farmhouse burned down and the Sherrods rented the property, complete with 14 milk cows and 60 laying hens.

"We were dirt poor," Helen recalls. But they paid for the cows and chickens with cream checks and egg money, borrowing family machinery to farm wheat. Because Bill liked ranching better than farming, after the 1946 harvest, they began searching for property around Denver, Grand Junction, Rifle and Meeker. Bill fell in love with Steamboat Springs and bought the Perry Clark Ranch on the Elk River Road when the old boys on the bench in front of the drug store told him it was available.

He ran cattle in Colorado and farmed wheat in Kansas, driving back and forth with the tractor for two years until the "Sherrod Place" was paid off. Bill Sherrod ran up to 200 head of Shorthorn cattle in Routt County until his death in 1982. His wife remembers how "particular" he was; the boys at the El Rancho remember his humor; and everyone remembers him as one of the best grain farmers in Routt County.

FRANK SQUIRE

F rank Squire was the eldest son of Albert and Mina Squire and raised on the Morgan Bottom homestead northeast of Hayden where they settled after leaving Devonshire, England in 1872. Frank was born there in 1890, the sixth child and eldest son of twelve children.

Frank pioneered innovative ranching in Northwest Colorado. He was one of the first to prove that sheep and cattle could be raised on the same property, that it was economically viable to raise Herefords and good horses and that educating children was essential to the survival of the family farm.

Frank, with his brother Rube, worked as a right-hand-man for James L. Norvell from whom he bought the "Denison Place" or Duquette Ranch in 1917. He was an expert horseman and roper, competed in many rodeos and served as State Brand Inspector for 20 years. He also owned General Pershing, a powerful gray-white bucking horse who became a rodeo legend in Northwest Colorado.

Frank married Annie Cullen, daughter of prominent homesteaders and an accomplished horsewoman, who helped train their string of champion relay horses. Annie was one of the first women in Northwest Colorado to race horses in local rodeos. Annie and Frank, who purchased the Maxwell Building at the corner of 9th and Lincoln, in Steamboat Springs, lived above the drug store and post office after 1944, when they retired from the ranch, until Annie was struck by an automobile a block away and died in 1964. Their apartment is still occupied by their grandson Frank. The building was placed on the National Register of Historic Places in 1995.

(Photo: Margaret Hogue)

The Hogue Ranch is currently operated by the fourth generation of Squires, grandson Michael Hogue and his wife Maureen. It is noted for an outstanding annual hay crop, the bloodlines of its registered Red Angus cattle and an annual Rocky Mountain Oyster Fry.

49

FRANK STETSON

Frank Stetson was born on a ranch in Taos, New Mexico in 1908 and came to Moffat County as a youngster. The Stetson family ranched on land near Bears Ears, and Frank graduated from high school in Craig.

As a young man he worked every kind of ranch job, including a stint for Coke Roberds. In 1931 he married Lucienne and the couple raised three children on their own ranch on the Yampa River east of Oak Creek. Lucienne still lives on the ranch, now run by family members.

In addition to raising cattle, Frank was involved in the sheep industry. Always active in community affairs, he served on the school board and later became County Commissioner, a position he held for 24 years (1949-1972). During his tenure many major improvements were made to the Routt County Fairgrounds. Bobby Robinson says "Old Frank Stetson was a tough, a fine man, a good bronc rider and one of the prettiest ropers there ever was."

Robinson is fond of telling how, back in the 70s, County Commissioners Ed Moore from Hayden and Andy McDermott from Steamboat Springs suggested moving the Routt County Fair to Steamboat Springs. He says Stetson made it quite clear, "They'll have to whip me till I can't get off the floor if they ever mention it again." No one ever did.

The 1983 Fair book dedicated to Frank describes him as "a respected community leader, County Commissioner, livestock man, Fair supporter and friend of 4-H." Like his friends, it hails him as "an active contributor to the quality of life in Routt County."

(Photo: Bob Temple)

JOHN CHARLES (J.C.) TEMPLE

Charlie Temple came to Northwest Colorado as a 14-year-old ranch hand, driving his uncles' cattle to Maybell where he worked for several years on their ranches. He was a son of Scottish immigrants attracted to Colorado by "gold fever."

Although born in Blackhawk, Colorado in 1867, Charlie grew up in Colfax County, New Mexico where he was acquainted with "Billy the Kid" and Pat Garrett. He was fond of telling a story about another notorious outlaw he knew from his ranching days in Brown's Park. When asked whether Butch Cassidy ever stole any of his horses, Temple explained, "He never stole any. Borrowed a few and never returned 'em. But never stole any."

In 1891, Charlie bought ranch land west and south of Hayden. Four years later he married Daisy Dowden, a native Coloradan, and they had six children: Reid, Laura, Frank, Dora, Milton and Maynard. Following Daisy's premature death, he married a local school teacher, Melva Day, who remained with him until her death in 1935.

J.C. Temple was always proud of being a cattleman from Hayden and lay claim to being the first cowman from Routt County to ship cattle on the railroad from Wolcott to Denver over Corona Pass. He raised purebred Shorthorn bulls prior to switching to purebred Herefords. He was also instrumental in the formation of the Colorado Stock Growers Association and remained active in that organization until his death in 1950.

Frank's son Bob, who now lives in Winter Park, is related to the Routt County Fair on his mother's side of the family as well. His mother's grandfather was Ezekiel Shelton, one of the first homesteaders in the valley and founder of the Congregational Church at Hayden. Her father, Byron (B.T.) Shelton, was the first secretary of the Routt County Fair; he raised hay and cattle on a ranch two miles east of Hayden, serving as Hayden's mayor and postmaster and organizing the Yampa Valley Bank.

Bob Temple describes the Routt County Fair's special place in the memories of his family in the Fair's 75th Anniversary Program, published by the Hayden Heritage Center, in 1989:

"It was the time when you'd see people from Twentymile, Williams Fork, Breeze Basin, Morgan Bottom, Elk Head and the areas of the country to the east and south that you'd seldom see through the year...It came at a bad time of year for those still haying or cutting grain but most of us could find time even if it meant "shutting down" for a day or two! And, believe it or not, the Almighty usually made it easier by having heavy thunder storms during the Fair. 'Couldn't have hayed or cut grass anyway.' Those heavy rains lasted about half an hour, always right in the middle of "head and heelin'!"

GEORGE KENNETH WHITEMAN

The Routt Fair was the highlight of every year for Kenneth who served on the board of directors for many years. He enjoyed the kids and their projects, encouraged many of them to participate and worked closely with the 4-H program in Routt and Moffat Counties. He was a strong supporter of Junior Livestock Sales in both counties and believed that kids and animals were a positive combination.

Kenneth was born in Hayden in 1908, the oldest child of Olive and Clayton Whiteman. At the age of 15 he moved with the family to California where he graduated from high school. After attending the University of Colorado at Boulder and returning to Hayden to work, he married Berenice Meeker in 1933.

Kenneth Whiteman at the Junior Livestock Sale in the early 1970s (Photo: Larry Whiteman)

The Whitemans spent a brief period in California and in 1937 returned to Hayden to ranch in the Breeze Basin area. To supplement ranching, his life's ambition, Kenneth served as a field representative for the Rifle Production Credit Association for 35 years until his death in 1975. He was highly respected as an agricultural banker and made many close friends throughout Northwest Colorado.

In 1947 the Whitemans traded for the Lower Cary and Kleckner Ranches west of Hayden, along US 40, where their Whiteman Hereford operation produced registered and commercial cattle. The commercial operation was expanded to summer rangeland acquired in Wyoming in the early 1960s and the ranching operation continued until it was sold in 1972.

MAX WILLIAMS

Max Williams came to Northwest Colorado to rodeo during the late 1920s. While working as a hand at the Durham Ranch on Waddle Creek, he met and married Dorothy Durham. Before they began a family, which eventually included six children, the couple worked together breaking horses. A newspaper article described the process: "Max would take the rough off while Dorothy would rein them."

(Photo:
Dorothy Williams)

Max worked at many different jobs during the Depression, including feeding cattle on various ranches in the area, helping build a bridge across the Williams Fork and a stint at the oil refinery in Craig. In 1940 he settled with his family on the lower Cary Ranch near Hayden. A spark from a passing train caused a fire on the property that burned their house to the ground. In 1948 the family bought a ranch just west of Ferry Carpenter's property and members of the Hayden Roping Club helped them move to their new quarters in less than a day.

Max always enjoyed roping and won numerous competitions throughout the area in related events, often winning money but always having fun. In a newspaper interview, Dorothy recalled that one year Max was roping in the July 4th rodeo at Steamboat Springs. There were no shoes for his three little boys so Dorothy and the children stayed home. "Well Max won on the 4th and used the money to buy shoes for the boys so the family could all go and watch him rope again on the 5th. He won that day too."

Max and Dorothy remained on their ranch until 1965 when they bought a house in Hayden on Washington Street. Max worked for Colorado Ute for several years and then at the courthouse in Craig. He was working as a caretaker for the Routt County Fairgrounds when he died on March 31, 1976, 69 years after his birthday on March 30, 1907.

Friends of the Fair

The enthusiasm and generosity of Routt County Fair superintendents, exhibitors, parents, children and visitors is, according to Fair Board President Robin Lighthizer, one of the reasons our Fair is thriving at a time many counties are struggling to keep the tradition alive. The Fair has been enriched by a "hands on" board which actively designs educational and recreational exhibits and competition and an enormously supportive Board of County Commissioners.

County Agent Bill Culbertson remembers the Commissioners telling him "Whatever Home Agent Jean Chandler and the ladies want, they get, regardless of the budget. They even plowed open the road to Twentymile School so Calla Appel, Billy Appel's mother, could hold a program." That was in 1952. In 1989 another group of commissioners earmarked all county income from Colorado lottery funds for Fairground maintenance and improvements.

Everyone loves the Fair and has a story to tell:

• *Val Gary had been married a month and had never cooked oatmeal, when her husband suggested she the enter the Fair. She bought a bushel of peaches and made one jar of jam. "I didn't know what I was doing. His Mom made jam and I was trying to be like his Mom," says Val. She won the Grand Championship and is now a member of "We B Jammin," a cooking clatch which always enters "something tasty."*

• *After all the folderall about paying a Seattle artist big bucks to erect the Steamboat Springs Art Council's first art-in-public places sculpture, Sureva Towler and cabinetmaker Bob Moore put a cowpie in a mahogany frame, labeled it Art In Public Places #2 and took a blue ribbon in Mixed Media.*

• *Fair Board President George Simonton fell through the floor in the old Exhibit Hall loft after a heavy rain.*

• *When the Horse Show judge failed to show up, County Attorney Bob Gleason located him in the County Jail and bailed him out just long enough to assure that 4-H kids were not disappointed.*

• *Seth Copeland rode the sheep in the Mutton Bustin' contest until it got tired and lay down.*

• *Beth Sundberg is remembered for being the last one through the Exhibit Hall doors with her fresh cut flowers.*

• *Ida Booco remembers standing in the ditch helping her husband repair a broken water line in front of the steer sheds.*

No one quite remembers what year these things happened. No one really cares. Because everyone and his cousin and his dog has a story about sweeping the grandstands, competing for a trophy or sharing a caper. The special friends described here are among many who have made unique long-term contributions to the Fair.

GEORGE D. COOK (1892-1960) served as a member of the Routt County Fair Board and Director of Sports for rodeos for 24 years between 1935 and 1959. He was also president of the Western Slope Rodeo Association, a position he used to bring in talented competitors. For more than 30 years he was chairman of the Steamboat Springs Cowboys Roundup and readily admitted that putting together rodeo programs was his favorite pastime.

Cook came to Routt County from Denver with his parents when he was 18 and left only to serve in the 78th Infantry Division in France during World War I. He married Verna Gear in 1919, soon after the Armistice was signed, and they had four children, none of whom remained on the family ranch in the Sidney area.

He was a charter and active member of American Legion Leo Hill Post No. 44. He also helped organize the Yampa Valley Electric Association, serving as its treasurer in 1949. His death from a heart attack in 1960 was mourned by race horse owners, bronc riders, calf ropers and rodeo participants throughout Colorado and Wyoming.

(Photo: Norma Gilroy)

1983

HOWARD ELLIOTT, a Routt County banker for more than 30 years, served as secretary of the Routt County Cattlemens Association for 10 years, and was long-time treasurer of both the Routt County 4-H Foundation and Routt County Wool Pool. His level of expertise in agricultural lending would be extraordinary even by today's standards.

Born in Oklahoma, Howard was raised on a farm in Kansas, and when he went off to college at Kansas State University in Manhattan, he decided to major in agricultural economics. It was 1939, the end of the decade of the Great Depression, when he began working in Ness County, Kansas as a supervisor for the Farm Security Administration, now the Farm Home Administration.

Howard was transferred by the FSA in 1942 to Colorado Springs, and a year later, to Steamboat Springs, bringing his young wife Maxine, whom he had met while in school in Manhattan. Howard continued to work for the FSA in his office in the Annex across from the courthouse, until 1947, when he was invited to join Routt County National Bank as an agricultural field man, appraising and inspecting ranches on which the bank held loans. Through the years he continued to rise in the ranks of the banking industry, retiring from Routt County National Bank in 1977 as a senior vice president and director.

Howard and his wife Maxine headed the computations committee for Winter Carnival for many years. He also was a member of the boards of the Chamber of Commerce, United Methodist Church, the Steamboat Springs Cemetery District, and the Routt Memorial Hospital. Maxine worked for many years for the Yampa Valley Electric Association. Howard and Maxine, both of whom died in 1996, raised two sons. Both boys were Olympic skiers: Jere, now a businessman in Colorado Springs, on the 1968 Alpine Team; and Jon, who designs cross-country trails in Montana, on the 1960 Jumping Team.

BILL GAY is the only Routt County Quarter Horse breeder sustaining the foundation line established by Dawson, Roberds, Peavy, Semotans, Stetson, Lighthizer and his father, Bob Gay. His 20-year-old brood mare out of Spanish Cashier, a daughter of Spanish Cash out of Lassie Gay, is the closest living descendant by Champagne, bred by Roberds. "It all ties together," he says. "It's our heritage and no realtor can put a dollar value on it."

"This valley produced two great teams which complimented each other, ironically, on the same land five miles east of Hayden. In the 1920s Si Dawson owned the land and Coke Roberds was the horseman he partnered with to produce foundation stock that became the American Quarter Horse. In the 1960s Ferry Carpenter owned the land and Mel Williams was the herdsman he teamed up with to breed the greatest herd of maternal giants in the Hereford breed."

Bill says Routt County breeders raised horses to fulfill a purpose. "They bred real horses. Now it's show and glow. Horses have no useful purpose. Their breeders are Rexall Wranglers. They have more money than Drugstore Cowboys but, like them, have never been dirty a day in their lives. Horse breeding has become razzmatazz showbiz, so we've pretty much quit it in this country."

The Gay Ranch is still in the horse business because, as Bill explains, "We are still in the cattle business and horses are an integral part of our ranching operation." Geldings produced on Gay's ranch have carried cowboys to the PCRA pay window from Madison Square Garden to the Cow Palace in San Francisco. Their Quarter Horses have been sold and shipped from coast to coast.

(Photo: Jill Montieth)

Gay left the Pleasant Valley Ranch where he was raised to obtain a degree in Agricultural Journalism at Colorado State University in 1969, the only one of 4,500 students awarded the degree that year. Like so many local youngsters, he was born in the Band Room, of a building which successively housed the Colorado Apartments, Dr.Willett's Clinic, high school music classes, and now the 7th Street Players.

He rode horseback to the Pleasant Valley grade school his Dad attended. When the building fell into disrepair 30 years ago, the Gays mounted it on a sled and pushed it down the frozen river to their ranch where it is used as a storage shed. Like his father, Bill attended Steamboat Springs High School and, after a stint as a foreign exchange student in the Philippines, toured Europe promoting the Marlboro Man for Philip Morris International. "It's not that I condone smoking," he grins, "I was the only one they could find who could drive a four-horse team."

In 1980 Gay moved to Petaluma, California to develop land trusts and draft conservation easements for the Trust for Public Lands. He spent the first half of the 1980s designing long-term programs to preserve productive agricultural land, wildlife habitat and open space, and wrote the first agricultural conservation easement in Colorado for the Carl Kleckner Ranch near Pagosa Springs. Unlike the 20 brood mares he took with him to California, Bill had no problem adjusting to the return to the ranch on a cold November morning in 1985.

Long-time 4-H advocate Bill Gay shared these thoughts in a 1995 *Routt County Livestock News:*

4-H is a life-long experience. It is rewarding to share Fair, Achievement Day and the Junior Livestock Sale with multi-generational 4-H families. What fun to visit with proud grandparents watching from the stands, help mom and dad worry about whether the "kids" are old enough to do "all the things they are doing" and watch 4-Hers survive quite nicely in spite of all the unsolicited advice, instructions, and coaching from the "grown ups."

Many of us began our 4-H experience through projects. A baby lamb, a little bunny or a bum calf grabbed our childhood want for such companionship. Thus began an education, from responsibility to bookkeeping.

4-H is an ever expanding experience. project participation lends itself to competition at the local, state, and national level as well as subject-related team competition. This groundwork made it possible for many of us "country bumpkins" to participate in activities from collegiate judging teams to international studies through the IFY program.

Yet in the final analysis it has been the opportunity to be involved with 4-H youngsters and this community that has brought me the greatest enjoyment. At the same time, it has given me a chance to put back just a little of what volunteer leaders, CSU Extension personnel, junior livestock purchasers, and friends of 4-H made possible for me. Working with 4-H youth helps us all stay 4-ever younger. Thank you Routt County for inviting me along.

1987

ERNEST GRAHAM had very special powers: He could make things grow. He grew so many varieties of vegetables and flowers in his garden on Butcher Knife Creek that Fair Superintendents were frequently forced to expand exhibitor classifications. "We've got everything that grows, you better believe it," Ernie said of his Eden, "Don't believe the people who say you can't grow tomatoes in Routt County," he told a visitor, gesturing to a single plant laden with 40, you better believe it, tomatoes.

Ernie was born in Tennessee and spent 50 years laboring among his prize-winning garlic, berries, potatoes and onions in Strawberry Park before he died in 1988 at the age of 81. He received a Green Thumb Award for the most blue ribbons for several years running and spent hours arranging them on a piece of cardboard.

On a summer tour he'd share stories about the history and habits of every plant: Grape Hyacinths, Devil in the Bush, Canterberry Bells, Ozark Beauties, Massadonias and countless types of daisies, some of them waist-high. Despite painful arthritis, Ernie grinned as he tiptoed through his flowers. The voice from under the floppy crushed beige hat, decorated with fish hooks, was low.

"There's 500 daffodils in that run, you better believe it. I got too much to do around here to rest one minute. Those Golden Glows make me mad they come up so fast. No, you can't say I favor one more than another. See that red leaf with the yellow bloom, that's wild spinach. The Black Pansies are special too, cost $1.40 for just 12 seeds."

Ernie bought most of his seed from the G. W. Parks Company in Pennsylvania but his goal was to produce all of his own. His sister Daisy, only surviving widow of a Civil War veteran, made jelly from currants and wild rosebuds while Ernie set out strawberry plants. For many years they produced traditional strawberry barrels, stuffing seeds in holes in earth-filled barrels which "yield enough berries for a whole lot of people for a whole lot of summer."

Through the years Ernie worked as a cook at the Harbor Hotel, in the coal mines and at construction. He sold his house plants at Boy's Market and stocked the local restaurants with a wide variety of greenery. He was quick to share medicine plants, Christmas cactus and advice – everything but his breeding stock.

"Copper and brass pots kill plants so cover their insides with paraffin. The other killers are paint, fly spray and natural gas, you better believe it. The hot days are good but the cool nights are not. But if you water a plant once a week and keep it out of the way of mice, it'll do OK."

Everyone in Routt County agreed that Ernie could grow anything and the vegetable patch, beyond the sweet peas clogging his front door, contained "everything that grows." Six geese and two peacocks patrolled the two golden willows in the front yard, defined by a wild variety of fencing which kept his garden from falling into the Strawberry Park Road.

Ernie drove a beat up little jeep with flapping plywood doors and always came to town to pick up the newspaper, mail and slop for the pigs on Wednesday afternoon. "We've never had any trouble from nobody, not rabbits, not people flogging around. This is good land," he confided, "You can make anything grow here, you better believe it."

BILLY GRAVES loved the Routt County Fair. He attended every one of them from 1914 until his death in 1970. He was a "fixture" in Hayden and it was not uncommon to see him walking the three miles from his home on the E.C.Signs farm, now the Yampa Valley Regional Airport, into town with a gunny sack for his purchases.

William E. "Billy" Graves was born in 1884 in Cove, Arkansas on a farm from which his 90-year-old mother later wrote, "I am thinking of giving up farming as my mule is getting too old and I do not think I am able to break in a new one." His schooling ended at the age of 12 when his father died.

He came to Routt County in October 1909 and worked for Ed Smith at the Pilot Knob Sawmill and for Dr. D.K. Detwiller near the Williams Fork Valley. He took up his own homestead in 1911, selling it to the Preece Brothers in 1953. He never married and never drove a "gas powered" vehicle.

Billy raised sheep, hay and potatoes and always had a large garden from which he canned all the produce, even radishes. While selling potatoes door-to-door in Mt. Harris in 1918, he observed, "At three cents a pound, a fellow really earns his money." Although a small man he was an excellent hay stacker and known as a "good hand." He worked for area ranchers, the Omholt-Johnson and Beale Sawmills, and the Cozad Coal Mine on Dry Creek.

1977

$\mathbb{S}$AM HASLEM was born in Vernal in 1930. a survivor of the Depression, poverty, drought and Mormon crickets. His family wintered Hereford cattle on the desert below Jensen, Utah and summered them on Blue Mountain. He attended first grade at the Mantle Ranch School, taught by his mother, in a single room built from logs on three sides and by the canyon wall on the fourth. His classmates were Pat Mantle and Charles "Potch" Mantle.

His mother Ruth had been a Congregational missionary abroad and had taught school on the west coast of Smyrna, now Turkey. His father Joe (1895-1987), a World War I veteran and charter member of the American Legion, grew up ranching without a tractor or electricity, carrying water from the Green River by horse and sled. The family took great pride in buying an $11 Montgomery Ward radio in order to listen to news during World War II. According to Sam life was quite simple, "If we didn't have the money for something we went without it."

Sam carried this heritage into college at Colorado State University's School of Animal Husbandry, and through his years in an Air Force B-36 Squadron. He joined the Colorado State Extension Office in March 1955 and retired from it 32 years later. He served a three-year term as CSU's State Sheep and Wool Superintendent and has been a pilot since the age of 16, flying ambulance flights. Sam became the Routt County Extension Director in 1970 and in 1987 left the courthouse to spend time at home in Hayden, with his wife Louise. They purchased the Haslem homeranch at Jensen.

It takes at least two tons of hay to keep a cow in this valley, Sam explains, "It's very expensive. So if you want to succeed, you've got to do a very good job." He laments Routt County's special obstacles: distance from the markets; severe climate; the need to import corn and grain in order to fatten livestock; and new land owners who don't know that pretty blue and yellow flowers may well be noxious weeds.

"We used to say that what we're doing in Northwest Colorado is merchandising grass. The cheapest way to sell it and get it out of here is in a four-footed animal...it's the only way to beat the soaring cost of machinery, debt loads, interest rates and depreciation schedules."

Sam is renowned for his energy, laughter and optimism. He'll interrupt himself to make the call to get the answer right now. He is never too rushed to tell a story on himself, on a friend or on a county commissioner. "When I came to Routt County, I had just done my masters in Animal Science, with a lot of emphasis on meat science, so Joe Rossi and I had some real strong arguments about the merits of a carcass contest at the Fair, but we are still friends. "

"My greatest accomplishment was helping get water lines to the Fairgrounds in the 1970s. The kids were washing calves with ditch water loaded with effluent from Red Steffens' septic tank...That might have been what put such a shine on 'em."

Sam beams describing other "favorite" projects: starting Wine and Carcass Contests; hosting workshops; building the Exhibit Hall, Lockhart Sales Arena, restrooms and showers; getting electricity on to the Fairgrounds and the County Shop off of it and, always, working with 4-H kids. He donated the seed for the Fairgrounds' first lawns, and helped build the new chain link fence on the north side of the grounds. He remembers how hard the Fair board tried to convince the County Commissioners that hog pens were essential to the Fair and how, failing to make the point, they simply bought them with the year-end fund balance.

"We have the best 4-H Program in the state," says Sam, "Always have had."

SHIRLEY PORTOUW, in a lifetime of assisting women and families through education, most frequently focused on the practical realities of teaching children to take care of themselves: "As soon a child learns to walk and talk, he or she should be made to be responsible," she told a newspaper reporter during her longtime career as home economist, including 12 years with the Routt County Extension Service. "You don't want to end up," she said, "with any 25-year-old crybabies."

She practiced what she preached with her own three children, making them learn to do things at an early age. "The more things you learn, the better prepared you are to get along in the world." Although this advice from Shirley was given well over a decade ago, it may be even more appropriate today. Her advice to women just starting their careers then: "Work hard, learn as much as you can about your chosen field, and be prepared for the prejudices of the 'real world.'"

The information Shirley has doled out through the years could fill volumes – how to make jam, mend a camping tent or sew a man's workshirt. She was widely proclaimed for increasing the number of exhibits at the Fair, outstanding upholstery classes and extraordinary sourdough starter. In fact, how to make sourdough bread in high altitudes was subject of one of many booklets Shirley authored for the Colorado Extension Service.

1985

Raised on a ranch in Eastern Oregon, Shirley often attended meetings for country extension officers as a child. After graduation from Oregon State University, she went to work as a home economist. Over the next decade, Shirley moved with her husband to Tucson, where she obtained a master's degree in clothing and textiles from the University of Arizona and gave birth to the couple's three sons. The family then moved to New Jersey for four years, but they missed the Western lifestyle.

When the opportunity for Shirley to become extension specialist for Routt County was offered in 1972, the entire family moved to Steamboat Springs, her husband Wally giving up his engineering job in New Jersey to serve as Steamboat Springs' favorite Animal Control Officer. Over the years Shirley has practiced just about everything she has ever taught to her constituents, emphasizing the importance of continuing education, especially for women. As she confided to a newspaper reporter: "This job is always a continuous education for me!"

Each move brought new challenges and opportunities for Shirley and she in turn shared her extensive knowledge with thousands of Colorado residents. In 1986 Shirley accepted a position as director of the Grand County Cooperative Extension Service, headquartered in Kremmling, where she worked until retiring in Colorado Springs in July 1991. "Retirement" involves a busy schedule teaching how to use breadmaking machines.

BOBBY (R.N.) ROBINSON SR. presided over the barbecue at the Routt County Fair for 73 years before deciding that he's "not the horse he used to be" and retiring five years ago.

"The Barbecue King of Routt County," now 85, still hosts the sumptuous feed prior to the Saturday night Junior Livestock Sale and supervises preparation of his legendary sauce for 300 pounds of barbecue and 700 guests. Robinson, who says he can do anything that requires 44 bib overalls and a size five hat, is built like a ranch hand. He has no hips to hold up his jeans. His bright blue eyes are

1982

shielded by a well-trompled cowboy hat which he never removes, and he will not hesitate to tell you when "you're fuller of shit than a hummingbird is songs."

His father came into Routt County from Kansas and homesteaded a quarter of a mile above the juncture of Cottonwood Creek and the Dry Fork of Elk in 1908. Robinson was born two years later, a product of the frontier: delivered by Dr. John Solandt, for whom the Hayden Hospital was named, and educated at the Rock School at Elkhead. He left school after the eighth grade, left home at 15 and has lived in Hayden since the town installed water and sewer lines.

"I was there when they dug the Bear River," he grins. "I worked ever since before I was big enough and I did it all on horseback. I could build a stack that never leaked. I could ride a pretty good bucking horse. Came in second in a wild horse race at Oak Creek...'course there was only two of us in the race."

Robinson, who retired in 1978, worked for the Colorado State Highway Department and the State Patrol before he bought a Cat and began building ditches and reservoirs throughout Routt and Moffat Counties. The outfit is currently run by his son Bob Jr.

He credits Marguerite "Mac" Dunckley, granddaughter of one of the first settlers in Dunkley Park, with being "the best thing that ever happened" to him. They were married in 1934 and the walls of their home are littered with community service awards from the Masons, Shriners, Colorado Cattlemens Association and Tread of Pioneers Museum. Bobby was also instrumental in getting Peabody Coal Company to donate the five-acre tract for The Haven Senior Assisted Living Facility and has long-served on the board of Hayden's Babson-Carpenter Foundation.

Bobby collects and restores treasures including a 1912 Republic truck with wooden wheels and hard tires; one of the first Hamilton watches made; a gun carried by the Marshal of Trinidad in the late 1860s with notches on the handle representing nine dead men and a bucket for slew water presented to him by 4-H youngsters.

Bobby Robinson epitomizes the spirit of Routt County and the Fair, which he has been attending since he was nine years old. He was there for what he calls "the big picnic" in 1913, when the town turned out to meet the first train into Hayden, and the following year when Coke Roberds roped the longhorn who charged the nickel-plated jackrabbit on the radiator of an Apperson Jackrabbit automobile.

"Let's be honest," he smiles "Hayden's fine men liked to race horses. That's why the Fair has always been a good time. It's what this valley is all about: raising cattle, putting up hay, growing coal, rodeoing, racing, having a few laughs and telling a few lies."

60

BOBBY ROBINSON'S BARBECUE SAUCE

1 bottle Worcestershire   1 gallon water
1 bottle lemon juice   1 bucket slew water
1 gallon vinegar   6 pounds salt and 1/4 pound pepper

Strain slew water through gunny sacks to get rid of the microbes and frog eggs. Cut beef, buffalo, elk, moose or deer into 20-pound #1 top round boneless roasts. Slop on the sauce. Cover with three layers of clean, wet gunny sacks. Cook 1 hour over a scrub oak fire pit. Remove the gunny sacks. Turn the meat, preferably with a pitchfork. Wet and replace the gunny sacks. Cook 1 hour. Repeat every hour for 16 hours, beginning at 8 pm in order to serve at noon the next day.

GUSTATORIAL PRECAUTIONS FROM THE CHEF:

"Never forget to wet the gunny sacks, which is a chore especially after your buddies go to bed and leave you all alone in the smoke. Be sure you're cooking over coals and that flame never touches the meat or any derelicts who fall into the fire. Slew water is not the secret ingredient. It is a quart of whiskey or any other alcohol but you can't say that in front of 4-H kids. The real secret to the sauce was that the cooks were drunker than waltzin' pissants. There was a whiskey bottle behind every truck tire and there was trucks everywhere. If someone left a can of beer lying around, we threw it in too."

(Photo: Nancy Ellis)

Jack SPRENGLE still raises chickens at his Pine Street spread—more than an acre of land, a handsome 1920s log home, barn and chicken house—shielded by 50-year-old trees. A dozen hens provide fresh eggs for the families of three of his five children who still live in Steamboat Springs, but an abundant supply of local foxes carefully monitor his rabbits and geese.

Jack remembers installing the Battery Brooder in the corner of the Fair's steer barn in the early 1960s and serving as Superintendent of Small Animals for the next dozen years. When pedigreed rabbits were introduced to judging ten years ago, he moved over to supervise beer and wine exhibits. He was the familiar face at the podium, cashier and clerk for the Junior Livestock Sale, first with Howard Elliott and then with Pat McClelland. His cousin Barbara Hudspeth, whose grandfather D. H. Trogler owned the local brickyard, began clerking the sales in 1984 and still does.

Jack still shakes his head when he recalls the year he plugged in the calculator and there was no electricity. "Cookie kept asking me for averages, average price per pound of this sale, of the class, of the total sale. I amazed myself by doing it all with a pencil, but it was scary."

Born in Pueblo, Colorado, in 1930, Jack was four years old when his father became the first county extension agent for Rio Blanco County, and moved his family to Meeker. In 1941, Ray Sprengle became Routt County Extension Agent and moved his family to Steamboat Springs. Jack was 13 when he bought a 4-H lamb from John S. Wright who ranched on the land where the gondola sits today. His mother was a 4-H leader in cooking and his father, who left Steamboat Springs to serve as livestock specialist in Ft.Collins, became a field representative for the American Hereford Association. He was elected to the Hereford Heritage Hall of Fame posthumously for significant contributions to the breed.

While at Steamboat Springs High School, Jack got a part-time job working for Chuck Lyon, who had acquired the original Chamberlain-Gray Drug Store. After a stint in the Army in Korea, Jack graduated from Colorado State University in Ft.Collins and returned to Steamboat Springs with his wife, Carolee Gordon, whom he married in 1956. The couple had five children, all raised in the log home where Jack still resides. Carolee died in a tragic automobile accident in 1985.

Jack began working at Routt County National Bank in 1957 as a teller, and stayed on over the next 34 years, retiring as a senior vice president of the bank, then known as United Bank of Steamboat Springs. He spent most of his long banking career involved in commercial and agricultural loans. Everyone in town has been associated with him in some community service: 15 years on the city and 9 years on the county planning commissions; active member of Holy Name Church; generous volunteer for the Salvation Army, Northwest Colorado Aid Support Group, Steamboat Springs Cemetery District and the Tread of Pioneers Museum.

JIM STANKO retired from 11 years at the helm of Routt County's 4-H Program in 1996 in order to return to ranching. He held the post longer than any other Youth Agent and acquired an enviable track record: the best shooting sports team in the state, healthy scholarship and exchange programs, and increasing countywide enrollment.

County Extension Agent C. J. Mucklow says Jim built "one of the top 4-H Programs in the state." During his tenure he organized hundreds of community and highway cleanup days, dances, pizza projects, gymkhanas, parade floats, field days and field trips and exchange trips. He says the most important part of 4-H is watching people help each other, and the most satisfying experience is seeing youngsters turn into successful adults. High Valley Club member Kaycee Samuelson says, "He's the best. He helped me tons of times."

Jim's idea of Heaven is sitting in the Bud Werner Library crawling through old newspapers. He is a local history buff. He teaches it to Colorado Mountain College students, to Elderhostels and to 4-H Clubs. This is the third book reflecting his love of Routt County. He helped create the Routt County Archives at the Bud Werner Memorial Library and spearheaded the Tread of Pioneers Museum board from 1977 to 1992.

If you can't find what you are looking for in any of those places, just call Jim. He has a photographic memory, insatiable curiosity and dogged determination to fill in missing pieces. He also loves putting together exhibits with scotch tape, bailing wire and pieces and parts from the ranch, where he keeps one of everything, and two of some things, ever hauled into Routt County.

Jim was born and raised in Routt County and obtained degrees in history and political science at Western State College. His son Patrick, a 10-year 4-H member recently obtained a masters degree in electrical engineering, and his wife Joanne has taught elementary school for 28 years.

Since 1974 the Stankos have ranched on the homeplace established in 1907. He taught state and local history at elementary schools in Oregon, New Mexico and Colorado. He was a founding member of the Steamboat Springs Rural Fire Protection District board and currently serves on the Steamboat Springs Cemetery District board.

Rodeo at the Routt County Fair

Rodeo is the product of great open range cattle operations which required cowboys to break and train horses for roping, sorting and handling livestock on unfenced ranges. It was created by cowboys eager to prove themselves and their outfits better than the neighbors. This was most frequently demonstrated at impromptu matches after a round-up or trail drive. Contests to prove who could rope the fastest or ride the rankest bronc in the horse string developed into "events" collectively known as a rodeo.

Because the term rodeo has such a wide range of definitions, it is difficult to determine where the first rodeo took place in Routt County. We do know that Routt County cowboys, like every cowboy on the frontier, did not shy from the opportunity to test skills at any campsite or corral.

By the turn of the century most towns in the Yampa Valley had a 4th of July celebration or some special community event which offered, at very least, a bucking horse contest with some sort of purse or prize to draw participants. Early rodeos took place at Hayden, Steamboat Springs, Oak Creek and Mt.Harris in temporary arenas formed by circling horses and later automobiles. In Yampa sections of the main street were blocked off.

By opening the Routt County Fair in 1914, the county created an identifiable site, facilities and tradition for an annual rodeo and races. A rodeo program has been an integral part of the Fair ever since, with the exception of 1930 which had only a stake race; 1932, 1933 and 1934 when all fair events were cancelled; 1942 and 1943 when men were at war; and 1951 when the Fair was cancelled.

THE STAKE RACE, featured on the first day of the first Fair, was followed by BUCKING HORSE RIDING on the third day. It was the forerunner of today's barrel race and it remained an annual event until 1959 when it was replaced by the Cloverleaf Race. The first winner of the stake race was Coke Roberds who collected a $20 purse.

SADDLE BRONC RIDING is a long-standing Fair tradition. In the early days riders were awarded points for the ease and speed with which they saddled and mounted prior to "making time" instead of mounting in the bucking chute as they do today. The mounted cowboy was required to hold the buck

63

rein in one hand while holding the other hand in the air. He was required to keep both feet in the stirrups, spur the horse in the shoulder on the first jump then continue with a spurring stroke from the shoulder to the saddle skirts throughout the ride while not touching the horse with his free hand. The ride ended when judges fired a shot into the air. Winner of the first bucking contest was G.F.

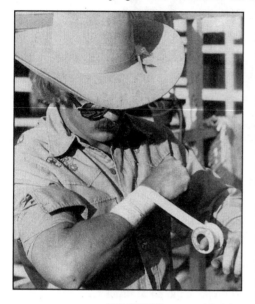

Brown who took home a $60 purse.

Bronc riding claimed the spotlight in 1918. First a three-way tie for the championship was ridden off by Jim Clark, Walter Bennett and Tex Waters who won it. Then all the riders repeated the event while a hat was passed and $136 was collected for the Routt County Red Cross. Between 1925 and 1929 every rider was required to provide a horse, an unusual rule which may or may not have been enforced. It is also unclear whether the horse was to have been a bucking horse for use by other contestants or a mount for other rodeo functions.

STAKE RACES and SADDLE BRONC RIDING were the only rodeo events until 1922 when eight years of testing new events began. CALF ROPING took place most of these years with the memorable exception of 1925 when the stock contractor failed to show up with the calves and goats were used instead. BAREBACK BRONC RIDING and BULL-DOGGING were added in 1928 and 1929. Purses during the roaring 1920s soared to $200 for bronc riding (1928) and $115 for calf roping (1929).

Two other novelty events entertained rodeo fans at different times between 1929 and 1949: COW RIDING, a popular spectacle at most rodeos and, at three rodeos, a WILD COW MILKING CONTEST required cowboys who had never milked a cow to tangle with cows that had never been milked. The cow had to be roped from a horse, held by a "mugger" while getting a few drops of milk, and the milk delivered by both men after a footrace to a judge at the end of the arena.

The Depression left its mark upon rodeo. Old guard cowboys from local ranches, who bucked and roped to pit their skills against animals and neighbors, began competing with a new breed of cowboy, more interested in points, purses and overall standings. Automobiles made travel to rodeos across the country possible and gave rise to the "professional" cowboy.

Professional rodeo circuits were established in the 1940s and 1950s. The Western Slope Rodeo Association, formed in 1941, helped establish several circuits, and the Fair thrived as part of a circuit which included the Steamboat Springs 4th of July Cowboys Roundup, Meeker's Range Call and Craig's Ride N Tie Days in addition to annual celebrations in Debuque, Kremmling, Rifle, Rangely and Toponas. Six towns on the circuit contributed to a $300 purse for the Best All Around Performer based on points earned at these rodeos.

Although war cancelled the Fair between 1942 and 1945, a Fair rodeo was held in 1944 and 1945. The advent of roping clubs in Hayden and Toponas made CALF ROPING and TEAM TYING fiercely competitive and by 1948 they became major rodeo events at the Fair beginning in 1948; Calf Roping for Boys under 14 was added in 1949.

BAREBACK BRONC RIDING was introduced in 1947 when it was described vividly in the Fair Book: "Riding a bucking horse while seated in a saddle is one thing. Trying the same stunt without a saddle, on the slippery, uncovered back of a jumping, twisting wild bronc, with no aid but the grip on a surcingle around the horse's body is still another. A fast colorful, exciting event is bareback riding, with the cowboy required to remain aboard for eight seconds to make a qualified ride."

Several events held today were added during the 1950s and early 1960s. STEER WREST-LING, commonly called bulldoging, began in 1958; LADIES BARREL RACING in 1959; BULL RIDING in 1960. CUTTING HORSE CONTESTS, held between 1956 and 1967, were revived as demonstration events in 1994 and 1995. Calf Roping for Boys under 18, started in 1949, was discontinued in 1969.

Auctioneer Homer Wilson from Craig in 1958, riding Archie.

Designating a single event champion, winner of the most points over a two day rodeo or winner of a single go-round, began during the 1960s. The most remarkable feat of that decade and the Fair was Lonnie Mantle's winning streak. He took the bronc riding championship for five consecutive years (1961-1965), the longest on record at the Routt County Fair.

A Junior Rodeo, part of the Fair in 1954 only, included bareback bronc riding won by Bob Valasques; Jerk or Break-Away Roping won by Lynn Whiteman; a Stake Race won by Betty Williams; Calf Roping won by Duane Tabb; Team Tying won by Jerry Green and Jim Lindsey; a Bundle Race won by Larry Whiteman; an Eighth Mile Race for Boys won by Eddie Lighthizer and for Girls won by Kay Conyers who also won the Quarter Mile Free-For-All.

DALLY TEAM ROPING replaced Team Tying in 1966. Dally roping requires that the steer be caught by the head and one or both hind legs and brought to a stop or dropped, differing from Team Tying in which the steer has to be tied after it is caught. Several Hayden Roping Club members have had winning years in this event.

GOAT TYING, a ladies event tried in 1961 and 1963, became a regular contest in 1970 and lasted until 1984. It was dominated by Judy Green, a college goat tier who took championships in 1970, 1971, 1973 and 1975.

During the past ten years the Fair Rodeo has featured Saddle and Bareback Bronc Riding, Bull Riding, Steer Wrestling, Calf Roping and Team Roping and Barrel Racing. Recent additions include Kids Barrel Racing (1983), Mixed Team Roping and Old Timers Roping (1985). The variety has attracted cowboys from areas outside of Northwest Colorado who, since the mid-1960s have dominated the winners circle in all events.

The Routt County Fair has been a member of several different rodeo associations: the Western Slope Rodeo Association (1940 into the 1960s); the Amateur Cowboys Association (1955-56); Professional Rodeo Cowboys Association (PRCA) when the rodeo was billed as a Pro-Am event (1972-75); Colorado State Rodeo Association (CSRA) sanctioned (1977 through the 1980s); Colorado Professional Rodeo Association (CPRA) sanctioned (1994-95); Professional Rodeo Cowboys Association (PRCA) again (1996). Open rodeos were held in 1970 and 1990-93. The Routt County Fair Rodeo was voted the Best New Western Slope Rodeo by the CPRA in 1994.

BRONC RIDERS

The following cowboys and champions pitted their skills against the strength, speed and smarts of animals with a strong distaste for being ridden. These local riders occupied the winners circle on more than one occasion.

Between 1914-1939

WALTER BENNETT, Hayden, was raised on Williams Fork. He rode the rough string on the Cary Ranch and won the Fair's 1915 bucking contest. His reputation earned him a spot in Buffalo Bill's Wild West Show in Chicago in 1912.

Edgar Bobbitt on Canahejo. First money, 1920. (Photo: Tread of Pioneers Museum)

GEORGE BIRD, Yampa, two-time winner of the Fair bucking contest in 1916 and 1919, had one of the better rides on Pershing at Yampa in 1924 and was a top competitor in rodeos at Yampa, Mt. Harris and Steamboat Springs.

EDGAR BOBBITT, Hayden, cleaned up in 1920 with spectacular rides in Steamboat Springs, Oak Creek and at the Fair and was one of the few to ride General Pershing.

JIM CLARK, Hayden, two-time winner of the Fair in 1917 and 1921, and involved in a dramatic ride-off for a three-way tie in 1918.

CLAYTON DANKS, Snake River, was the first and only World Champion bronc rider from this area. He earned the title by riding the famous Wyoming bucking horse, Steamboat, twice in the early 1900s at Cheyenne's Frontier Days. He became a rodeo judge (1908 to 1930), judging at the Routt County Fair.

STANLEY LARSON, Clark, was the only four-time winner of the saddle bronc contest, only one win behind Lonnie Mantle's five-win record. He was also the first cowboy to win the contest on both the first and second days in 1929; his other wins were back to back in 1924 and 1925.

PHIL LECKENBY, Steamboat Springs, in 1926 won the Routt County Fair and at the Moffat County Fair became one of the of the few cowboys to ride Pershing to a finish.

TUFFY WREN, Steamboat Springs, was one of the top bronc riders of this era and renowned for the somersault pictured on the cover of this book.

TEX WATERS, Hayden, was the first back to back winner of saddle bronc riding at the Fair, in 1917 and 1918, a record made while breaking a three-way tie.

Other bronc riders who made memorable rides at rodeos throughout the country, even though they did not win at the County Fair: Emory Clark, Clarence Decker, Ivan Decker, Fred Fairbanks, Walter Laughlin, Walter Long, Lawrence "Doc" Marshall, Streeter Reinhart, Otto Summers, Charlie Tipton, Leonard "Kid" Vaughn, Marion Yoast.

66

In the 1940s

ED UNCAPHER, Toponas, two-time winner in 1940 and 1948

CARL UNCAPHER, Toponas, two-day winner in 1944 and second day winner in 1946

DELBERT SCOTT, Hayden, bareback champion in 1947, 1948 and 1949

HAROLD SCOTT, Hayden, first Routt County cowboy to win championships in saddle bronc in 1950 and 1952, and in bareback in 1947 and 1953

In the 1950s

PAUL BONNIFIELD, Yampa, bareback champion in 1956

GRANT BRYANT, Steamboat Springs, saddle bronc champion in 1953; bareback champion in 1954

COURTNEY FAIRBANKS, Steamboat Springs, one of few second generation bronc riders in 1957 and the last Routt County cowboy to win a saddle bronc championship in 1959

NORM FRENTRESS, Hayden, a first day win in saddle bronc riding at the 1950 Fair

DARWIN LOCKHART, Steamboat Springs, last Routt County cowboy to win both saddle and bareback bronc events and the second four-time winner: saddle bronc in 1955 and 1958, and bareback both days in 1958

In the 1990s

TRACEY LAWTON, Steamboat Springs, a 1988 winner and last Routt County cowboy to win a bareback championship in 1990

JIM SCRAFFORD, Steamboat Springs, only Routt County cowboy to win a bull riding championship in 1992

BUCKING HORSES

Good bucking horses, like good cowboys, attract a following. How the horse bucks riders off or insures high points prompts as much discussion as technique and style displayed by the rider. In early rodeos a horse with a good reputation could draw as large a crowd as a top name cowboy. Because stock contractors supply bucking horses and move from rodeo to rodeo, it is harder to get to know today's horses. Prior to the 1940s most bucking stock came from local ranches and participated in rodeos year after year so everyone was familiar with horses as well as riders.

Two Routt County horses, Pin Ears and General Pershing, attracted attention throughout Northwest Colorado from the turn of the century until well into the 1920s.

Jim Corbett on Pin Ears. (Photo: Tread of Pioneers Museum)

PIN EARS, whose career spanned the years from the turn of the century to around 1910, never bucked at the County Fair. His legacy spawned rodeo recognition for the Worst Bucking Horse, an award for the hardest horse to ride presented at early rodeos and the Fair. Pin Ears, named for the scars left by frostbite at birth, was owned by Lou Long of Twentymile Park. On the ranch he was a gentle old plug and a children's pet, but as soon as he was taken to town and let out in an arena he became a bad one.

Before Pin Ears retired just about every cowboy in the valley had a try on him. Most saw a lot of sky and felt hard ground. In fact in one afternoon he threw three of Routt County's best riders, Kid Vaughn, George Marshall and George Wright. However on September 11, 1903, Marion Yoast from Dunkley won the Northwestern Colorado Bronco Riding Championship at Steamboat Springs when he rode Pin Ears.

Because he frequently would rear up on his hind legs and paw the air after throwing a rider, he gained a reputation for being a killer. This caused quite a stir at the 1906 rodeo in Steamboat Springs when, after the rider had been thrown, Long walked out to catch the horse which reared; Long stuck out his hand and Pin Ears extended a paw as if the two were shaking hands for a job well done. There is no record that Pin Ears ever struck or hurt a rider.

Two attempted rides on Pin Ears entered Routt County legend. The first involved Kid Vaughn who took on the horse behind Wagner's Saddle Shop in Hayden. As soon as the Kid was mounted, Pin Ears took a dozen jumps, fish tailing his rear end around before hitting the ground while spinning like a top. Kid Vaughn bit the dust but immediately announced that he was going to try it again. When his next attempt ended the same way and Kid emerged from the dust, there was no talk about another ride.

The second "classic" ride was made by Pete Laphan who, after getting a little liquored up at a Steamboat Springs rodeo, boasted he could ride Pin Ears. Other cowboys were ready to accommodate him and had the horse ready before Pete could find his boots so a young cowboy lent Pete his boots. After two fish tailing jumps, Pete was airborne and gone but the boots remained stuck in the stirrups until the horse quit bucking. Old timers still joke that Pete's boots made time even if Pete failed.

Pershing's High Dive.
(Photo: Helgesen)

GENERAL PERSHING was another force to contend with on rodeo circuits in Colorado and Wyoming from 1919 into the mid-1920s. He was a grey gelding, renowned for the antics of a kangaroo, and owned by Frank Squire. According to long-time bucking judge Reuben Squire, no bronc in the Yampa Valley soiled so many rodeo shirts. Typically he would make several jumps and land on his hind feet, coming within an inch of toppling over backward, before jumping straight up like a sky rocket, doubling over like a jack knife, straightening out like a coiled spring, and again landing without his forefeet ever hitting the ground.

Pershing threw five men on Memorial Day afternoon in 1921. The following year a confident Streeter Rinehardt announced that he would donate 80% of the purse to the winner of his ride. History does not record how the horse spent his winnings. By the mid-1920s Pershing was rarely used for main events because no one would draw for him.

In 1926 he was recognized as the Worst Bucking Horse at the Routt County Fair. Cowboys would attempt to ride Pershing only in exhibition for special purses or side bets. In one of these rides at Oak Creek in 1924, Fred Fairbanks found out just how much force Pershing could exert. Fairbanks was making a very good ride and looking like he could beat Pershing, when the horse shot straight up. Fairbank's boots were shoved into the stirrups so hard that the leather, strong enough to pull a sled, gave way forcing him to take the fall.

Fred Fairbanks on Pershing in mid-20s. First money. Seconds later he was thrown. (Photo: Tread of Pioneers Musuem.

WORST BUCKING HORSE AWARDS

At early Fairs the meanest bronc was recognized with an additional $25 purse. Newspaper accounts, probably incomplete, include the following horses with owner or rider.

1915	Lightning Rod, ridden by Clay Clark
1916	Chili, ridden by George Bird
1920	Ace High, ridden by Leonard Vaughn, and Mile High
1922	General Pershing, owned by Frank Squire
1923	Cutie, owned by Bill Green
1924	General Pershing, SkyLark and Viva Skiva
1926	General Pershing
1935	Wild Fire, owned by Ralph Reeves and Ten High, owned by Peck Wilson

Other well know broncs and owners of this era were Bad Whiskey; Black Diamond (Al Coulter); Carrie Nation (Lou Long); Cactus Kate (Virgil Marshall); Cork Screw (Lawrence "Doc" Marshall); Duke (George Cook); Dynamite (George Crawford), Fox Squirrel (Charlie Yust); Hired Girl (George Bird); Midnight (Benton Livestock Co.); Nancy Hanks; Prohibition (Al Padgett); Spot (Stanley Bruno); Tiger Tom and Geronimo.

ROPERS

In the 1920s and 1930s

DENNY CULLEN, Steamboat Springs, Calf Roping in 1929

ELMER MACK, Moffat County, a major Fair participant, stock contractor and Calf Roping Champion in 1929

In the 1940s

LEONARD LIGHTHIZER, Hayden, Calf Roping in 1947

GLENN TABB, Hayden, record holder for most wins in Routt County Roping events; most wins in Calf Roping, 1948, 1950, 1952; winning both days and tying for first on the first day of 1958. He also won Team Tying with Vernon Williams in 1949, 1953, 1955 and 1956, and finished off his career 20 years later with a win in 1975 with Burt Rakestraw.

MAX WILLIAMS, Hayden, first Calf Roping Champion in Routt County in 1929, winning on the 1st day; in 1940, winning both days, and in 1944; Team Tying in 1948 with Dewey Savage and in 1949 with Dorsey Lighthizer

In the 1950s

JACK AND BILL BARNES, Hayden, first Routt County brothers to win Team Tying in 1959

LEON AND JERRY GREEN, Hayden, first father-son combination to win a Team Tying event in 1959 and 1960

STETSON AND STETSON, Oak Creek, Team Tying in 1950

VERNON WILLIAMS, Hayden, Calf Roping in 1953; Team Tying Champion with Glenn Tabb in 1949, 1953, 1955 and 1956, and with Lawrence Drake in 1961

In the 1960s

LEON GREEN, Hayden, Team Tying with Lynn Sideway in 1963

In the 1980s

GARY FAGG, Hayden, Calf Roping in 1983

JERRY GREEN, Hayden, Calf Roping in 1986

TIM REYNOLDS, Steamboat Springs, Dally Team Roping with Thane Bacon in 1988

OLD TIMERS TEAM ROPING AWARD

This event, started in 1985. Competitors over the age of 40 and winners, between 1985 and 1994, received a special award, spurs handmade by Bobby Robinson. Each award was presented in honor of a major contributor to Routt County's Western heritage. In 1984 the spurs were presented to the Champion Saddle Bronc Rider in memory of Elmer Mack. No contest was held in 1995.

		In memory of
1985	Homer Wilson and Gary Fagg	Frank Stetson
1986	Tony Tonozzi and Jim Mazuchi	Coke Roberds
1987	Gilbert Lazor and Gary Fagg	Ferry Carpenter
1988	Homer Wilson and Joe Brown	Si Dawson
1989	Pome Camilletti and Don Rutherford	Frank Squire
1990	Gilbert Lazor and Dan Michaels	Si Dawson
1991	Gilbert Lazor and Dan Michaels	J.C.Temple
1992	Homer Wilson and Frank Weidner	Bill Green
1993	Wayne Workman and Doc Allen	Pat Mantle
1994	Frank Weidner and Steve Kinney	80th Anniversary

SPECIAL CONTRIBUTORS

STOCK CONTRACTORS, who frequently furnish secretaries, announcers, pick-up men and clowns, develop a string of animals known for their distemper and distaste for being ridden or caught. Among the local ranchers who furnished rodeo stock during the early years of the Fair were Bill Green and sons Leon and Raymond (cows and calves in 1940 and 1941), and Elmer Mack and Isadore Bolten (stock in 1944 and 1945). Pat Mantle, one of the region's first real stock contractors (stock in 1972) sold his Rocky Mountain Rodeo Company to Carl Murphy (stock from 1973 to 1975). Since then Jerry Berentis, H&H Rodeo Company, Edker Wilson, Dean Drake and Eddy Lang have furnished livestock for the Fair.

RODEO ANNOUNCERS included local favorites Clarence Horton, Timer Heid, Darwin Lockhart and Lynn Whiteman who have shared the mike with Ed Bingham, Gabby George, Stan Johnson, Bud Knafple, Stan Johnson, Les Mergleman, and Glenn Winters.

But Routt County's premier sound man, at both Winter Carnival and Fair, was Walt Weber who brought in the first electrical sound system in 1938, and initiated a tradition of playing John Philip Sousa marches before and during the Fair. Weber mounted his sound system on his Ford panel truck and drove it up and down the streets of Hayden announcing events and playing Stars and Stripes Forever, loud. Speakers perched high atop the announcers stand also promoted a festive atmosphere with deafening but rousing marches.

RODEO SECRETARIES AND TIMERS, on whom the Fair depends for starts, finishes, results and the processing of complaints, represent local talent. Secretaries: George Cook, Diane Taylor, Sylvia Flores, Barbara Fagg, Rhonda Guard, Jerry Green, Kenneth Simpson, Wilma Smith. Timers: Joan Anderson, Fran Byers, Rosemary Crosthwaite, Caroline Dodo, Myrtle Dixon, Pauline Dunn, Sue Eding, Barbara Fagg, Betty Fagg, Chris Graham, Mabel Green, Pauline Haller, Judy Hayes, Fran Meacham, Dorothy Mergleman, Linda Signs, Wilma Smith, Didi Stone, Dorothy Taylor, Cheryl Whiteman, Karen Wilkinson, Sally Williamson, Judy Wise, Pep Winters, Mildred Yoast.

In 1958 Darwin Lockhart took two first places in bareback and first in bareback bronc riding. No one can remember whether this was the year he and Ray Weber celebrated life by stealing the Trailways Bus while it was idling in front of the Harbor Hotel.

Rodeo Champions

The following lists of rodeo and race champions have been painstakingly compiled by Jerry Green, many for the 1989 and 1994 anniversary tributes to the Routt County Fair produced for the Hayden Heritage Center. Variations in dates and spelling reflect incomplete, inaccurate and inconsistent newspaper accounts rather than his long hours of research.

BAREBACK RIDING CHAMPIONS

Year	Day	Winner	Year	Winner
1928	1st	Dan Lovisone	1960	Bud Massey
	2nd	Dutch Foster	1961	Kenny Latham
	3rd	Dutch Foster	1962	Dick McIntyre/Larry Rohrig
1929	2nd	Jack Spratt	1963	Gene Hollenbeck
	3rd	Ted Larson	1964	C. W. Williams
1947	1st	Harold Scott	1965	Butch Myers
	2nd	Del Scott	1966	Dick Claycomb
1948	1st	Del Scott	1967	Dick Aronson
	2nd	Arden Stewart	1968	John Mahaney
1949	1st	Del Scott	1969	John Mahaney
	2nd	Marvin Laman	1970	Larry Rohrig
1950	2nd	Dick Dorrell	1972	Bruce Ford
1952	1st	Phil Weber	1973	Glen Ford
		Dick Nassau	1974	Larry Collins
	2nd	Dick Dorrell	1975	John Harbour
1953	1st	Harold Scott	1976	Pat Kessler
	2nd	Jack Lucas	1978	Greg Baldwin
1954	1st	Dick Nassau/Sam Morgan	1979	Rick Marsh
	2nd	Grant Bryant	1981	John Capraro
1955	1st	Dick Nassau	1982	Jesse Hill
	2nd	Dick Nassau	1985	Lynn Lyons/Casey Smith
1956	1st	Dick Nassau	1986	Rick Marsh/Todd Copenhaver
	2nd	Paul Bonnifield	1987	Lynn Lyons
1957	1st	Dick McIntyre	1988	Tracey Lawton
	2nd	Chuck Disney	1989	Joe Abbatangelo
1958	1st	Darwin Lockhart	1990	Tracey Lawton
	2nd	Darwin Lockhart	1991	Eddie Relaford
1959	1st	Sam Morgan/Dave Catoor	1992	Eddie Relaford
	2nd	Ray Weber	1993	Kenny Heinze
			1994	Travis Greenlee
			1995	Steve Hillman/Chuck Colletti

SADDLE BRONC RIDING CHAMPIONS

Year	Day	Winner	Year	Day	Winner
1914		G. F. Brown	1954	1st	Dick Nassau
1915		Walter Bennett		2nd	Joe Salisbury
1916		George Bird	1955	1st	Darwin Lockhart
1917		Jim Clark/Tex Waters		2nd	Harold Scott
1918		Tex Waters	1956	1st	Pat Mantle
1919		George Bird		2nd	Pat Mantle
1920		Edgar Bobbitt	1957	1st	Courtney Fairbanks
1921		Jim Clark		2nd	Chuck Disney
1922		Dutch Myers	1958	1st	Darwin Lockhart
1923		Gus Kracht		2nd	Sam Morgan
1924		Stanley Larson	1959	1st	Courtney Fairbanks
1925		Stanley Larson		2nd	Sam Morgan
1926		Phil Leckenby	1960		Joe Salisbury
1928		Dutch Foster	1961		Lonnie Mantle
1929	1st	Stanley Larson	1962		Lonnie Mantle
	2nd	Stanley Larson	1963		Lonnie Mantle
1935	1st	Church Williams	1964		Lonnie Mantle
	2nd	Ward Watkins	1965		Lonnie Mantle
1936	1st	Jim Stanley	1966	1st	Jim Hammer
	2nd	Earl Lusk		2nd	Larry Burgess
1937		Warren Francis	1967		Jack Mitchell
1939	1st	Vern Meeks	1968		Harry Watt
	2nd	Ed McMahan	1969		Nial Robinson
1940	1st	Ed Uncapher	1970		Harry Watt
	2nd	Ed McMahan	1972		Jerry Gaddis
1941	1st	Dick Miller	1973		Glen Rodewald
	2nd	Lex Crawford	1974		Randy Hoffman
1944	1st	Carl Uncapher	1975		Jim Rogers
	2nd	Carl Uncapher	1976		Chip Hall
1945	1st	Don Myers	1978		J. D. Hamaker
	2nd	Andy Jackson	1979		Eddie Schmidt
1946	1st	Bill Whitney	1981		Fidel Olivas
	2nd	Carl Uncapher	1982		Kirby Werner
1947	1st	Bob Terrill	1985		Clay Keller
	2nd	Mac Ayers	1987		Dale Haskins
1948	1st	Ed Uncapher	1988		Dale Haskins/Fidel Olivas
	2nd	Bob Terrill	1989		Dale Haskins
1949	1st	No riders	1990		Mark Henderson
	2nd	Don Myers	1991		Ramos Benny
1950	1st	Norman Frentress	1992		Eddie Schmidt
	2nd	Harold Scott	1993		Eddie Schmidt
1952	1st	Harold Scott	1994		Fidel Olivas
	2nd	Don Dorrell	1995		Matt Sliwkowski/Spikes Davis
1953	1st	Grant Bryant			
	2nd	Dick Nassau			

BULL RIDING CHAMPIONS

Year	Winner	Year	Winner
1960	John Mahaney	1978	Aaron Bickley
1961	Paul Lupcho	1979	Mark Wade
1962	Larry Rohrig/Lonnie Mantle	1981	Kevin Bates
1963	Lonnie Mantle	1982	Gary Hiler
1964	Dwight Springer	1985	Paul Gallegos
1965	Warren White	1986	Randy Lopez
1966	Garland Hayes	1987	Cody Hall
1967	Don Smith	1988	Lot Robinson
1968	Tom Seewald	1989	Gary Walter
1969	John Mahaney	1990	Clint Dorscher
1970	John Mahaney	1991	Myron Duarte
1972	Harry Watt	1992	Jim Scrafford
1973	Hal Meredith	1993	Bob Coen
1974	Kenny Gee	1994	Travis Greenlee
1975	Britt Givens	1995	Wayne Alderman
1976	Brad Brewn		

TEAM TYING CHAMPIONS

Year	Day	Winner
1948	1st	Russell Yount/June Graham
	2nd	Max Williams/Dewey Savage
1949	1st	Dorsey Lighthizer/Max Williams
	2nd	Glenn Tabb/Vernon Williams
1950	1st	Stetson/Stetson
	2nd	Jim Dodo/Bill Laramore
1952	1st	Bill Green/Ab Johnson
	2nd	Jim Dodo/Wayne Allen
1953	1st	Bus Norell/Bud Norell
	2nd	Glenn Tabb/Vernon Williams
1954	1st	Jay Gentry/Phil Sheridan
	2nd	Russell/Jay Yount
1955	1st	Glenn Tabb/Vernon Williams
	2nd	Russell/Jay Yount
1956	1st	Jack/Bill Barnes
	2nd	Glenn Tabb/Vernon Williams
1957	1st	Homer/Ellis Wilson
	2nd	Lawrence Drake/Duane Tabb
1958	1st	Ellis Wilson/Don VanTassel
	2nd	Jay Gentry/Phil Sheridan
1959	1st	Jerry/Leon Green
	2nd	Jack/Bill Barnes
1960		Jerry/Leon Green
1961		Vernon Williams/Lawrence Drake
1962		Bob Crosthwaite/Millard Dixon
1963		Lynn Sideway/Leon Green
1964		Lee/Gary Goodrich
1965		Bob Crosthwaite/Homer Wilson

DALLY TEAM ROPING CHAMPIONS

Year	Winner
1966	Lee/Gary Goodrich
1967	Bob Jones/Conway Irick
1968	Babe Haller/Bill Laramore
1969	Dave Prather/Vern Wagner
1970	Allen Rogers/Wes McKay
1972	Tom Latham/Jake Milton
1973	Gerald Eichelberger/George Devore
1974	John/Ken Bell
1975	Glenn Tabb/Burt Rakestraw
1976	Bus/Dee Norell
1978	Jeff Mitchell/Keith Watson
1979	Shane/Homer Wilson
1981	Dee/Ken Norell
1982	Jacy Dickens/Rick Lauridsen
1984	Lee Lancaster/John Jolly
1985	Kent Mahoney/Randy Schriebvogel
1986	Clay Leonard/Mark Hill
1987	Wade Masters/Rick Lauridsen
1988	Tim Reynolds/Thane Bacon
1989	Rick Lauridsen/Wade Masters
1990	Frank Weidner/Jack Cobb
1991	Jim Mazuchi/Wayne Workman
1992	Grant Sheer/Cody Carver
1993	Monte Atkinson/Joe Roderick
1994	Dustin Dunfee/Dennis Hathcock
1995	Brian/Chad Espenscheid
	and Wade Kreutzer/Grant Sheer (tie)

MIXED TEAM ROPING CHAMPIONS

Year	Winner
1985	Becky Mahoney/Brady Chapman
1986	Melanie Watt/Kevin Norell
1987	Tammy Ellerman/Kevin Norell
1988	Becky/Kent Mahoney
1989	Tammy/Jay Ellerman
1990	Sammi Gilbert/Jim Mazuchi
1991	Ci Ci Kinney/Roger Wilde
1992	Sammi Gilbert/Ray Gilbert
1993	Sue Weidner/Joe Roderick
1994	Ron/Laura Nauta
1995	Larry/Dana Irwen

CALF ROPING CHAMPIONS

Year	Day	Winner	Year	Day	Winner
1922		Bob Gray	1958	1st	Lawrence Drake/Glenn Tabb
1924		Roark		2nd	Homer Wilson
1925		Elmer Mack	1959	1st	Leland McNeil
1926		Charles Miller		2nd	Leland McNeil
1928		Elmer Mack	1960		Jay Gentry
1929	1st	Max Williams	1961		Dave Prather
	2nd	Denny Cullen	1962		Allen Rogers
1935	1st	Casey Davis	1963		Bob Crosthwaite
	2nd	Ward Watkins	1964		Earl Haller
1936	1st	Jerry Litterill/A.J.Holder	1965		John Lecky
	2nd	Lin Perkins	1966		Jim Mazuchi
1937		Orville Thomas	1967		Marcel Gros
1939	1st	Dell Owens	1968		Dick Aronson
	2nd	Walt Alsbaugh	1969		Dale Thompson
1940	1st	Max Williams	1970		Jerry Kraft
	2nd	Max Williams	1972		Mac Jesson
1944	1st	Max Williams	1973		Myrl Goodwin
	2nd	Ab Johnson	1974		Myrl Goodwin
1945	1st	Tom Watt	1975		Dale Thompson
	2nd	Russell Yount	1976		Bill Sixkiller
1946	1st	Russell Yount	1978		Mark Cain
	2nd	Russell Yount	1979		Jacy Dickens
1947	1st	Leonard Lighthizer	1981		Jacy Dickens
	2nd	Tom Watt	1982		Ben Grave
1948	1st	Tom Watt	1983		Gary Fagg
	2nd	Glenn Tabb	1985		Lory Merritt
1949	1st	Marble Parker	1986		Jerry Green
	2nd	June Graham	1987		Clay Lenard
1950	1st	Ralph Chrisler	1988		John Ashley
	2nd	Glenn Tabb	1989		Jacy Dickens
1952	1st	Glenn Tabb	1990		Ken Norell
	2nd	Glenn Tabb	1991		Kevin Kobza
1953	1st	Jim Sheriden	1992		Dick Carroll
	2nd	Vernon Williams	1993		Mike Hadley
1954	1st	Jay Gentry	1994		Levi Polich
	2nd	Jim Sheriden	1995		Mike Hadley
1955	1st	Babe Haller			
	2nd	Bus Norell			
1956	1st	Homer Wilson			
	2nd	Jay Mitchell			
1957	1st	Homer Wilson			
	2nd	Phil Sheriden			

BOYS' CALF ROPING CHAMPIONS

Year	Day	Winner
1949	1st	Jack Orr
	2nd	Tom Watt Jr.
1950	1st	Phil Sheridan
	2nd	Dutch Williams
1952	1st	Phil Sheridan
	2nd	Herb Ingersoll
1953	1st	Larry Whiteman
	2nd	Duane Tabb
1954	1st	Jay Yount
	2nd	Phil Sheridan
1955	1st	Larry Whiteman
	2nd	Jay Yount
1956	1st	Jay Yount
	2nd	Jay Yount/Lynn Whiteman
1957	1st	Jerry Green
	2nd	Gary Whitmer
1959	1st	Lynn Whiteman
	2nd	Lynn Whiteman
1960		Leon Fedenic
1961		Wes McKay
1962		Wes McKay
1963		Frank Sheehan
1969		Wes Cook

CUTTING HORSE CONTEST CHAMPIONS

Year	Day	Winner
1956	1st	Troy Lindsey
	2nd	Troy Lindsey
1957	1st	Troy Lindsey
	2nd	Ellis Wilson
1958	1st	Ellis Wilson
	2nd	Lucienne Stetson
1959	1st	Bert Powers
	2nd	Bert Powers
1960		Bill Wright
1961		Dee Salisbury
1962		Troy Lindsey
1963		Woody Searle
1964		Austin Beebe
1965	1st	Ben Reary
	2nd	Ellis Wilson
1966		Ellis Wilson
1967	1st	Ellis Wilson
	2nd	Ben Reary

STEER WRESTLING CHAMPIONS

Year	Day	Winner	Year	Day	Winner
1958	1st	Lane Decker	1974		Randy Staley
	2nd	Doug Pearce	1975		Ralph Betz
1959	1st	Babe Haller	1976		Ken Norell
	2nd	Jay Mitchell	1978		Vaughn Cook
1960		Ed Pickering	1979		Norman Thacker
1961		Frank Hewes	1981		Kent Hall
1962		Bob Buckley	1982		Kurt Hall
1963		Harold Loyd	1985		Jesse Hill
1964		Del Jackson	1986		Jon Hotchkiss/Mike Lazor
1965		Tom Burwell	1987		Kelly Chamberlin
1966	1st	Butch Myers	1988		Jon Hotchkiss
	2nd	Dick Aronson	1989		Larry Swain
1967		Dick Aronson	1990		Jock Campbell
1968		Steve Lange	1991		Ron Fritzlan
1969	1st	Larry Allen	1992		Ron Fritzlan
	2nd	Dwaine Morey	1993		Dave Upchurch
1970		Jon Hotchkiss	1994		Dick Aronson
1972		Danny Jackson	1995		Jimmy Ferguson
1973		Lee Kimzey			

GOAT TYING CHAMPIONS

Year	Day	Winner
1961		Ilda Booco
1963		Cheryl Whiteman
1970	1st	Judy Green
	2nd	Judy Green
1971	1st	Judy Green
	2nd	Judy Green
1973		Judy Green
1974		Bonnie Blasingame
1975		Judy Green
1978		Robyn Funkhouser
1981		Traci Hayes
1982		Becky Fuchs
1984		Traci Hayes

COW RIDING CHAMPIONS

Year	Day	Winner
1928	2nd	Cecil Kennedy
	3rd	George Bird
1929		Jim Smith
1935		Ken Hargiss
1941	1st	Bob Groth
	2nd	Walt Alsbaugh
1944	1st	Wilbur Luark
	2nd	Wilbur Luark
1945	1st	Tom Watt
	2nd	James Sellers
1946	1st	Tom Watt
	2nd	Tom Watt
1947	1st	Andy Peroulis
	2nd	Rod Hinman

WILD COW MILKING CHAMPIONS

Year	Day	Winner
1928		Orville Heck
1929		John Hynd
1947	1st	Jim Dodo/
		Wilbur Pretti
	2nd	John Chivington

LADIES' BARREL RACING CHAMPIONS

Year	Day	Winner
1959	1st	Melva Lou Drake
	2nd	Melva Lou Drake/Kay Montieth
1960	1st	Dorothy Korts
	2nd	Sally Williamson
1961		Kay Montieth
1962		Sharon Dixon
1963		Betty Lyons
1964		Cheryl Whiteman
1965		Elaine Ewing
1966		Pauline Haller
1967		Pauline Haller
1968		Pauline Haller
1969	1st	Kay Merrill
	2nd	Mim Buckley
1970		Kay Brennan
1974	1st	Jean Young/Becky Carson
1975	1st	Becky Carson/Vicki Callicrate
1976		Sharon Hammer
1978		Colleen Behrman
1979		Donna Krening
1981		Mary Anderson
1982		Julie Haskins
1984		Melanie Watt
1985		Tina Lenard
1986		Tina Lenard
1987		Tina Lenard
1988		Radene Spears
1989		Maggie Adams
1990		Corrine Thurston
1991		Rhona Boettler
1992		Dianne Binder
1993		Monique Mallory
1994		Dianne Binder
1995		Dianne Binder

STAKE RACE CHAMPIONS

Year	Day	Winner	Year	Day	Winner
1914		Coke Roberds	1946	1st	Bud Daugherty
1915		Si Dawson		2nd	J. T. Hudson
1919		George Bird	1947	1st	Jim Dodo/Quentin Semotan
1920		Arch Ryan		2nd	J. T. Hudson/Glenn Tabb
1921		Arch Ryan	1948	1st	Wilbur Luark
1922		Woodall		2nd	Ivan Daugherty
1923		John Chambers	1949	1st	Jim Dodo
1924		John Chambers		2nd	Raymond Green
1926		Charles Miller	1950	1st	Jim Dodo
1928		Frank Squire		2nd	Jim Dodo
1929		John Chambers	1952	1st	Clarence Wheeler
1930		John Chambers		2nd	Duane Tabb
1931		John Chambers	1953	1st	Millard Dixon/Bob Perry
1935	1st	George Mills		2nd	Millard Dixon
	2nd	Marshall Peavy	1954	1st	Ernest Bridges
1936	1st	Marshall Peavy		2nd	Millard Dixon
	2nd	Marshall Peavy	1955	1st	Vernon Williams
1937		Marshall Peavy		2nd	Babe Haller
1939	1st	Don Dodo	1956	1st	Millard Dixon
	2nd	Russell Yount		2nd	Babe Haller
1940	1st	Dell Owens	1957	1st	Leon Green/Lawrence Drake
	2nd	Dell Owens		2nd	Pauline Haller*
1941	1st	Marshall Peavy/Dell Owens	1958	1st	Millard Dixon
	2nd	Marshall Peavy		2nd	Harold Harper
1945	1st	Dewey Savage	1959	1st	Millard Dixon
	2nd	Ivan Daugherty		2nd	Daryl Hatch

*NOTE: Pauline Haller was the only woman to win the Stake Race.

The first Northwest Colorado cowpunchers to become World Champion Bronco Riders were Clayton Danks, foreman of the Reverse Four who became Sheriff of Wyoming's Freeman County, and Kid Vaughn, who was raised on a ranch near Cross Mountain and was a long-time hand at the Two Circle Bar.

According to Patty Vaughn, Kid's granddaughter-in-law, Kid bought Pin Ears from a widow woman on Wolf Creek near Mt. Harris and was bucked off the first time he saddled the horse who jumped the fence at Uncle Eph and Aunt Fanny Riders's ranch.

Old-timers still speculate on why Kid shot himself in a barn behind his house on May 18, 1906. He was 33. Everyone agreed it was because he was in pain but no one knew whether the pain was caused by problems with his wife or stomach. Kid's son Virgil cowboyed until he was 87 years old, as did Virgil's son Leonard and his grandsons Boone and Lowell, but none took up bronc riding.

From John Rolfe Burroughs' *"Where The Old West Stayed Young"*:

...The city dads of Steamboat Springs found it necessary to pass an ordinance (August 2, 1903) making it a misdemeanor for cowboys to hold bucking contests and horse races on Main Street Sunday mornings because it frightened the ladies on their way to and from church...

Section 2: (A) No person shall break or attempt to break, ride or attempt to ride any wild, vicious, pitching or bucking horse, ass broncho, or other animal or animals within the streets of said town;

(B) No person or persons shall, within the streets of said town of Steamboat Springs break or attempt to break any horse or horses, ass or asses, to drive or work with any wagon, cart, buggy, or other vehicle...

Section 4: The term 'horse'... (and) the term 'ass' as used herein shall be taken to include both the male and female of the species.

Early Cow Horse Race at the Routt County Fair (Photo: Margaret Squire Hogue)

Racing At The Routt County Fair

Like the Ute Indians, who loved racing on the flats near Steamboat Springs, Routt County pioneers were excellent horsemen. Testing the strength of a bronco, the speed of a cow pony or the quality of a Quarter Horse was an integral part of life in Northwest Colorado. Competition for speed, skill and derring-do built the legends of the West. What was unique to the Yampa Valley was the intense interest of pioneers, herdsmen and cowboys in breeding horses that fit the special needs of the cattle industry.

Developing bloodlines and raising horses which displayed enough intelligence and stamina to work both stock and land was essential to survival. Their quality was demonstrated in horses shown and raced on straightaways at town celebrations prior to the turn of the century, and at the County Fair since its inception.

The excitement of seeing locals and "outsiders" compete, while wagering a dime or two, provided the momentum which turned Hayden's Railroad Day into the County Fair and the County Fair into a racing tradition. Phippsburg's Lila Rider remembers sitting in the grandstands holding the "pot" for $15 bets between her husband Bud and Emma Reary which was, she explains "big money" back in the 1950s.

Racing at the County Fair began in 1914 when Si Dawson sent his hired hand and a team of mules, Jake and Judy, to grade and slope the first oval track in Northwest Colorado. Eighty-two years later the same track is still in use, and many of the plank rails defining the inside and outside were not replaced until 1993.

The Fair has consistently provided a showcase for quarter, three-eighths, five-eighths and three-quarter mile races as well as relay and pony express races. The reputations of horses, strings of horses, and their breeders and owners were created and cultivated at the Fair. One of the earliest racers was Henry Kitchen's Red Bird, a bay cow pony with a white patch on his forehead who won his first race at the July 4th celebration in Steamboat Springs in 1894 before taking 31 out of his next 35 races. Although Red Bird never ran at the Fair, he set the standard for racing in the valley.

Most early competitors hailed from Northwest Colorado and the countryside around Vernal, among them: Gordon Adair, J.S. Boyer, Sam Elmer, Ray Fisk, J.D. Grimes, Clayton Danks, Shorty Heguenin, John and Dick Kitchens, George Lobb, Tex McDowell, Guy McNurton and Roy Rheuland. Si Dawson and Coke

Roberds of Hayden did not win many races but most of the champions who did were the offspring of their breeding programs and stallion Peter McCue. Their most successful horse at Fair races was a cow horse named Water Dog.

I didn't know Si Dawson,
But I knew Coke Roberds well.
They built our famous race track
So I've heard people tell...

They always had good saddle broncs
Top riders rode them for the count.
The ropers tied big Hereford calves.
They each had a real good mount.

Sometimes there was a fight or two.
We always got our money's worth.
Barnum had the circus, but
We had the greatest show on earth.

—George Watts

County roads made good flat tracks in the 1930s. (Photo: Tread of Pioneers Museum)

Local owners included:

Bob Gray, Yampa, raced Miss McCue, Twilight, Undecided and Medicine Bow between 1914 and the 1920s.

Jack McPherson, Snake River, raced long-distance horses like Indian, Mary Brown, Dunbrobin and Roe Dear which dominated races in the late teens and early 1920s.

The Peavy Brothers, Deep Creek, were Lawrence, whose wife Evelyn owned Fleet, a strong competitor in the late 1920s, and Marshall, who entered nearly every cow horse and flat saddle race, frequently winning with Bob H, Mary McCue, Monty and Margie.

Fred Sayre, Hayden, dominated flat saddle competition between 1914 until his death in an automobile accident in 1931. The five-eighths mile free-for-all, was named to honor his love of racing (1935-1941) and his quality horses which included a pony named Trixie, and Montrose, Montana, Sundance and Dalston, considered one of the best long-distance horses produced in Northwest Colorado.

Jess Stringham, Hayden, raced until the late 1930s, owned CocaCola, Silver, Little Squaw and the renowned Billy McCue.

Herb Summer, Hayden, who raced for three decades prior to the 1940s, earned a reputation with Patches, Twinkle, White Cloud, Charlotte and Skeeter.

82

Jap Wyman, Meeker, dominated early Fair races with Wampus Cat, "a hard horse to beat," and ran a fine line of versatile flat saddle horses including Carter Johnson, Grace Denny and Denny's Best.

A new generation of owners and racers began frequenting the Fair after the Depression. Stimulated by mobility from better trucks, development of racing circuits, and creation of the Western Slope Rodeo and Racing Association in 1941, the Routt County Fair began to attract major performers. Because it was one of the last races of the season, contestants flocked to Hayden for a final attempt at points to qualify for "overall" money. Fair promotion said contestants came from as far away as Alabama, but most hailed from Colorado, Utah and Nebraska and other towns on the circuit with oval tracks: Craig, Kremmling, Meeker, Rifle and Steamboat Springs.

Between 1935 and 1941 the Fair was dominated by horses from "outside" and Alamosa's Frankie Burns who generally showed up with a string of 8 to 12 horses primed for flat saddle, relay and Roman races. Other prominent visiting competitors included: Philip Brossard of Cook, Nebraska; J.E. Haddon of Payson, Utah; and from Colorado Lawrence Allen, C.V. Hallenback, George Loesch, D. Owens, Jack Phelps, Date Scott, Hugh and Lowry Seely and Marion Tefft.

During the 1940s and early 1950s, Marshall Peavy, Jess Stringham and Herb Summer continued to make impressive showings even while sharing the spotlight with the next decade's owners: Gib Coyner, Kenneth Gray, Bill Green, Mabel Green, Wilber Luark, Dick Miller, Jim Rhodes and Gilbert Summer.

Local owners included:

Andy Black, Oak Creek, had good horses in Mattie S and Giggles.

Mike Hinman, Kremmling, dominated races between 1947 and 1950 with Mary Nile and Minerva.

Leonard Lighthizer, Hayden, influenced racing and Quarter Horse breeding during the era, first appearing at the Fair in 1923 and 1924. From the 1940s into the 1960s, he won horse and saddle events with Hi Ball, Playboy, Upset L, Dew Drop, Little Drip, Speedy Lark and Snuffy.

Quentin Semotan, Deep Creek, raced Brenda Star, Star Duster and Irish Molly at the Fair during the early 1950s.

Leonard Williams, Steamboat Springs, won the first of many Fair races in 1931 with a cow horse named Stockings and won during the late 1940s and early 1950s with Tabor, Dougan and Cinderella.

A new crop of owners carried the colors into the next three decades. The circuit initiated competition in Grand Junction and Vernal, prompting increases in the number of racers, owners and breeders. These included locals Joe Birch, Nick and Ruby DeLuca, John Hayes, Will Montieth, Daryl Rule, Steve Rohrbaugh, Ross and George Watts, Doug Wheeler and Gary Yeager; and "outsiders" Carl Allen of Vernal, Wayne Garrett and Chuck Shively of Craig, Charles McNutt and Ralph Sasser of Grand Junction. Among the most prominent:

Wilber Arnett, Hayden, became a frequent winner with Deep Sparkle, Humble Heart and Marvel.

Rusty Baker, Steamboat Springs, ran Rusty Vandy, Star Blend, Mary Hill, Snazzy Rip and Ant Coq to consistent applause.

Jim Camilletti, Hayden, starred with Bourbon Supreme, Leech Bar, Joker, Gill and Heel Fly.

Mike Dorr, Steamboat Springs, competed with Go Go Tex, Star Home and Easter Rock.

Ed and Kathy Duncan, Steamboat Springs, broke barriers with Badger and Carrie Nation.

Art Hudspeth, Steamboat Springs, earned kudos with Hang Ten, Sturdy and Slantner.

Leonard Lighthizer, Hayden, continued his 40-year winning record with horses like Chili, Skunk Tail and Two Medicine.

Walter Mann, Deep Creek, won with Honey Dew, Eddie M, Running Doll, Twinkle and War Policy.

Doug Monger, Steamboat Springs, was racing Mr. Big Boy, Baronet Jet and Indian Moonglow.

Clarence Wheeler, Steamboat Springs, has been galloping down Lincoln Avenue towing skiers during Winter Carnival competition since 1933 when he was 19. He initiated donkey jump skijoring in 1950, the same year he began coordinating Winter Carnival riders, many of them relatives. Clarence was born in a sod hut in Nebraska, schooled at Clark and educated at his father's livery at 7th and Yampa. A charter member of the Yampa Valley Cutter and Chariot Racing Association, he assured lively Fair races by running Barney, Dee Star, Night and Brune Dee.

Walt Wheeler ran Snazzy Fellow and Square Van Deck in the late 1970s and early 1980s.

The 1970s and 1980s were not kind to racers in Northwest Colorado. The last cow horse race at the Fair was held in 1978 and during the 1980s the only flat saddle races were quarter, three-eighths and one half mile free-for-alls and a one and one-half mile relay, all discontinued after the 1988 Fair. The other mainstay of the Fair, pony express races were last held in 1991 and 1994. The sole surviving racing traditions are kids races and chariot races.

Several factors contributed to the demise of flat and stock saddle racing from the Fair: the expense of owning, training and traveling with race horses; and the popularity of chariot racing, launched with formation of the Yampa Valley Cutter and Chariot Racing Association in 1960. Racing involved more risk and less prestige than breeding and showing. Costs outdistanced purses, especially at the Fair. At the first Fair in 1914, the purse was $100 for the three-eighths mile free-for-all and the entry fee 10 cents; at the last race in 1988 the purse was $100 and the entry fee $20.

Two types of races were popular: races for racing blood horses most frequently under flat saddles, run continuously until the 1960s; and races for working cow horses, which ran with a stock saddle and a curb bit, which ran from 1914 to 1978 and as a jackpot between 1970 and 1978. When enough horses were entered and enough money wagered, there were separate divisions for two and three year olds.

QUARTER MILE RACES, a free-for-all run continuously from 1914 until 1960, were always varied and popular. The Ladies quarter-mile cow horse race, popular from 1916 to 1926 and again from 1937 to 1949, drew wives and daughters of owners who raced the same horses in the quarter mile free-for-all for cow horses. Boys and girls also ran quarter mile races at the Fair between 1952 and 1955. From 1956 to 1959 it was run as a boys race, the girls race being one-eighth mile; from 1960 until 1969 it was a quarter-mile race open to both, and called a "kids race" between 1970 and 1977, and in 1988 when reinstated. Quarter mile races for ponies, horses under 14.5 hands high, were held at early Fairs; run as an eighth mile Shetland Pony Race between 1936 and 1940, and then run only sporadically until discontinued in 1955.

Special purses have attracted contestants to several quarter mile races: the Prey Brothers Special Cow Horse Race (1921 and 1922); the Western Slope Quarter Mile Derby won by local horses Mary Nile (1948 and 1949) and Minerva (1950) owned by Mike Hinman of Kremmling; a Palomino Race (1950); and a Hayden Free-For-All (1955).

Incomplete records make it impossible to reconstruct complete or accurate records of winning horses and their owners. The following list does, however, reflect the commitment and involvement of many consistent winners and the diligent research of Jerry Green.

Flat Saddles

1914	Cricket	
1916	Booger Red	Billy Winters
	Red Buck	Jim Lee
1917-18	Carter Johnson	Jap Wyman
1918	Duster	Billy Winters
1919	Jimmy	Tug Dale
	Indian	Jack McPherson
	CocaCola	Jess Stringham
1920-22	Bob H	Marshall Peavy
1920	Silver Tip	Jap Wyman
	Grace Denny	Jap Wyman
1922	Billy McCue	
1923	Red Lady	
	May O.B.	J. Grimes
1924	Jimmy Spinner	R. Mulkey
1925	Penny	Dick Kitchens
1925-26	Blue Boy	Dick Kitchens
1925-26	Little Squaw	Jess Stringham
1926-27	Patches	Herb Summer
1928-29	Fleet	Lawrence Peavy
1931	Jiggs	William Gray

Horses from other parts of Colorado dominated competition between 1935 and 1945, most notably those owned by Frankie Burns of Alamosa. No records are available after 1968.

1945	White Cloud	Herb Summer
1946-47	Charlotte	Herb Summer
1947	Lady Donna	Gib Coyner
1947-49	Mary Nile	Mike Hinman
1948	Little Buddy	Herb Summer
	Red and Hi Time	Leonard Lightizer
	Jitterbug	Jim Rhodes
1948-49	Minerva	Mike Hinman
1952	Dunkirk	Date Scott
	Brenda Star	Quentin Semotan
1953	Jimmy Spinner	Herb Summer
1954	Jerry Dunn	Herb Summer
1957	Little Drip	Leonard Lightizer
1967	Rock Issue	Kay Larson
1968	Slim Jimmy	Bill Laramore

One-eighth mile races for two-year-olds

1949	Dewdrop	Leonard Lighthizer
1949-50	Upset L	Leonard Lighthizer
1950	Bonnie K George	Loesch
	Little Buddy	Herb Summer
	Minerva	Mike Hinman
1968	Speedy Lark	Leonard Lighthizer

Cow Horses

1915-16	Ivey D	Sam Elmer
	Colonel	Jap Wyman
1919	Silver	Billy Winters
	Sandy	Jack McPherson
1920	Woolly	G. Laub
1920-23	Sugar Bill	Reece Horton
1923	Wheeler	Marshall Peavy
1923-24	Red Bird	Leonard Lighthizer
1924-25	Medicine Bow	Bob Gray
1926	Chuck Rider	Henry Hindman
1929-30	Twinkle	Herb Summers
1930-31	Papoose	C.D. McClelland
1931	Stockings	Leonard Williams
1935	Monte	Marshall Peavy
1937-38	Billy Whiskers	Jess Stringham
1938-40	Margie	Marshall Peavy
1939	Hi Ball	Leonard Lighthizer
1940	Hornet	Dick Miller
1941	Little Dutch	Jess Stringham
	Playboy	Leonard Lighthizer
	Dougan	Leonard Williams
	Charmer	Jess Stringham
1944	Hi Ball and Playboy	Leonard Lighthizer
	Brown Magic	Mabel Green
	Monogram	Bill Green
1945	Flicka	Bud Pitman
1947	Red Shick	Peggy Hinman
1948	Colus Landy	George Loesch
	Charlotte	Herb Summer
	Joe	Hazel Yount
1949	Peanuts	Buddy Hayden
1957	Little Drip	Leonard Lightizer
1968	Joker	Jim Camilletti

Ponies

1918-21	Trixy	Fred Sayre
1923-24	Peaches	Otto Horton
1926-27	Buelah	Jack McPherson

Shetland Pony Races were won by John Kitchens (1937 and 1938) and Bud Terrill (1939); a 55" high pony race by Darwin Lockhart (1945); a 52" high pony race by Milt Kitchens (1945); and both pony races by Nancy Hinman (1946).

THREE-EIGHTH MILE RACES, a free-for-all flat saddle race first run in 1914 was a feature race between 1923 and 1941 and run continuously between 1919 until 1931.

1914	Cinderella	
	Flying Dance	A.J. Whitlock
1915	Red Rock	Jim Lee
1918	Dalston	Fred Sayre
1919	Mary Brown	Jack McPherson
1920	Silver Dick*	Jess Stringham
	Brown Soyer	Shorty Huguenin
1921	Billy McCue*	Jess Stringham
	Montrose	Fred Sayre
1923	May O.B.	J.D. Grimes
1924	Mary Brown	Dick Kitchens
1926	Little Squaw	Jess Stringham
1929	See Me	Red Thomas
	Fleet	Lawrence Peavy
1931	Mischief and Jiggs	Jess Stringham
	Dennys Best	Jap Wyman
1935	Tabor	Leonard Williams
1937	Buddy Nile	G.T. George
	You & I	J. Grimes
	Muggins	F. Harris
		Scooter

Between 1935 and 1950 these races were won primarily by circuit riders with the exception of Lowry Seely's Windy Wee and Date Scott's Oney Bee (1952), and Dean Preece's Grafton and Wilber Arnett's Humble Heart (1968). A 580-yard race for two and three-year-olds in 1968 was won by Rusty Baker's Rusty Vandy on the first day and Ruby DeLuca's Roudy Lee Bar on the second.

Cow Horses

1919	Silver	Jess Stringham
1920	Sugar Bill	Reece Horton
1921	Lady Red	
1922	Sugar Bill	Reece Horton
1923	Trix	Marshall Peavy
1925	Medicine Bow	Ben Anderson
1926	Chuck Rider	Henry Hindman
1939	Hi Ball	Leonard Lighthizer
1941	Sue	Marshall Peavy
1945	Gold Hill	Ben Anderson
	Black Spade	Gilbert Summer
1947-48	Cold Deck	George Loesch
1948	Snuffy	Leonard Lighthizer
1949	Bonny K	George Loesch

HALF MILE RACES, popular because they start and finish in front of the grandstands, were free-for-alls run between 1914 and 1987 and sporadically between 1925 and 1941 when divisions for two and three-year-olds began. It too has been varied: cow horses (1918, 1921 and 1922), ladies (1919) and ponies (1922).

The first half mile special was run in 1921 and the most prestigious Fair trophy, the Si Dawson Cup (1937-1941), was presented to the horse with the fastest time in either of two races on both days. Winners included Herb Summer's Skeeter (1937), Andy Black's Mattie S (1938) and Frankie Burns' Panther (1939-41). Pat Holderness remembers the 1944 half mile free-for-all with terror. The new starting gate was hooked up to her father's tractor which stalled. An incredible hush fell over the grandstands as the horses approached seconds before his engine caught and Jack could pull the gates off the track.

The Western Slope Quarter Mile Derby, run between 1946 and 1950, was won by Carl Albert's Silver Dick (1946), Kenneth Gray's Gold Hill (1947-48), Lowry Seeley's Windy Wee and Dexter Hill (1949-50).

Flat Saddle

1914	Cinderella	
1915	Flying Dance	A.J. Whitlock
1916	Red Buck	Jim Lee
1917-20	Wampus Cat	Jap Wyman
1918	Diamond	Clayton Danks
1921	Mary Brown	
	Miss McCue	Bob Gray
1922	Red Bird	Leonard Lighthizer
	Dan	Roscoe Cozad
1923	Sir John	J. Grimes
1924	Penay	E. Smith
	Cry Baby	Doc McClelland
1926	Little Squaw	Jess Stringham
1926	Sun Dance*	Fred Sayre
1929	Mary McCue	Marshall Peavy
1930	Richard D	T.P.Mills
1937	Skeeter	Herb Summer
1938	Matti S	Andy Black
1939	Giggles*	Andy Black
1940	Playboy	Leonard Lighthizer
	Cinderella	Leonard Williams
1945	Scotty	John Chambers
1947-48	Gabb Hill	Kenneth Hill
1948	Mary Nile	Mike Hinman
1949	Bay Bum	Marion Tefft
	Ute Chief	Lowry Seely
1950	Black Beauty	Lawrence Allen
	Windy Wee	Lowry Seely
	Dexter Hill	Lowry Seely
1952	Black Beauty	Lawrence Allen
1967	Maple Lou	Leonard Lighthizer
	Tonda Loe	Chuck Shively
1969	Humble Heart	Wilber Arnett

Cow Horse

1918	Water Dog/Cow Horse	Coke Roberds
	Lebold/Ladies Race	Mrs. Williams
1919	Twilight/Ladies Race	
1921	Quick Silver/Cow Horse	Fred Sayre
1922	Tip/Cow Horse	Bob Gray
1922	Babe/Pony Race	

LONG DISTANCE RACES—five-eighths, three-quarter and one mile races and many varieties of special and novelty races—have not been run continuously.

FIVE-EIGHTHS MILE RACES

1918-19	Dalston	Fred Sayre
1920	Black Mink	Jap Wyman
1921	Mary Brown	Marshall Peavy
1922	Dalston	Fred Sayre
1925	Auditor	Marion Tefft
1926	Dunbrobin	Jack McPherson
1928-31	Mary McCue	Marshall Peavy and C.E. McClelland

Run as The Fred Sayre Memorial Race (1935-1941)

1935	Jefferson	Fred Grimes
1936-37	Mattie S	Andy Black
1938	Rose Marie	Andy Black
1940-41	Wally Warfield	J.E.Haddon

Run as The Hayden Special (1949)

1949	Gold Hill	Kenneth Gray
	Sundowner	Kenneth Gray
1949-50	Snuffy	Leonard Lighthizer
1968	Nas U Time	
1969	Gala Claim	Bud Blaskings

THREE-QUARTER MILE RACES, was run sporadically after 1947 when it started being run as The Hayden Special on the second day of the Fair.

1916	Fred Sayre
1917	Jim Lee
1918	Fred Sayre
1919	Jack McPherson
1922	Bob Gray
1923	J.D. Grimes
1947	Haefly and Phillips

ONE MILE RACES, two laps around the track, are the longest of and most strenuous of the flat saddle races.

1919-20	Dalston	Fred Sayre
1921	Mary Brown	Jack McPherson
1922	Sandy	Van Kitchens
1923	Sir John	J. Grimes
1924	Montana	Fred Sayre
1925	Auditor	Marion Tefft
1926	Dunbrobin	Jack McPherson
1929-30	Mary McQue	Marshall Peavy
1931	Roe Dear	Jack McPherson

Pat Barber, who is devoting retirement from the Yampa Valley Electric Association to developing a Prairie Dog Breeding Farm, remembers "freezing his butt off" racing Buddy Werner's '41 Ford convertible to the races with Buddy and Loris.

July 4th, 1983

RELAY RACES (1914-present) require the rider to change both horse and saddle.   They are run with stock saddles, often adapted to facilitate rapid change.   Early relays used a strings of five and four horses on a 2.5 mile track until, 1928 when the traditional three horse relay on a 1.5 mile track was instituted.

PONY EXPRESS/COWBOY RELAY RACES (1921-1995) differ from the standard relay by requiring riders to change from a running to a standing horse and to regain speed as rapidly as possible.   Called the Cowboy Relay when it began (1921), it was limited to Routt County horses (1939-1941) and became known as the Pony Express Race (1946) the same year a Boys Pony Express Race was added.

BOYS PONY EXPRESS CHAMPIONS

Year	Day	Rider
1944	1st	Darwin Lockhart/Jack Eckstine
1944	2nd	Ronald Cluff/Jack Eckstine
1945	1st	Darwin Lockhart/Jack Eckstine
1945	2nd	Darwin Lockhart/Jack Eckstine/Williard Etzler
1946	1st	Jimmie Stetson
1946	2nd	Jimmie Stetson
1947	1st	Jimmie Stetson/Frankie Stetson
1947	2nd	Doc Younger
1948	1st	Glen Stetson
1948	2nd	Wilbur Luark Jr.
1950	1st	Frankie Stetson
1950	2nd	Frankie Stetson
1952		Jimmie Stetson

RELAY RACE CHAMPIONS

Year	Day	Rider/Owner
1914	3rd	Rube Squire
1915	3rd	Frank Squire/Curley Watts
1916	3rd	Estis/Jap Wyman
1917	3rd	Curley Watts
1918	1st	Ralph Salisbury/Wilson
1918	3rd	Frank Squire/Watts
1919	3rd	Frank Squire
1920	2nd	Bob Gray
1920	3rd	John Chandler
1921	2nd	Frank Squire
1922	2nd	Dutch Meyers/Bob Gray
1923	2nd	Roscoe Cozad
1924	2nd	Bob Gray
1924	3rd	Roscoe Cozad/Bob Gray
1925	2nd	Bill Egry
1928	3rd	Red Thomas
1929	3rd	Red Thomas
1930	2nd	Roberts
1936	1st	Frank Burns
1936	2nd	Frank Burns
1937	1st	B. Wallace
1938	1st	Frankie Burns
1938	2nd	Frankie Burns
1939	1st	Frankie Burns
1939	2nd	Frankie Burns
1940	1st	Jack Phillips
1940	2nd	Frankie Burns
1945	1st	John Chambers
1945	2nd	Hall & Loesch
1946	1st	Wilbur Luark
1946	2nd	Hall & Loesch
1947	1st	George Loesch
1947	2nd	Wilber Pretti
1950	1st	George Loesch
1950	2nd	George Loesch
1953	1st	Wayne Allen
1953	2nd	George Loesch
1993	2nd	Justin Pierce/Jerry Garcia
1994	2nd	Mark and Aaron Huffstetler
1995	2nd	Clint Langerud/Brook Hodson

PONY EXPRESS CHAMPIONS

Year	Day	Rider/Owner
1921	2nd	Dutch Meyer/Jess Stringham
1923	3rd	Roscoe Cozad
1925	3rd	Bill Egry
1926	2nd	Miller
	3rd	Miller
1928	1st	Frank Squire
1929		Red Thomas
1930	3rd	Milton Temple/Ben Anderson
1936	1st	Frank Burns
	2nd	Frank Burns
1937	1st	Leonard Lighthizer
1938	1st	Herb Summer
	2nd	Herb Summer
1939	1st	Jack Condon
	2nd	Herb Summer
1940	1st	Herb Summer
	2nd	Luark Brothers
1944	1st	Leonard Lighthizer
	2nd	Leonard Lighthizer
1948	1st	Pat Patten
	2nd	Pat Patten
1949	1st	George Loesch
	2nd	George Loesch
1950	1st	George Loesch
	2nd	George Loesch
1952	1st	George Loesch
	2nd	Hugh Seely
1953	1st	George Loesch
	2nd	George Loesch
1954	1st	Ross Watts
	2nd	Jimmie Stetson
1955	1st	Larry Loesch
	2nd	Art Fredrickson
1956	1st	Jimmie Stetson
	2nd	Jimmie Stetson
1957	1st	Jack Wheeler
1958	1st	Frankie Stetson
	2nd	Clarence Wheeler
1959		Gerald Truax/Dean Wheeler
1960	1st	Jack Wheeler
	2nd	Clarence Wheeler
1961	1st	Jack Wheeler
	2nd	Jack Wheeler
1962	1st	Dean Wheeler
	2nd	Clarence Wheeler
1963	1st	Clarence Wheeler
	2nd	Clarence Wheeler
1965	1st	Jack Wheeler
	2nd	Doug Camilletti
1966	1st	Art Hudspeth/Rusty Baker
	2nd	Art Hudspeth/Rusty Baker

(No results found since 1966)

CHARIOT RACES (1924-present)

Typically a quarter mile "controlled runaway" for the driver of a two-horse team, chariot races were approved as an exhibition race in 1924 (Henry Hindman and John Hitchens) and 1941 (John Chambers and Dick Kitchens) and have been at the Fair since 1971. Early chariots were made from 55-gallon drums mounted on a Model A frame with motorcycle or bicycle wheels. Today they are lightweight aluminum or fiberglass designed to pull easily, take curves and protect drivers.

The Yampa Valley Cutter and Chariot Racing Association formed in 1960 attracted many of the best racers in the area: Darwin Lockhart, Leo Snowden, Jim Thompson, Doc Utterback, Clarence, Walt and Linda Wheeler, and Rusty Baker who took five consecutive state championships.

Competition throughout the region kept them too busy to concentrate on the Fair although they have been active particpants since 1971. Their ranks include: (in the 1970s) Ike Anderson, Rusty Baker, Jim Camilletti, Art Hudspeth, Dwight Huffstetler, Otis Lyons, Pat Robson, Leo Snowden, Doc Utterback, Clarence and Dean Wheeler; (in the late 1980s and early 1990s) Donna Brenton, Ed and Kathy Duncan, Dick Green, Cinda Wheeler Garcia, Jason Graham, Curt McIlvaine, Doug Monger, Clarence and Doug Wheeler, Barbara Yeager Wheeler and Linda Wheeler.

SPECIAL RACES

Early races which drew enthusiastic participants and audiences involved timed stunts with nightshirts (1921-1924), beer mugs (1922-1923), cigars (1919-1920), hats (1921), musical chairs (1923), parasols (1929-1931) and mules (1930-1931). Those described here endured the test of time.

Roman Race (1923-1950), featuring a rider standing astride two horses racing around a half mile track, was a major event between 1937 and 1941 when Frankie Burns took on all challengers. Local Ross Watts was a spectacular performer at the last race in 1950.

1923	Roscoe Cozad
1926 and 1929	Red Thomas
1931	William Gray
1937	Billy Walker
1938	Frankie Burns and H. Humphries
1939 and 1940	Frankie Burns and Jack Philips
1946	Chet Hall and George Loesch
1947	Bud Pitman
1948 and 1949	Pat Patten

Wild Horse Race (1922-1993), requires a two or three member team to saddle and ride a wild horse and can be held in an arena or on a track. Always popular and always dangerous, this race has generated more than its fair share of what Dan Knott calls "elbow-bending" stories.

Barbara Green, proprietor of the Yarnyard in Steamboat Springs, says she always went to the Fair to sit in the stands with Pat Fulton and gossip. Their favorite subject was a local chap who insisted that all he wanted in life was a redheaded woman and a pink Cadillac with a pink horse trailer. He got all three in the 1950s when Hayden farmers "made a million" in wheat, but confessed "none of 'em were worth a damn."

WILD HORSE RACE CHAMPIONS

Year	Day	Winner	Year	Day	Winner
1922	2nd	Frank Squire	1954		Lee Williamson
	3rd	Bill Egry .	1956	1st	Jim Lindsey
1923		Bill Rynell		2nd	John McIntyre
1928	1st	Dan Lovisone	1957		Dick Miller
	2nd	Cecil Kennedy	1958		Dave Cattoor
	3rd	Glen Gates	1981	1st	Bill Lee
1929	1st	Max Williams		2nd	John Hayes
	2nd	Elmer Getty	1982		John Hayes
1948	1st	Doug Salisbury	1990		Clay Gray/John Shellhart
	2nd	Jay Gentry			

Cowboy Race (1926-1931) requires the contestant to enter a corral, saddle a horse, race around the track and repeat the performance two more times. Frank Stetson Sr. took first place money ($30) three of the six years and Dick Kitchens, who won the first year, was the only other Routt County champion.

The Novelty Race (1935-1940), which replaced the Cowboy Race, required the cowboy to change horses every eighth mile, walking the first, trotting the second and running the last leg.

1935	Leonard Lighthizer
1936	Denny Cullen
1937	Leonard Lighthizer
1938	Harold Wixson
1939	Marshall Peavy

Potato Race (1914-1931), a "favorite" of local horsemen, was run continuously from the first Routt County Fair until 1931. It required riders to spear potatoes on a six-foot stick and move them, one-by-one to the opposite end of the arena and was often won by Si Dawson, Coke Roberds, Emory Clark, Clayton Danks, Marshall Peavy, Bill Egry, Arch Ryan and Leonard Lighthizer.

Mike Robson, Shane Yeager and Bobby Yeager head down the homestretch. Lockhart Sale Barn, built in 1974 seen in background.

Bed Race (1919-1931) requires the contestant to get out of a bed, put on boots, roll and tie the blanket to his saddle, mount and ride to a second horse which he then leads around a half mile track. The race enjoyed a brief revival in 1988, 1989 and 1991.

1930	Bill Gray
1931	Walter Dalpez
1923	Dick Kitchens
1924-26	John Chambers
1929-30	Frank Stetson Sr.
1931	Tex Waters

Bundle Race (1924-1931) required the cowboy to race to a bundle of clothes, don the attire and race the clock back.

1924	Jack Brown
1925-26	Gilbert Summer
1930	Dorsey Lighthizer
1931	Arch Ryan

Slow Horse Race (1988-1994), suggested by Fair Board President Bill Gay, invites local politicians to quite literally "run for office" and, mercifully, results were not recorded.

Routt County Riders

Young men and women who loved fast horses, had the ability to remain aboard, and built reputations for getting the most out of a horse. They raced for the sake of racing regardless of the make or model horse or type event and their ranks include:

1914 to 1931: John Chambers, Bill Egry, Frank and Rube Squire, Curley Watts

1935 to 1950: Denny Cullen, Jack Ecstine, Willard Etzler, Mildred Lighthizer, Darwin Lockhart, the Luark Brothers

1950s: Kay Conyers, Jack Harper, Anton Frederickson, Joanna Stevenson, Leo "Squeek" Snowden, Danny Younger, Frank, Jimmie and Glen Stetson

1960s: Fred Camilletti, Doug Camilletti, Doug Wheeler, Clare Wheeler, Chester Wheeler, Jack Wheeler

1970s: Carla and Teri Fry, John Hayes, Doug Monger, Sharon Sheridan, Terry Green and Dorinda Valdeck

1980s: Mike Robson, Shane Yeager, Bobby Yeager

Relay and Pony Express stars included: Arch Ryan, Denny Cullen, Guy Bergman, Dick Kitchens, Leon Green, Lane Decker, Paul Hertzog, Kay Perry, Art Fredrickson, Jocko Camilletti, Mike Robson, Kenny Gee, Shane Yeager, Monty Youngland.

Steamboat Springs Junior Livestock Show

From 1949 until 1958, 4-H and FFA members exhibited livestock at a Fall show, separate from the Fair, in Steamboat Springs. The first Junior Livestock Sale and the first Round Robin Showmanship Contest took place at this show.

Becky Ward, 1983

BEEF DIVISION

	Champion Male	Champion Female	Market Animals	Champion Showman
1949	Douglas Sherrod	Donald Trull	Douglas Sherrod	Douglas Sherrod
1950	Douglas Patton	Douglas Ross	Willie Stender	Willie Stender
1951	Billy Brown	Douglas Ross	Doris Kuchera	Douglas Ross
1952	Douglas Patton	Douglas Ross	Ed Buchanan	Sheila Reagor
1953	Stuart Ross	Sheila Reagor	Sheila Reagor	Sheila Reagor
1954	Stuart Ross	Stuart Ross	Jackie Sherrod	Sheila Reagor
1955	Boyd Powell	Aaron Huffstettler	Marian Hinman	Sheila Reagor
1956	Shirley Stender	Maraian Hinman	John Hoelsher	Sheila Reagor
1957	Donna Hinman	Boyd Powell	Aaron Huffstettler	Marian Hinman
1958	Georgia Jones	Aaron Huffstetler	Charlotte Martensen	Aaron Huffstetler

SHEEP DIVISION

	Champion Male	Champion Female	Market Animals	Champion Showman
1949	Willie Stender	Willie Stender	Dean Look	Willie Stender
1950		Donna Guees Columbia		
		Lee Williamson Corriedale		
		Frank Selbe Suffolk	Patsy Truax	Patsy Truax
1951	Frank Selbe	Lee Williamson	Patsy Truax	Patsy Truax
1952	Lee Williamson	Shirley Stender	Lenore Ekstrom	Frank Selbe
1953	Shirley Stender	Frank Selbe	Shirley Stender	Frank Selbe
1954	Lee Williamson	Lee Williamson	Ronald Woodcock	Lee Williamson
1955	Shirley Stender	Leroy McLaughlin	Shirley Stender	Shirley Stender
1956	Kathleen Cogshill	Leroy McLaughlin	Leroy McLaughlin	Leroy McLaughlin
1957	Leroy McLaughlin	Shirley Stender	Leroy McLaughlin	Glen McLaughlin
1958	Shirley Stender	Glen McLaughlin	Glen McLaughlin	Glen McLaughlin

HORSES

	Saddle Horse	Colt	Showman
1949	Douglas Ross	Betty Cullen	Douglas Ross
1950		Mary Cullen	
1951		Betty Cullen	
1952	Joanne Semotan	Betty Madison	
1953	Douglas Ross	Josie Ekstrom	
1954	Joanne Semotan		Joanne Semotan
1955	Boyd Von Fleet		Gary Whitmer
1956	Gary Whitmer		Kay Conyers
1957	Gary Whitmer		Gary Whitmen
1958	Roy Tufly		Sharon Arnett

Junior Livestock Showmanship

Beef, Sheep and Horse Showmanship began at the Routt County Fair in 1959; swine was added in 1974.

BEEF SHOWMANSHIP

	Seniors	Intermediates	Juniors
1959	Shirley Stender		
1960-63			
1964	James Morgan		
1965			
1966	Dwight Huffstetler		Mavis Stees
1967	Don Sherrod		Jocko Camilletti
1968	Nancy DeGanahl		Gordon Booco
1969	Nancy DeGanahl		Allen Booco
1970	Eileen Klumker		Randy Booco
1971	Nancy DeGanahl		Valeen Jacobs
1972	Nancy DeGanahl		Guy Stees
1973	Nancy DeGanahl		Valeen Jacobs
1974	Valeen Jacobs		Judd Jacobs
1975	Kim Frentress		Shane Jacobs
1976	Guy Stees		Larry Booco
1977	Guy Stees		Shana Ely
1978	Grace May		Darcy Lackey
1979	Grace May		Greg Barns
1980	Jody Kayser		Lora Camilletti
1981	Lorrae Camilletti		S. Hammer
1982	Ty Zabel		Darcy Camilletti
1983	Ty Zabel		Darcy Camilletti
1984	Ty Zabel		Chip Herold
1985	Ty Zabel		Brad Carnahan
1986	Ty Zabel		Jason Dorr
1987	Ty Zabel		Brad Carnahan
1988	Brad Carnahan		Kody May
1989	Chip Herold		Todd Camilletti
1990	Brad Carnahan		Ty Camilletti
1991	Jay Whaley		Jody Booco
1992	Lonnie Shoemaker		Ty Camilletti
1993	Dusty Whaley		Patrick Peterson
1994	Ty Camilletti	Jessica Booco	Tyler Knott
1995	Jessica Booco	Jamie Booco	Cassidy Kurtz

SHEEP SHOWMANSHIP

	Seniors	Intermediates	Juniors
1959	Glen McLaughlin		
1960	Jackie Crawford		
1961			
1962	Arloa Knott		
1963			
1964	Kent Franz		
1965	Jackie Crawford		
1966	Bert Franz		
1967	Debra Hamill		
1968	Earl McLaughlin		Coleen Kirby
1969	Coleen Kirby		Kerry Kirby
1970	Kenny Brenner		
1971	Kenny Brenner		Shelia Barnes
1972	David Kuntz		
1973	Judi Zehner		Kevin Zehner
1974	Barbara Brenner		John Maneotis
1975	John Maneotis		Jody Kayser
1976	Shayne Rienks		Sheri Nelson
1977			
1978	Kirk Zabel		Billie Jo Duff
1979	Queeda Chew		Chad Bedell
1980	Jody Kayser		Ted Carnahan
1981	Cheryl Hoaglund		Stacy McCusky
1982	Jody Kayser		Travis Bedell
1983	Jody Kayser		Robin Haight
1984	Tad Carnahan		Janet Baker
1985	Janet Baker		Robin Haight

96

Year	Seniors	Intermediates	Juniors
1986	Joseph Haslem		Janelle Hoglund
1987	Nick Maneotis		Mark Haight
1988	Nick Maneotis		Shawn Hockaday
1989	Nick Maneotis		Julie Whittingham
1990	Rod Wille		Julie Whittingham
1991	Rod Wille		Wyatt Flanders
1992	Jeffie Duncan	Nichole Rickman	Hobey Early
1993	Lindsey Early	Hobey Early	Natalie McDonald
1994	Jeffie Duncan	Melissa Meade	Kaycee Samuelson
1995	Aleah Hockin	Brandi Rickman	Candice Moore

SWINE SHOWMANSHIP

Year	Seniors	Intermediates	Juniors
1974	Joann Weng		
1975	Tina Jacobs		Robie Jacobs
1976			
1977	Justin Sidwell		Cindy Weng
1978	Fred Wegenor		Alisa King
1979	La Dean Chew		Alisa King
1980	Ceena Truax		Tad Carnahan
1981	Ceena Truax		Tad Carnahan
1982	Suzanne Hockett		Ron Hockett
1983	Darcy Camilletti		Fred Kayser
1984	Darcy Camilletti		Brad Carnahan
1985	Pat Stanko		Brad Carnahan
1986	Mike James		Tyson James
1987	Pat Stanko		Susie Ficke
1988	Pat Stanko		Jay Dee Hockaday
1989	Brad Carnahan		Jay Dee Hockaday
1990	Lonnie Carnahan		Jody Booco
1991	Lisa Shoemaker		Jody Booco
1992	Jody Booco	Amy Appel	Nick Camilletti
1993	Jeannie Zimmerman	Jody Babcock	Travis Newbold
1994	Jeffie Duncan	Nick Camilletti	Keith Bell
1995	Jeffie Duncan	Sara Ann Greenberg	Kelly Carlson

1984

HORSE SHOWMANSHIP

Year	Seniors	Intermediates	Juniors
1962	Elvin Hibbert		
1963	Bill Gay		
1964	Bill Gay		
1965	Bill Gay		
1966	Joanna Gilroy		
1967	Ted Gilroy		
1968	Joanna Gilroy		Deobrah Zehner
1969			
1970	Linda Moore		Randy Booco
1971	Eileen Klumker		William Montieth
1972			
1973	Lonnie Morton		Vickie Morton
1974	Vickie Morton		Sheri Nelson
1975	Vickie Morton		Brian Musick
1976	Vickie Morton		Chad Bedell
1977	Jolene Stetson		Brian Musick
1978	Brian Musick		Dawn Bedell
1979	Brian Musick		Kip Kihlstrom
1980	Roxanne James		Travis Bedell
1981	Roxanne James		Travis Bedell
1982	Debbie Link	Kip Kihlstrom	Leon Shupp
1983	Chad Bedell	Travis Bedell	Jolynn Vetter
1984	Rebecca Weaver	Margaret Weaver	Brian DeGanahl
1985	Rebecca Weaver	Kenny Meyer	Brenda Hogue
1986	Kip Kihlstrom	Wanda Meyer	Brenda Hogue
1987	Ken Meyer	Wanda Meyer	Franklin Case
1988	Kip Kihlstrom	Franklin Case	Sheri McNeal
1989	Wanda Meyer	Sunny Booco	Amanda Appel
1990	Wanda Meyer	Shawneen Guire	Lindsey Early
1991	Tim Williams	Lindsey Early	Nathan McDonald
1992	Sheri McNeal	Amanda Appel	Nathan McDonald
1993	Keri Wilson	Lisa Pascetti	Jamie Rapp
1994	Keri Wilson	Amanda Appel	Jessica Moody
1995	Shawneen Guire	Casey Sopkowich	Janie Montieth

Round Robin Showmanship Contest

The Grand Champion and Reserve Grand Champion in each Division – swine, sheep, dairy cattle, beef and horses – are judged on grooming and showmanship. The event was inaugurated in 1958 as part of the Steamboat Springs Junior Livestock Shows, and continued as a Fair event. For many years it was featured as entertainment at the Junior Livestock Sale Barbecue until 1991, when it was moved to Friday following the Junior Shows. Results have been reconstructed from incomplete newspaper records but are complete since 1978.

At the Junior Livestock Show in Steamboat Springs

1956	LeRoy McLaughlin
1957	Glen McLaughlin
1958	Aaron Huffstetter

At the Junior Livestock Show and Sale at Fair

1959	Shirley Stender
1960s	Bill Gay, Elvin Hibbert, Delbert, Dewy and Don Sherrod
1970s	Kenny Brenner, Nancy DeGanahl, Valeen Jacobs, David Kuntz, Vickie Morton

	Seniors	Juniors
1978	Mary Barber	Lane Kihlstrom
1979	Justin Sidwell	Jennifer Harding
1980	Judy Kayser	Jennifer Harding
1981	Lorrae Camilletti	Darcy Camilletti
1982		
1983	Judy Kayser	Tad Carnahan
1984	Ty Zabel	Katrina Harding
1985	Ty Zabel	Kenny Myers
1986	Mike Robson	Kenny Myers
1987	Brad Carnahan	Wanda Meyers
1988	Brad Carnahan	Kody May
1989	Brad Carnahan	Jay Dee Hockaday
1990	Lonnie Shoemaker	Jody Booco
1991	Lisa Shoemaker	Jeffie Duncan

	Seniors	Intermediates	Juniors
1992	Lonnie Shoemaker	Ty Camilletti	Nick Camilletti
1993	Jeffie Duncan	Sophie Holly	Nick Camilletti
1994	Jeffie Dunca	Nick Camilletti	Kaycee Samuelson
1995	Jeffie Duncan	Brandi Rickman	Cassidy Kurtz

Dairy goats replaced dairy cattle in the mid 80s but returned in 1989 when dairy goats were eliminated; rabbits were added in 1994.

Fred Kaiser, 1979

GRAND CHAMPION LIVESTOCK

	Market Steer	Market Lamb*	Market Swine**
1930	Enid Fetzler		Harvey Muirhead (Fat Hog)
1931	Willett (Bud) Rider		
1931-34		No Fair	
1935	Alice Peavy		
1936	Mary Peavy		
1937	Mary Peavy		Robert Lyons (Fat Hog)
1938	Francis Peavy	James Lauffman	
1939			Warren Annand (Burrow) and Bob Lyons (Sow)
1940	Mary Peavy	John Sinden	
1941	Francis Peavy		
1942-45		No Fair	
1946			Mary Cullen
1947	Douglas Sherrod	Willie Stender	Kenneth Robes
1948	Vern Stees	Willie Stender	
1949			
1950	Sheila Reagor	Willie Stender	
1951		No Fair	
1952	Larry Whiteman	Lenore Ekstrom	
1953	Melva Drake	Lee Williamson	
1954	Sandra Sherrod	Garry Bird	
1955	Marion Hindman	Shirley Stender	
1956	Marian Hindman	Rita Moore	Lee Hoelscher
1957	Aaron Huffstetler		
1958	Shirley Stender	Glen McLaughlin	John Hoelscher
1959	Aaron Huffstetler	Jackie Crawford	
1960	Dewey Sherrod	Jackie Crawford	John Hoelscher
1961	Dewey Sherrod	Elvin Hibbert	John Hoelscher
1962	Delbert Sherrod	Joella Gilroy	Jan Crawford
1963	Charolette Martensen	Elvin Hibbert	Elvin Hibbert
1964	Donald Sherrod	Kent Franz	Elvin Hibbert
1965	Delbert Sherrod	Ted Gilroy	Jan Crawford
1966	Mavis Stees	Jan Crawford	Jan Crawford
1967	Clay DeGanahl	Marty Hamil	Amy Gilroy
1968	Jocko Camilletti	Barbara Brenner	Jacque Wheeler
1969	Cindy Hewes	Barbara Brenner	Terry Green
1970	Wayne Kruse	Kelly King	Terry Green
1971	Jocko Camilletti	Suzie Barnes	Lewis Moon
1972	Jocko Camilletti	Rhonda Zehner	Joseph Komive
1973	J May	Shayne Rienks	Barry Barnes
1974	Sherri Haslem	Patty Brenner	Joseph Komive
1975	Wade Look	Jody Kayser	Joann Weng
1976	Julie Frentress	Jerry Murphy	Jim Anderson
1977	Brian Musick	Kirk Zabel	Cindy Weng
1978	Jona Ely	Wendy Meacham	Shannon Bangs
1979	Jody Kayser	LaDean Chew	Fred Kayser
1980	Fred Kayser	Neil Chew	Brad Carnahan
1981	Fred Kayser	Jody Kayser	Fred Kayser
1982	Lorrae Camilletti	Jody Kayser	Nina Cloven
1983	Jody Kayser	John Redmond	Fred Kayser
1984	Philip Rossi	Julie Redmond	Eliza Cloven
1985	Darcy Camilletti	Janet Baker	LaDawn Bruggink
1986	Ty Zabel	Julie Redmond	Teffanie Truax
1987	Darcy Camilletti	Julie Redmond	Nick Maneotis
1988	Todd Camilletti	Julie Redmond	Debra Wagner
1989	Todd Camilletti	Ty Camelletti	Debra Wagner
1990	Chip Herold	Brad Carnahan	Lonnie Shoemaker
1991	Lisa Shoemaker	Graver Pryor	Nick Camilletti
1992	Jody Booco	Rod Willie	Tyler Knott
1993	Jamie Booco	Tommy Rossi	Andy Kurtz
1994	Jessie Booco	Terry Whaley	Jamie Booco
1995	Jamie Booco	Cara Coster	Nathan McDonald

* There were no Market Lamb Classes at the Fair until 1938 and only occasionally until 1954.

** Since 4-H Classes began in 1929 there have been several types of Swine Classes. Early results are sketchy but were most frequently for burrows, sows and sows with litters. Until the late 1950s there was little interest in showing 4-H hogs and no results were publicized between 1948 and 1955. Between 1956 and 1970s Market Swine Classes were small.

SONOFABITCH BURRITOS

From Tom Kleman, proprietor of the Fifth Street Cafe, and manager of Steamboat Springs' El Rancho (1975-82) for Ray Sieverding. Kleman is remembered for introducing Mexican fare; no one can remember how many times Sieverding lost the restaurant to Frank Stetson in a Bar Booth game.

Season ground or shredded beef with salt, pepper, garlic and cumin and saute with diced onions. Wrap in a flour tortilla with shredded Monterey Jack and Cheddar cheese. Cover with red salsa or green chile and sprinkle with mixture of two shredded cheeses. Heat until cheese is melted and, right before serving, top with shredded lettuce, diced fresh tomatoes and green onions. The burritos can also be made with ground or shredded lamb, pork or chicken.

Make red salsa by mixing uncooked diced fresh tomatoes, green peppers, onions, green chiles and garlic. Make green chile by cooking cubed pork with onions, cumin, garlic, Anaheim and jalapeno peppers, chopped tomatilloes and diced red tomatoes.

LAMB ROAST

From John and Jeanne Maneotis who enjoy sharing this dinner with their children: Sara, Cayla and John Jr.

5-8 pound roast
6-8 cloves garlic, peeled
Sprinkle with salt, pepper, garlic salt and oregano, cubed or powdered beef boullion.

Stuff cloves of garlic into slits in the lamb roast. Place in pan fat side up. Pour 2 cups water in pan and sprinkle with boullion to taste. Sprinkle seasonings on top of roast and in the water. Place in 250 degree oven and bake several hours on low before increasing the temperature. This keeps the meat tender. At serving time, season to taste and return the slices to the pan to soak up the broth. Serve hot.

PORK ROLL-UPS

From Stephanie Temple who with husband, George, raises pigs 4.5 miles west of Hayden. "Temple's Hog Heaven," which, at one time had 200 hogs on the floor and four sows in the farrowing houses, still sells six-week old weaners to 4-H youngsters. George is the product of the Temple-Dunckley merger which related everyone in West Routt County: Three Temples (his father Pat, Harry and Kathryn) married three Dunckley's (his mother Eunice, Ethel and Ralph).

Local history is also confused by the fact that Dunckley families spell the name with a "c" but when the post office was established the name was spelled Dunkley. The two spellings still distinguish people from place.

Flatten, uncured, boneless ham cutlets. Roll them around the following stuffing: crumbled stale rolls or bread, celery, onions, mushrooms, butter, sage and poultry seasoning moistened with chicken broth. Secure with a toothpick and bake covered 30-40 minutes at 350 degrees. Makes its own gravy.

4-H Breeding Project Champions

BEEF

Prior to 1952 4-H members showed breeding stock in the Adult Division which was replaced by a 4-H Beef Breeding Division. Because criteria for selection varied, it is difficult to trace overall winners, but early Fairs recognized an Overall Male and Overall Female, listed below.

	Champion Male	Champion Female
1952	Shelia Reagor	Jeffery Martinson
1953	Sally Summer	Larry Whiteman
1954	Jeffery Martensen	Lee Hoelsher
1955	Shelia Reagor	Shelia Reagor
1956	Shirley Stender	Marian Hinman
1957	Aaron Huffstetler	Aaron Huffstetler
1958		
1960		
1961	Tom Klumker	Marion Hinman
1963	Ivan Shupp Jr.	
1963	Chuck Perry	Bill Gay
1964	Delbert Sherrod	Don Sherrod
1965	Jerry Norris	Bill Gay
1966		
1967	Marsha Gray	Michael Stender
		Nancy DeGanahl (Hereford)
		Jack Branseum (Angus)
1968		
1969	Mavis Stees	Michael Stender

Between 1970 and 1981 Beef Breeding Champions were recognized by species, class placing or both. Some of the 4-H members who consistently won in these classes included: Tom Barnes, Nancy deGanahl, Shane and Shirely Ely, Tony and Bobby George, Delbert and Jim Kemry, Kathy Kruse, David Kuntz, Tina Look, Scott May, Doug Monger, Lewis Moon, Lambert Pickney, Philip Rossi, Steven Stender, Frankie (Pud) Stetson, Ronda Zehner.

Since 1982 there have been two awards for Beef Breeding Champions: Don and Judy Sherrod present one, in memory of Bill Sherrod, for the Champion English Breed Female. Bill and Cynthia May present another for the Champion Exotic Female.

	English Female	Exotic Females
1982	David Sherrod	Shane Yeager
1983	Tony George	Shannon Yeager
1984	Audra Wagner	Leon Shupp
1985	Shelly McLaughlin	Kody May
1986	Debra Wagner	Kody May
1987	Shelly McLaughlin	Shannon Yeager
1988	Jay Dee Hockaday	Kody May
1989	Jay Whaley	Todd Camilletti
1990	Jay Whaley	Kody May
1991	Nikki Camilletti	Richard Green
1992	Nikki Camilletti	Kody May
1993	Kevin Sherrod	Lisa Epp
1994	Dusty Whaley	Mark Monger
1995	Brandon Craig	Mark Monger

SHEEP

During the 1950s a Champion Ram and Champion Ewe were picked; later a Champion White Face Ram and Ewe and a Champion Black Face Ram and Ewe were chosen. During the 1960s, 1970s and mid 1980s, sheep were judged by breeds. Since the mid 1980s breeding sheep have been judged as Meat Breed and Wool Breeds. In some years, each breed had a champion and in other years there was only a class champion. The following list includes consistent winners and the Best of Breed where known.

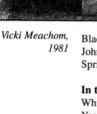

Vicki Meachom, 1981

In the 1950s

Kathleen Cogshill (Suffolk), Donna Guees (Columbia), Lynn Farrell (Suffolk), Glen and Leroy McLaughlin (Suffolk and Hampshires), Rita Moore (Suffolk), Frank Selbe (Suffolk), Willie and Shirley Stender (Suffolk), Lee Williamson (Corriedale and Suffolk).

In the 1960s

White Faces: Don Babcock, Bernard and Arloa Knott
Black Faces: Larry Appel, Susan Barber, Jan Crawford, Burt and Kent Franz, Mike Flanders, Bill Gay, Elvin Hibbert, Lydia Hockaday, Coleen Kirby, Eileen Klumker, David Kuntz, Rita Moore, Susan Signs

In the 1970s

White Faces: Mark Kagie, Jim Redmond, Guy Stees
Black Faces: Donna Fleming, Cheryl Hoaglund, Judy Kayser, Mark Kagie, Andy and John Maneotis, Jolene Pitney, John and Carol McLaughlin, Larry and Terry Nay, Russ and Spring Steele

In the 1980s

White Faces: Jeremy Kline, Jim, John and Julie Redmond, Rod and Tonya Wille, Shannon Yeager
Black Faces: Janet Baker, Brad Carnahan, Robin Duncan, Machille and Katrina Harding, Shawn and Jay Dee Hockaday, Cheryl and Janelle Hoaglund, Chip and Nita Herold, Joseph Haslem, Nick and Angela Maneotis, John and Julie Redmond, Julie Whittingham, Rod and Tonya Wille
Crossbreeds: Shannon and Shari Yeager. An unusual crossbreed between a wild Big Horn and a Suffolk sheep was shown by Joe, Shawneen and Trevor Guire. It was the only known attempt to breed wild and domestic sheep and gained national attention.

In the 1990s

White Faces: Audra and Melissa Meade, Tommy Rossi, Sheri McNeal, Rod and Tonya Wille
Black Faces: Megan and Rusty Baker, Misty Copeland, Robin Duncan, Lindsey and Hobey Early, Shawneen Guire, Wyatt Flanders, Aleah Hockin, Danny May, Nicole Richman, Tommy Rossi, Kaycee Samuelson, Johnathan Steele, Bonnie and Jessica Wright, Rod and Tonya Wille, Chris Williams, Shari and Shannon Williams

Fred Kaiser, 1979

102

HORSES

The Horse Breeding Project, launched in the 1979 by Olive Morton, required prior registration and a Record Book. Winners are determined by placing at the Fair and scoring on the book.

1979	Dawn Bedell	1988	None
1980	Brian Mosick	1989	Amanda Appel
1981	Brett Mason	1990	Amanda Appel
1982	Brett Mason	1991	Jeffie Duncan
1983	Shani Mason	1992	Shawneen Guire
1994	Rebecca Weaver	1993	Shawneen Guire
1985	Rebecca Weaver	1994	Shawneen Guire
1986	Rebecca Weaver	1995	Shawneen Guire
1987	Wanda Meyer		

CHAMPION HALTER HORSES

Although horses have been shown at the Fair since the end of World War II, results are available only since 1947.

1947	Iva Decker
1948	Gregory Linger
1950	Betty Cullen

	Saddle Horse	Colt
1952	Jeffery Martensen	Jack Wheeler
1953	Jeffery Martensen	Josie Ekstrom
1954	Jeffery Martensen	Joann Semotan
1955	Joann Semotan	
1956	Jerry Green	
1957	Jeffery Martensen	Georgia Jones
1958	Gary Whitmer	Carol Lodwick
1959	Sharon Jones	Barbara Infanger
1961	Charlotte Martensen	Bill Gay
1962	Charlotte Martensen (mare)	Charles Hogue
	Wesley Cook (gelding)	

GRAND CHAMPION HALTER HORSE

1963	Bill Gay	1980	Lee Chockley
1964	Bill Gay	1981	Chad Barker
1964	Bill Gay	1982	Roxanne Barker
1965	Bill Gay	1983	Chad Bedell
1966	Diane Borchert	1984	Lee Chockley
1967	Joella Gilroy	1985	Mike Robson
1968	Joella Gilroy	1986	Jerry Panepinto
1969	Cindy Hewes	1987	Levi Thompson
1970	Eileen Klumker	1988	Kip Kihlstrom (gelding)
1971	Nancy deGanahl		Franklin Case (mare)
1972	Lonnie Morton	1989	Molly Forsyth
1973	Lonnie Mortion	1990	Keri Wilson*
1974	Vickie Morton	1991	Keri Wilson
1975	Lonnie Morton	1992	Cody Samuelson
1976	Chad Bedell	1993	Casey Sopkowich
1977	Jolene Stetson	1994	Casey Sopkowich
1978	Chad Bedell	1995	Nicole Rickman
1979	Lane Kihlstrom		

*Reserve Champion moved up when Champion failed to complete horse project

DAIRY CATTLE

Although dairy calves were the first animals shown at the Fair, classes have varied greatly. Some years there were Champion Males and Females, others only Champion Females; some years there were no classes, others there were only class winners. But they have always been an important part of the Fair and always excel in quality and showmanship.

From the 1920s through 1940s
Dean Dale, Avis Dixon, Jean Conner, Thelma Margerum, Walter Moore, Billy Marshall, Jim Sellers, John Sinden

In the 1950s
Maurice Harvey, John Hoelsher, Lydia Hinkle, Dale Look, Linda Norris, Frank Selbe, Barbara Soash, Dick Soash, Roy Tufly, Francis Werner, Gary Whitmer, Allen Williams

In the 1960s
Kirk Blake, Doug Blake, Kent Franz, Bert Franz, Rita Hinkle, Arloa Knott, Kim Studer, Jacques Wheeler

In the 1970s
David Tipton

In the 1980s
Adonna Daughenbaugh, Nate Daughenbaugh, Stephen Green, Lori Jazwick, Paul Jazwick, Chris Miller, Chris Paquette

In the 1990s
Daleena Babcock, Jody Babcock, Casey Estes, Holly Estes, Travis Ettzler, Paul Jazwick, Lori Jazwick, Tami Willimas

1988

RABBITS and POULTRY

Small animals are an important part of the Fair for 4-H members who are young or living in urban areas. Because varied classes make it difficult to trace Grand Champions, the following list includes some of the consistent winners until 1980 when Meat Pen Rabbits and BBQ Chicken and Turkey exhibits began and Grand Champions were recorded.

In the 1950s
Rabbits: Phyllis Bird, Carl Herold, Barbara Gilland, Eliose Moore
Poultry: Newt Dorr, Jessie Simonton, Pamela Thurow, Davie Watts

In the 1960s
Rabbits: Mike Barnes, Elvin Hibbert, Frank Hogue, Ann Redmond
Poultry: Bill Gay, Paul Rossi, Bob Redmond

In the 1970s
Rabbits: Dawn, Jennifer and Machelle Harding, David Long, Malanie Sprengle, Erin Wilson, Spring Steele, Maro Jo Hoaglund, Nita Herold, Alissa King, Tony George, Bret and Judy Grandbouche
Poultry: Jackie Hellyer, Jennifer Sprengle, Sam Barnes, Spring Steele, Dawn Harding, Mark Ethridge

In the 1980s
Rabbits: Rusty and Megan Baker, Robin Duncan, Jennifer Covillo, Travis Etzler, Lisa Hogue, Becky Holloran, Chris Paquette, Anna Shupp, Shani and Brett Mason, Tyler Knott, David Moore, Tashe Dobbs, Jill Webb
Poultry: Rusty Baker, Tristan Covillo, Danielle Flowers, Reheen Northrup, Jay Dee Hockaday, Amy O'Conner, Kenny Meyer,
Leon Shupp, Philip Rossi, Julie Redmond, Dusty Whaley, Jared Herfurtner

In the 1990s
Rabbits: Duleen Babcock, Emily Barker, Justin Crofts, Jeff Clyncke, Amber, Crystal and Mica Fisher, Christian Kidd, Rickly Little, Crystal, leo and Kenny Muhme, Matt and Nick Poulin, Leann Walter, Erica Weinland, Keri Wilson
Poultry: Jeff Clyncke, Hobey and Lindsey Early, Tristan Covillo, Travis Etzler, Luke Nichols, Angelo Pascetti, Cody Samuelson

	Meat Pen Rabbits	BBQ Chicken	BBQ Turkey
1980	Katrina Harding	Leon Shupp	
1981	Katrina Harding		Philip Shupp
1982	Anna Shupp	Julie Redmond	
1983	Shani Mason	Julie Redmond	
1984	Brett Mason	Amy O'Connor	
1985	Robin Duncan	Rebecca Northrup	
1986	Tyler Knott		Danielle Flowers
1987	Rusty Baker	Dusty Wheeler	
1988	Rusty Baker	Dusty Wheeler	
1989	Tashe Dobbs	Tristan Covillo	
1990			
1991	Dahleena Babcock	Hobey Early	Tristan Covillo
1992	Justin Crofts	Hobey Early	Travis Etzler
1993	Emily Barker	Hobey Early	Travis Etzler
1994	Amber Fish	Lindsey Early	Cody Samuelson
1995	Mica Fish	Lindsey Early	Travis Etzler

1986

OTHER LIVESTOCK

Although numbers of entries, types of classes and methods of selecting champions vary, the Fair has enjoyed other livestock exhibits.

DAIRY GOATS, judged between 1973 and 1989, included excellent projects from: (in the 1970s) Cindy Hunter, Cindy Iacovetto, David Long, Russ and Spring Steele, Rich, Sam and Tom Wisecup, Dale Williams; (in the 1980s) Jonathan Aufterhide, Christian and Najia Keller, Tina Keller, Jennifer Harding, Wanda Meyer, Rebecca Northrup, Chris and Julie Roberts, Keri Searls

DOGS were first judged at the Fair in a show organized by Shannon Sparkman in 1976. By 1990 the Dog Show became part of Exhibit Day but returned to the Fair in 1995. Outstanding participants included: (in the 1970s) Todd and Gregg Greget, Michael Rigas, Christ Tipton, Margaret Weaver' (in the 1980s) Jennifer Covillo, Rebecca Northrup, John McCain, Julie Whittingham, Jared Herfurtner, Tasha Dobbs; (in the 1990s) Carrie DeGanahl, Jamie Denker, Sara Greenburg, Janie Montieth, Travis Nash, Lisa Pascetti, Jeremy Peed, Anna Poulsen

LLAMA PROJECTS, organized in 1992, include track and showmanship classes. The largest show was in 1993 when eight llamas participated. Members of 4-H who have distinguished themselves in the project include: Adam Black, Sarah Leonard, Stephanie Lickteig, Luke Nichols, Jennifer Peterson

BUCKET CALF PROJECTS, begun in 1991, are for younger members who learn to clean, halter break and show bucket calves.

1991	Lisa Epp
1992	Sophie Holly
1993	Sophie Holly
1994	Ann Lighthizer
1995	Chris Frentress

JUNIOR LIVESTOCK SALE PRICES

Raising livestock for market is an integral part of 4-H and FFA Programs and the Junior Livestock Sale is a highlight of the Routt County Fair. Participants may sell only one animal in the sale unless they have two champions, and once an animal enters the sale ring it is sold to the highest bidder. Proceeds from the sale go directly to the youngsters, enabling them to attend college or raise more livestock. All animals placed in the sale are slaughtered and entered in the Carcass Contest.

Every effort has been made to complete the following records which reflect sale prices from the Steamboat Springs Junior Livestock Show 1949-1958 and the Routt County Fair Junior Livestock Sale 1959-1996.

	GRAND CHAMPION			AVERAGE PRICE		
	Steer	Lamb	Hog	Steer	Lamb	Hog
1949	.31	N/S		.275	N/S	
1950	.36	N/S		.33	N/S	
1951-54 N/S						
1955	.22	.24		.205	.215	
1956	.34	.26		.32	.24	
1957	.365	.31		.32	.29	
1958	.48	.345	.29	.39	.295	
1959*	.66	.44	.38	.405	.415	
1960	.64	.46	.38	.42	.44	
1961						
1962	.43	.365	.32	.405	.335	
1963	.60	.545	.30	.54	.50	.30
1964	.69	1.10	.27	.435	.62	.27
1965	1.02	1.90	.42	.40	1.42	.38
1966						
1967	.63	1.50	.75	.45	.58	.56
1968	.85	2.50	1.00	.58	1.05	.75
1969	1.00	2.50	.60	.58	1.20	.58
1970		.935	1.06	2.50	.63	1.07
1971	.82	1.25	.90	.62	1.10	.88
1972	.90	1.44	1.29	.78	1.20	1.00
1973	1.45	3.00	1.50	1.31	1.38	1.31
1974	1.38	3.75	1.70	1.00	1.42	1.70
1975	1.30	4.75	1.75	.875	1.68	1.50
1976	1.55	4.20	3.00	.90	2.30	1.70
1977	2.06	6.00	3.30	1.06	2.97	2.77
1978	2.40	6.10	7.25*	1.65*	3.53	4.33
1979	3.10	5.00	3.60	1.38	1.62	1.42
1980	3.20	8.00	2.75	1.25	2.38	1.70
1981	3.00	5.00	2.20	1.50	2.30	2.30
1982	2.20	5.50	1.70	.75	1.56	1.50
1983	2.15	7.00	2.60	1.00	2.50	2.67
1984	2.50	4.50	2.75	1.30	3.00	3.35
1985	2.00	5.25	2.60	1.10	2.20	2.32
1986	1.75	4.00	3.25	.86	2.55	2.48
1987	2.20	4.50	3.00	1.02	2.28	2.04
1988	2.25	9.00*	3.10	1.36	3.22	2.73
1989	3.25*	5.25	2.90	1.14	2.11	2.02
1990	2.50	7.50	6.00	1.19	4.32	4.38*
1991	1.60	5.60	4.00	1.15	2.97	2.32
1992	1.80	6.50	6.60	1.61	4.45*	3.94
1993	2.20	7.50	4.50	1.62	3.71	2.13
1994	2.00	8.00	5.50	1.39	3.42	2.89
1995	2.00	5.50	2.50	1.42	3.25	2.11

Champions:
Steer (1989) Todd Camilletti $3.25
Lamb (1988) Julie Redmond $9.00
Hog (1978) Sharron Bangs $7.25

*Record highs

Average:
Steer (1978) $1.65
Lamb (1992) $4.45
Hog (1990) $4.38

106

4-H

I pledge
> *My head to clear thinking,*
> *My heart to greater loyalty,*
> *My hands to larger service,*
> *My health to better living,*
> > *for my club, my community, and my country.*

Funding from the Department of Agriculture prompted school and civic leaders to begin organizing 4-H clubs in 1917. Within 10 years, the clubs were involved in state and county fair activities throughout the country. The first clubs in Routt County were created in 1929.

Today's 4-H members are between 8-18 years old and work on individual and group projects in a variety of areas: agriculture, forestry, wildlife, crafts, homemaking, health, and career skills.

Growth in Routt County 4-H programs warranted a full time 4-H Agent by 1979 when Sue Bell was hired. Between 1979 and 1984 the county has had three different agents. Jim Stanko assumed the position as a county-employed youth agent in May 1984 and held the job until 1995.

Future Farmers Of America

The owl symbolizes knowledge,
the plow labor,
the rising sun the promise of the future,
the eagle the national status of the program.

FFA was formed during the 1920s so that young people could study agriculture as a vocation in high school. They typically become involved with small crop or livestock breeding projects and may stay involved until three years after high school, or age 21.

When Steamboat Springs High School hired its first Vocational Agricultural Advisor, Robert Leighton, and formed a Future Farmers of America chapter in the 1950s, the program was for boys, and most FFA members also belonged to 4-H and showed their livestock as 4-H projects. Mack Jones, who became the advisor in 1951, ran a successful program until 1959.

Yampa had a thriving FFA program from 1957-1960, until the schools combined. George Morris was the advisor.

SoRoCo High School instituted an FFA program, still in existence, in 1963; and from time to time Hayden High School has offered vocational agricultural programs.

Jerold Truax was the first Routt County FFA member to receive one of the highest FFA honors, the Star Farmer Award.

Between 1964 and 1979 FFA had its own Division at the Fair for farm mechanics. Classes focused on large and small metal projects, large and small wood projects or projects combining wood and metal. SoRoCo FFA became increasingly involved in the Fair during the 1990s when several members entered beef breeding and swine divisions. Lonnie Shoemaker showed the

Grand Champion Swine in 1990 and Cara Costner, winner of the Kamar Scholarship, participated in the Farm Bureau Heifer Project.

FFA has made major contributions to the Fairgrounds by building portable panels, pens for livestock barns, and sound buffer panels for the Exhibit Hall. It started Farm Days at local elementary schools to promote knowledge of agriculture, an effort shared by 4-H members who supplied livestock for their program at the Steamboat Springs Elementary School in 1994 and at the Hayden Elementary School in 1995.

4-H Council

The 4-H Council, formed in 1940, plays an important role in the direction of 4-H programs. It was composed of two members and one leader from every club in the county until 1994 when the membership changed to include two members from each club and two leader/advisors from the county at large, voted upon by 4-H members, and a separate Leaders Council was formed.

The first 4-H Council members were President Charles Ward of Steamboat Springs, Vice President Joan Peters of Phippsburg, and Secretary-Treasurer Jack Williams of Hayden. The first leader/advisors were Alice Sprengle and Evelyn Semotan.

The Routt County 4-H Council is responsible for:
- Setting dates for various 4-H activities
- Establishing committees to conduct Exhibit Day, Fashion Revue and Achievement Day
- Conducting the St.Patrick Day Dance and other fundraising events, such as sales of license plates and plat books, candy and fireworks
- The barbecue prior to the Junior Livestock Sale
- Selection of Fair royalty
- The Routt County 4-H Exchange Program
- The Routt County 4-H Marketing Committee which helps promote the Junior Livestock Sale
- Funding and selecting participants for local and state junior leadership programs
- Monitoring the Howard S. Elliott Memorial 4-H Fund and the Don and Eileen Lufkin Cattle Breeders Fund
- Helping the Routt County Scholarship Committee which supervises three scholarship funds established in the 1990s

    The Kamar Company Scholarship (1992), a $1,000 award for using artificial insemination to improve the quality of a breeding project

    The Jared Herfurtner Scholarship (1993), two $1,000 awards in memory of the former Fairplay 4-H Club member

    The James Milligan Scholarships (1995), two $1,000 awards

History of 4-H and FFA

Because it offers young people and club leaders an opportunity to build friendships, to develop life skills and to fail and try again, 4-H has always been one of the most prominent youth programs in Colorado.

Routt Country 4-H started in the late 1920s as a result of efforts to involve youth in agriculture. Oddly enough, the Moffat Tunnel League (an organization of businessmen in Denver, Grand, Moffat and Routt Counties) played a major role in its development. The League's goal was to promote agriculture and business in order to bolster profits for the Denver Salt Lake and Pacific Railroad, better known as the "Moffat Road." If youngsters became involved in agriculture at an early age, they reasoned, they would continue ranching and farming as adults.

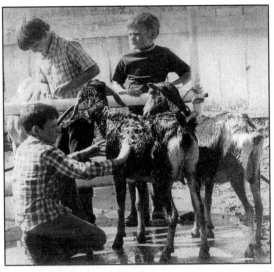

1978

In 1927 the League began providing dairy calves to youth. The first five milking Shorthorn calves arrived in the fall. These forerunners of 4-H projects went to Jean Conner and Claude Roper of Clark, and Sema Dale, Jim Sellers and Robert Whitham of Hayden. The next year, Routt County hired its first County Agent, Percy Ingram, whose combined salary and operating budget was $2,500. He put together three dairy clubs to receive the 1928 calves from the Moffat Tunnel League.

The First Clubs

On October 5, 1928 the DS&L train brought 21 calves into Routt County. The first stop was Yampa, where seven Dairy Shorthorns were delivered, making the **YAMPA DAIRY CALF CLUB** the first Routt County 4-H club. It was led by C.E.Margerum, who would become the first 4-H Fair Superintendent in 1929.

1983

Routt County's First 4-H Club:
The Yampa Dairy Calf Club

From Rita Herold

Members of the first Calf Club at Yampa included Walter Bennett, Eileen Elgin, Fred Elgin, Leo Hawley, Buford Huffstetler, Dan Knott, Thelma Margerum and Walter Peters. C.E. (Elmer) Margerum was the Club Leader and Floyd Moon was the County Agent.

Huffstettler placed first with his heifer and second with his calf. In a recent visit he recalled that first project:

"The calves were delivered to Yampa on a railroad car. We all went down to meet it. The railroad company had placed numbers on the different calves. We then drew numbers out of a hat to see which calf we would each receive. I got the number 6 calf. These were all Shorthorn heifer calves, what we called dual-purpose cows. They were used both for dairy and for beef.

Some of the animals leaned more to the dairy side and some looked more like beef animals. It was just the luck of the draw which type animal we received. We paid $90 apiece for those calves. That was a lot of money in those days. Each recipient paid $22.50 each year for a period of four years. This was paid to the Moffat Road Calf Club Fund."

His Lease and Agreement with the railroad, dated October 4, 1928 required Huffstetler to keep careful records of all proceeds derived from the sale of milk and cream, which had to be sold even to his own family, in order to apply proceeds toward payments for the heifer.

Huffstettler, who lived four miles south of Yampa, remembers showing his calf at the Fair in Hayden. He also remembers a Field Day at Ferry Carpenter's ranch later in the year.

Rita Herold, granddaughter of C.E. Margerum, grew up in Yampa 4-H programs and will receive her 20-year pin in 1996. She helped organize the 4-H Leaders Council and has served on the State Leaders Council, receiving state recognition in 1993, the year she was president. Her husband, Carl, has served on the Fair Board.

The Fairplay 4-H Baby Beef Club, organized at Trull in 1929 is the oldest club using the same name. Percy Hitchens (left) was the leader and members included Gilbert Hitchens, John Monger, Roy Woodcock, Enid Etzler and Delphia Butts.

The next stop on the Moffat Road was Steamboat Springs where members of the **ELK RIVER DAIRY CALF CLUB**, led by Glen Root, received their calves. Members were Frank and Robert Howard, Vaughn and Lawrence Powell, Charles Whitmer, Charles Roper and Beatrice Smith (later Mrs. Jay Kelton).

The last of the shipment, Holsteins, went to the **HAYDEN DAIRY CLUB**, under the leadership of H.K. Bailey, for members Dean Dale, Henry Gorman, Glenn Moore, Harold Smith, Neva Summers, Carl Wagoner and Mina Watts (Fredrickson).

In May 1929 Routt and Moffat County jointly hired Frances Jones as Home Demonstration Agent. She joined County Agent Ingram in organizing 4-H clubs throughout the county. The first girls' home economics club was the Stitch & Chatter Clothing Club, created the same month by the wives of Leo Connor and A.M. Powell in Clark. As the list of clubs indicates, three more clubs were organized in July.

The Steamboat Lions Club, involved from the beginning, sponsored calves for an Ayshire Club in Clark as well as for organizing a May 1928 Dairy Calf Show for animals delivered in 1927 and 1928. The best calf from each club belonged to: Jean Connors (Tufly) (Clark), Dan Knott (Yampa) and Jim Sellers (Hayden) who won the Overall Championship, the first 4-H champion animal in Routt County.

Early 4-H focused on a single project: livestock, under the direction of the County Agent, or home economics under the direction of the Home Demonstration Agent. This resulted in a proliferation of small clubs throughout the county, especially in home economics. There were separate clubs for first year sewers, first year food, second year sewers, second year food among others. Because canning was a separate project, it merited separate clubs. Membership ranged from 4 to 12 youngsters in each.

In the 1930s

During this decade 4-H programs flourished. The efforts of County Agent Floyd Moon and Edison Barr and Home Demonstration Agents Josephine Chambers, Ester Elliott and Helen Prout resulted in more than 20 active clubs. By 1939 there were 166 members enrolled in home economics projects and 127 in livestock projects.

Home economics clubs were devoted to sewing, cooking and canning, five in the Steamboat Springs area, four in Hayden, three in Yampa, two in Clark and others in Milner and McCoy.

The first Steamboat Springs sewing club, the Busy Stitchers, was headed by Anne Van Cleave. Baby beef clubs began at Deep Creek, Clark, Fairplay, Sidney, Hayden, Yampa and as far away as Slater and McCoy, totalling 27 by 1936. There were also attempts to form pig clubs in Toponas and on the Mesa.

The era was marked by several "firsts":

Yampa launched the first multi-project club in 1937, featuring projects in beef, sheep, pigs and gardening. Members included the Redmond Brothers (Bill, Dean and Jack) and Vincent Carnahan.

Madoline Bradburn became Routt County's first champion at a national fair in 1935 when her preserved strawberries took honors at the Colorado State Fair and received a $6 premium at the Chicago International Livestock Exposition. Keith Yount became the first Routt County 4-H member to attend the statewide 4-H Western Round-up when his potatoes won at the State Fair in 1940 after dominating special potato growing projects County Agent Floyd Moon started in the mid-1930s.

A Forestry Club began in the 1930s as did Livestock Judging, still a popular project.

Seed House Camp, a week-long summer camp between 1929 and the early 40s opened at the Seed House above Clark with 26 girls and 25 boys. Although it survived the Depression, when so many other 4-H events were curtailed, the joint Routt and Moffat County 4-H project was finally killed in 1942 by wartime food and gas rationing.

Bud Rider, Don Lufkin, Mary Peavy and Enid Etzler entered the National Western Stock Show's first Calf Scramble in 1935 but Mary Peavy and Enid Etzler were told girls did not "fit into bulldogging calves" when they attempted to participate. Bud Rider caught a calf.

However, the Peavy sisters opened new records for women when they began showing steers from Marshall Peavy's registered Hereford herd in the 1932 Winter Calf Show. After Marshall Peavy and A.R.Brown helped establish the Deep Creek Blue Ribbon Baby Beef Club in the 1930s, Marshall's daughters, Mary and Frances, his brother Lawrence Peavy's daughter, Alice, and Bud Rider "owned" winning circles at 4-H steer shows. In 1935 Mary took the County Fair Championship for Fat Steer and Alice had two steers in the top ten at the National Western Stock Show.

At the 1936 Routt County Fair, Frances upset Mary by winning the steer class; in 1937 Mary's steer placed third at the National Western. Only nine calves were sent to the 1939 National Western Stock Show, and a steer shown by Frances Peavy placed third. By the 1941 Winter Calf Show, first and second place steers belonged to Frances and Alice. Glen Barber stopped a Peavy family sweep by placing third but Mary came in fourth.

The War Years

The war impacted 4-H in many ways. Several new clubs formed and others adopted patriotic names such as Victory Canners, Patriotic Bakers and Uncle Sam's Sewers. Members immediately became involved in victory gardens, war bond sales and recycling projects.

At the 1941 Achievement Day, held right after the attack on Pearl Harbor, the second 4-H Council was elected and immediately adopted "Food For Victory" as their 1942 theme. The 1943 theme was "Production, Preservation and Conservation." To support the war effort a new project, Farm and Home Enterprises, was started in order to free adults for war-related duties.

4-H members assumed responsibility for household and farm chores, kept detailed records and wrote essays about their activities. Participation reached a fevered pitch: Helen and Ila Grace Weber had the best demonstration in the County Contest entitled "Rabbits for Victory" and ten Mount Harris boys sold the produce from their victory garden in the Colorado-Utah Supply Company Store.

With the increase in food and gas rationing in 1944 and 1945, 4-H activities were curtailed to an Exhibit Day in August which included demonstrations from club members. The 1945 4-H slogan was "Produce for Today, Prepare for Tomorrow" and the annual Extension Office report shows only ten active clubs: four in livestock, four in home economics, a garden club and a forestry club. Margaret Canaday took the first post-war award, for Grand Champion Fleece at State Fair, becoming the second Routt County 4-H member to attend Western Round-up in Denver.

Controversy shrouded 1947 when new County Agent, Guy Robbins, hoping to address declining numbers of leaders and members, proposed reorganizing 4-H so there would be one club in each of the county's three districts: South Routt, Steamboat Springs and Hayden. When the smoke cleared, there were 15 clubs, five for livestock, seven for home economics and three for gardening.

In the 1950s

A Soil Conservation project, started in 1950 with members Buddy Gumprecht, Dale Look, Douglas Patton, Willie Stender and Jackie Wheeler. The group planted trees and conducted grass tests on eight grasses in various parts of the county. Three new livestock clubs were formed in 1952 bringing the number of clubs in the county to 31, the most recorded to date. Some of the new

clubs were: the Hayden Livestock Club led by George Simonton; The Sidney Livestock Club led by Art Hudspeth and Bob Gay; and the Yampa Livestock Club led by E.S. Starbuck.

Two more new events sent Routt County 4-H members to the annual 4-H State Conference, a home economics judging team of Alice Selch and Patsy Truax, and a square dancing team of Chris Andrews, Sylvia Cook, Gene Cravins, Roberta Gay, Bonnie Rehder, and Dale, Francis and Ray Werner. By 1957 Yampa

Jess Hale, a Meeker horticulturist judging for a school fair, 1987 (Photo: Linda Long/ Susi Crowner)

started a 4-H talent contest in which eight clubs competed in square dancing and one-act plays and sent winners to the State 4-H Conference in Ft.Collins. The first drama contest was won by the Snap & Tacks 4-H Club, led by Jack May's wife, and the Bear River Ramblers from the Yampa area won the talent contest. This event continued until 1965.

A delegation of 46, the largest ever, attended the 1955 4-H State Conference, judging teams for livestock, dairy, home economics and range. The C&S 4-H Club had members in the talent contest; eight members of the Lucky Diamonds Square Dance Club were in the dance contest; and the Merry Mixers 4-H Club of Steamboat Springs did a one-act play. The Routt County home economics judging team, Sylvia Cook and Roberta Gay, placed fifth in the state and Sylvia was the top foods judge.

Donna Belton, Evelyn Schirr and Arlene Wattele participated in the first Routt County exchange, a 1957 trip to distant Boulder County where they stayed on dairy farms.

During the 1950s, 4-H members began attending the State 4-H Camp near Gould in Jackson County, an annual sojourn enjoyed by Routt County 4-Hers into the 1970s. Rita Herold was ten years old when she first went. She reminisces: "It was on the Western side of Cameron Pass. I arrived with Vickie Elkins and two other girls, riding in the back seat of the Extension Agent's car over a road that was neither graveled nor oiled. I was extremely car sick when we arrived at 10 pm. I roomed with two girls from Rio Blanco County and spent most of my time on the rifle range or in the craft hall. The camp had leadership activities and good programs in softball, horseshoes, archery, riflery and crafts."

In the 1960s and 1970s

During these years 4-H programming expanded into broader areas such as electricity, leathercraft, entomology, first aid, garden, and forestry; and in the 1970s photography, woodworking, vet science, and range management were introduced.

A Junior Leaders Association was formed in 1962, expanding for a brief period into a tri-county (Routt, Moffat and Rio Blanco) area in 1963. It was revised and renamed the Junior Leaders Council in 1972.

Window displays, Demonstration Day Shows and Talent Contests were popular during this era. Range Judging was added to livestock, dairy and home economics judging projects in the early 1960s, joined by Wool Judging in the mid 1970s. It was also a time when 4-H members became more involved with activities outside the county. Members like Bill Gay, Sandy Green, Marsha Gray, David Kuntz, Cheryl Signs and Kenneth Monger became active at District and State levels. Increased activity created a need for a summer agent, a position which became full-time Assistant County Agent in 1979 when Sue Bell became the first 4-H Youth Agent.

Weigh-in at the new scales, 1984

The era was marked by increased interest in national conferences and in the late 1960s Routt County began sending a delegation to Washington Focus. During the 1970s, when local 4-H members also became involved with national reports, six members won trips to Chicago for National Congress.

Two new contests were added to Market Livestock Projects. A Beef Production Contest, begun in the 1960s, was based upon rate of gain which sparked the idea of a Weigh-In Day. For steers this event was scheduled for December and usually fell on the coldest and snowiest day of the year. When carcass data was added to the computations, the Carcass Contest was established. It was also during the 1970s that placings at Fair and Record Book scores became part of these contests and sheep and swine were added to Production and Carcass Contests.

In the 1980s

As enrollment increased two new clubs—Southside (1984) and High Valley (1986)—joined 14 existing clubs although Arena Cleaners, Egeria Park, Wheeling Homesteaders and Yampa Valley 4-H dissolved.

Interest in projects began to shift. The intense focus on general projects manifest in the early 1980s, when 300 projects were shown on Exhibit Day, narrowed to specialized fields such as leathercraft and sewing. Two of the most successful current activities—the Exchange Program, started in 1983, and the Shooting Sports Program, started in 1984—were organized during this period and are described elsewhere in this chapter.

Contests remained popular. The Demonstration Contest again became an annual event in which local winners went on to show at the State Fair. The first of these were Nita Herold and Raylene Vetter who placed first in the County and first at State and won a trip to Western Round-up; Addona Daughenbaugh and Krista Monger earned trips to State Fair where they won Reserve Championships. Tasha Dobbs, Jennifer Covillo and Crystal Muhme also had top

114

demonstrations at the State Fair.

Mary Kilhstrom organized a Horse Bowl Team in 1986 which also competed in the Front Range Judging Contest and State 4-H Conference where it placed sixth in 1987, and third in both in 1988 when Jodi Link was one of the top scorers. Cherilynn Wallace started a Home Economics Judging Team which did extremely well at both Front Range and State 4-H Conference. It placed second in the Front Range contest and fifth at the State 4-H Conference in 1988, and fifth in both contests in 1989.

In the 1990s

Community projects were the hallmark of the 1990s. Clubs started highway and county road clean-up campaigns. The Elk River Wranglers, the first club to receive a State Community Pride Grant, helped restore the historic Moon Hill School and the Fairplay Club received another grant to beautify and restore the Elk Mountain Cemetery. The Steamboat Springs Rotary Club, which began sponsoring a Community Pride Award in 1994, gave it first to the Flat Top 4-H Club in South Routt for beautification of Snowden Park in Yampa and holiday visits to senior citizens.

Enrollment broke 300 in 1993, the same year the Elk River Wranglers became the first club in the Clark area since the 1950s. Shannon Sparkman returned to Routt County and revived the Dog Club she had created in Hayden in the late 1970s. The first Dog Show at the 1995 Fair was well attended and Jeremy Peed earned recognition for Senior Novice Dog Showman at State Fair. A Llama Club formed for eight members who entered showmanship and trail classes at the Fair between 1993 and 1995. Revived interest in clothing prompted a new Decorate Your Duds Project.

4-H Goes To The Fair

As early as 1926 the Routt County Fair had a Boys and Girls Exhibit. Early classes featured garden produce, livestock and needlework for youth under 17. By 1929 C.E. Margerum was supervising a 4-H Department for youngsters who wore special caps, purchased by the Fair Association, to promote the Fair. According to The Steamboat Pilot these first 4-H exhibits attracted attention and compliments and were won by Jim Sellers (dairy heifer), Hazel Long and Avis Dixon (clothing), and Foidel Canyon Morningstar Club (achievement).

1981

When the Routt and Moffat County Fairs joined forces in 1930, a special Overall Award was set up for the county with the best beef 4-H projects. Moffat County 4-Hers bought most of their project stock from the Dawson-Carpenter herds while Routt County 4-Hers tended to favor cattle from Deep Creek and Clark ranches. Enid Etzler had the first Grand Champion Steer but Moffat County walked away with the first Overall Award.

Although 1930 was the first year for 4-H Beef Projects, there were 23 animals in dairy classes, most from Routt County, won by Avis Dixon (Ayrshire), Thelma Margerum (Milking Shorthorn), Walter Moon (Holstein) and Jean Connor (Dairy Shorthorn). Hogs were first shown in a class won by Harvey Muirhead (Champion Barrow) and Catherie Carnahan (Champion Sow).

Routt County 4-Hers redeemed themselves the following year when Bud Rider (steer), Avis Dixon (Ayrshire) and Dean Dale (Holstein) took championships. Routt County turned the tables on Moffat County and won the Overall Beef Project Award as well as the Class Champion.

After the Depression 4-H classes were limited to a fat lamb and a fat steer class, which were divided by weights over and under 800 pounds. There were no premiums and it was not until 1938 that livestock species were filled and won by Frances Peavy (steer), Jack Sinden (dairy), James Kauffman (lamb) and Robert Lyon (hog).

Although 4-H activities continued during World War II the Fair and Camp Tobin were cancelled. After the war there were fewer 4-H market livestock projects at the fair because so many members were taking their animals to the Intermountain Livestock Show in Grand Junction which featured a Livestock Sale. The Fair's 4-H livestock contests did not begin to generate spirited competition until 1949 when youngsters from several Elk River families started showing livestock. Douglas Sherrod, Willie Stender, Frank Selbe, Doug Ross, Darlene Truax and the Look twins became strong competitors.

THE JUNIOR LIVESTOCK EXHIBIT AND SALE, first held in Steamboat Springs in 1949 had nothing to do with the Fair. It was started because the Fair was not held until September and many thought feeding livestock through haying season was expensive, inconvenient, and impractical. Another problem was that the Routt County Fair was held after the State Fair which required traveling and fattening steers and lambs during the winter months.

The Steamboat Pilot headline for coverage of the first Livestock Show and Sale held in Steamboat Springs announced that 37 head of cattle, sheep and colts were exhibited at the Rodeo Grounds. Prize money for beef cattle was $15 (first), $10 (second) and $5 (third). Lambs, calves and colts paid $5 (first), $3 (second) and $2 (third). The first champions were Donald Trull (beef female), Douglas Sherrod (beef male and steer), Willie Stender (ewe and ram), Dean Look (fat lamb), Darlene Truax (pen of three), Barbara Soash (dairy cow), and Douglas Ross (colt).

1981

Si Lockhart conducted the sale that followed the show. Boys Market, the Harbor Hotel, the Hi-Way Locker Plant and Henry Martin were the big buyers. Douglas Sherrod received 31 cents a pound for his champion steer from Boys Market, and Jerold Truax received the next highest price, 27.5 cents a pound from the Harbor Hotel.

The second Livestock Show and Sale was the highlight of 1950. This time the Routt County Commissioners gave $300 for prize money and the Steamboat Springs Stock Growers Association contributed a trophy for Show Champion.

A newly formed Routt County Livestock Growers Association also endorsed the effort. Douglas Ross had the champion steer and Patsy Truax the champion lamb. Willie Stender received the top price, selling his steer to Boys Market for 36 cents. No sheep were sold.

Two major changes were made in the show the following year: all exhibitors were judged for showmanship and the sale was dropped. The first champion showmen were Douglas Ross (beef), Patsy Truax (sheep), Dale Look (dairy) and Mary Cullen (horse). Boys Market, the Harbor Hotel and Safeway purchased several steers though there was no sale.

The Steamboat Springs show strongly impacted the Fair where only five head of dairy cattle, five colts and no sheep or hogs were shown. This helped justify the Commissioners' decision to cancel the 1951 Fair on grounds that interest did not justify the expense. In a move to bolster participation, the Fair was moved to the third week in August. This forced the Steamboat Junior Livestock Show to move to September in 1952. Another advantage to holding the County Fair in August was that Exhibit Day could be eliminated and all the home economic, general projects and style revue judging could take place at the Fair.

Even though it followed The Fair, the 1952 Junior Livestock Show in Steamboat Springs drew 55 exhibitors and 100 head of livestock. The big attraction was the showmanship class, which the Fair did not have, and Boys Market and Safeway continued to purchase some of the fat animals. The 1953 Junior Livestock Show moved to corrals on Yampa Street owned by Rusty Baker and Si Lockhart. Prizes totaling $450 drew 66 exhibitors and 121 head of livestock and attracted participants from clubs in Egeria Park, Sidney, Saddle Mountain, Hayden, Round Mountain, Elk River and Steamboat FFA.

By 1953 the Fair was back in full swing, expanded to three days, and activities involving livestock and home economics increased in number and popularity. A Junior Rodeo and Tractor Driving Contest, added in 1954, was first won by David Joe Zehner. Fat Steer and Beef Breeding Divisions drew competition and the Sheep Division pitted Shirley Stender against the McLaughlin Brothers, Glen and Leroy.

Steamboat's Livestock Show expanded to 70 exhibitors and 114 head of livestock in 1954 when the first Overall Showman Champion, Sheila Reagor of Yampa, was picked. The next year, the Steamboat Springs Chamber of Commerce began sponsoring a parade of animals down main street. Tiny Cook's Yampa Valley Livestock Sale Barn conducted the sale, but the real emphasis continued to be on showmanship. Maurice Harvey, Champion Dairy Showman, was Overall Champion Showman.

In 1956 interest in the Junior Livestock Show in Steamboat Springs waned. There were only 59 exhibitors and, while no sale was held, a Round Robin Showmanship Contest for the Showmanship Champions in each species was organized. The first Round Robin Showmen were Marian Hinman (beef), Maurice Harvey (dairy), Leroy McLaughlin (sheep) and Kay Conyers (horse). McLaughlin was the first Overall Round Robin Showmanship Champion.

When the 1957 Fair moved to the first week of September, followed the next weekend by the Steamboat Junior Livestock Show, members and parents practically lived with their animals for 12 days. The Fair provided competition in the fat classes and breeding stock, while the Junior Livestock Show emphasized showmanship and sales. Si and Darwin Lockhart conducted the 1957 sale, which set new records for prices. Steers averaged $32.05 cwt. and Aaron Huffstetler's 940 pound Grand Champion Steer was purchased for $36.50 cwt. by J.C.Penny & Co. and the Luekens and Boggs garages. The average price of lamb was $28.30, exceeded when Howard Elliott paid $31 cwt. for Leroy McLaughlin's champion.

Back-to-back shows took their toll on 4-Hers and their parents and 1958 was the last year for the Steamboat Junior Livestock Show. Turnout was light, only 11 steers and 8 lambs. Tiny Cook conducted the sale in which Shirley Stender and John Hoelscher tied for top price of $40 cwt. Lambs averaged $29 cwt. and McLaughlin again took the top price, $34.20 cwt.

In 1959 the first Junior Livestock Sale was held at the Fairgrounds on Saturday morning after the Livestock Show. Animals for this first sale had to be consigned and selling the animal was not mandatory as it is today. The sale included 16 steers, 6 lambs and 2 hogs and set the framework for future sales.

Judge Don Lorenz began running a successful Catch-A-Calf Contest for what quickly turned into 20 years. Eleven boys and one girl, Penny Wheeler, entered the first Catch-A-Calf Contest in 1959. When Penny failed to catch one of the seven calves, Frank and Lucienne Stetson saluted her effort by giving her one. The Routt County Farm Bureau took over the program in 1971 and in 1977 dropped the Catch-A-Calf Contest in favor of awarding a steer to members who applied for animals. To perpetuate the program 20% of proceeds from the Junior Livestock Sale were returned to the Farm Bureau in order to purchase animals for the following year. The Farm Bureau changed the program in 1982 when it began giving four heifer calves to 4-H or FFA members to raise for three years at the end of which the recipient returns a heifer calf to the program for another member to raise.

The late 1950s and 1960s saw an increase in interest in the sheep breeding project. This was due to the fact that two organizations sponsored small flocks for 4-H and FFA members. The first was Sears & Roebuck, which furnished breeding ewes during the late 1950s. Two Routt County recipients were the McLaughlin brothers, Glen and Leroy, who used the flock to dominate the Sheep Division at the Fair and Steamboat Springs Livestock Show. Dave McWhorter of Yampa also received a Sears flock in 1957 which he showed at the State Fair, placing in the top of his class.

The Routt County Farm Bureau established Columbia and Suffolk farm flocks in 1968. Each flock consisted of six ewes and recipients kept the flock for two years before returning six ewes for the next recipient. Many 4-H and FFA members established their own flocks from the offspring of these projects.

1984

Changes in the livestock classes in the 1970s saw the steer classes being judged as either English or Exotic, rather than by breeds. By the later 1970s hog classes were growing from 19 hogs shown in 1979 to 76 shown in 1989.

The 1972 Junior Livestock Sale toppled all records, reflecting an increase of 34% over the previous year, and grossing $35,268.37. Twenty-four steers sold for an average of $.90 a pound, 28 lambs averaged $1.44 and six hogs sold for an average of $1.29.

THE 4-H BARBECUE was the brainchild of Frank Stetson Jr. who suggested that 4-H should sponsor a feed before the Junior Livestock Sale in addition

118

to the traditional Sunday barbecue. So Bobby Robinson, head chef for the community barbecue, in 1975 began to host the extraordinarily popular pre-sale feast. The Sunday barbecue, sponsored by the County Commissioners since the 1960s, was dropped in favor of the pre-sale barbecue in 1990. The wonders of this gustatorial tradition are described in the sketch of "Bobby" Robinson elsewhere in this book.

A Dairy Goat Show was added in 1973 and a Dog Show in 1976. Market Lamb classes continued to grow until they became the largest classes at the Fair in the 1980s. Performance classes in the Horse Division grew to include Western Riding and Western Horsemanship. A Horse Breeding Project, including special classes at the County Fair and its own record book, was launched.

The Steamboat Pilot in 1972 began printing a Fair Supplement, with pictures and results, which continues until today; between 1991 and 1994 it printed a pre-Fair supplement which also served as the Fair Program. The largest classes were in the Horse Division. Numbers of livestock projects continued to increase, balancing modest declines in general and food projects, although clothing projects and Fashion Revue continued to draw as many as 50 exhibitors.

Jim Stanko attributes much of the strength of Routt County's 4-H programming to former 4-H members who return to serve as leaders and Fair Superintendents. "They are veterans. They know what they're doing and they are tireless workers," he says. Several of these prime movers, not mentioned elsewhere in this chronicle, are Joe Zimmerman, Hog Superintendent, who has assured a well-organized program in the face of soaring numbers. Larry Monger, Beef Superintendent, and his wife Mary Kay Monger who, with Nancy Peterson and Luke Studer, assure the Beef Show is a premiere event. David Kuntz, Sheep Superintendent, until his retirement in 1994, assured well run events in the face of expanding numbers.

University of Wyoming graduate students judged the carcass contest in 1992. It is possible, as David Ethridge found out in the 80s, to come in last in the market class but first in carcass judging.

The 90s have featured strong competition in livestock divisions.

Beef: The Beef Breeding Division continued to hold its status as the premiere division. Participation jumped from 9 members showing in 1990 to 18 showing 34 animals in 1995. New interest was sparked when Don Lufkin donated $1,200 to the premiums for breeding classes, and in 1995 established a fund which will award premiums of $1,500 for the next five years.

Swine: A Junior Swine Show attracted more than 100 hogs. The Swine show continued to grow to over 120 hogs and in 1994 was split into two days, one for showmanship and another for market classes.

Sheep: Although interest in sheep breeding waned, market lamb classes continued to draw around 100 entries.

Small animals: Patty Muhme, who took over when Jack Sprengle retired from ten years as Superintendent of rabbits and poultry, stressed quality and rules and, with Karin Covillo, involved 4-H members in shows in other counties. Starting an Open Rabbit Show at the Fair attracted rabbits from other counties and turned the show into a major event for Northwest Colorado.

Others: Diary Goat Projects were discontinued in 1988 but Dog Projects, a part of Exhibit Day until 1995, returned under the direction of Shannon Sparkman, and a Llama Project was started in 1993 with track and showmanship classes.

119

"The Fair is a learning experience. It teaches kids and their families responsibility and commitment. It truly is a family affair." — *Joe Zimmerman*
Steamboat Springs

"It teaches some basic lessons in life: survival skills, sure grit, salesmanship, competition and responsibility." — *Bev Bruggink*
Oak Creek

Special Programs

THE WINTER CALF SHOW interrupted the stillness of snowcovered main street in Steamboat Springs every December from 1930 until World War II. It was a "happening" – 4-H members loaded their calves onto sleds fitted with stock racks and hauled them into town to be paraded and judged. The Lions Club sponsored several early shows, sometimes called the Winter Steer Show.

The first year 12 owners marched their steers between 7th and 8th Streets to be judged in front of the Crosswhite Livery on 8th. The top five steers in the first show belonged to Enid Etzler, Doris Scott, Lola Robinson, Willett (Bud) Rider and Gilbert Hitchens. All were shipped to Denver in a covered railroad car to protect them from steam engine smoke and ash. For more than a decade all Routt County steers shown were sold at the National Western Stock Show.

The Depression impacted activities until 1934 when the Winter Calf Show regained its former luster. Isadore Bolton offered a $5 cash award for the best calf and 20 steers were entered. Winners belonged to Mary Peavy, Bud Rider, Enid Etzler, Don Lufkin, and Alice Peavy whose two steers placed in the top 25 at the National Western and sold for almost 12 cents a pound.

By 1936 the show was the bright spot in a long winter, boasting 27 steers and sponsored by the Lions Club and the newly formed Steamboat Springs Stock Growers Association, which donated a silver trophy. The top three steers were shown by Mary Peavy, Louis Ward and Don Lufkin. Mary Peavy's steer, a 1,025 pound Hereford, placed third at the National Western and sold for almost 15 cents a pound and the rest of Routt County steers sold in a lot for 12 cents a pound.

We didn't believe in "lean beef" in the 60s, says Lynne Sherrod. Darwin Lockhart, Delbert Sherrod and Del Scott with Delbert's Grand Champion steer in 1962. Delbert also had the Grand Champion in 1961 and 1963. (Photo: Sherrod Family)

The next year 14 steers were shown, all Herfords except for one Shorthorn. *The Steamboat Pilot* reported, "All were very well behaved and seemed to enjoy showing off for the crowd of onlookers." Mary Peavy placed first and second with Maxine Trull third. However, at the National Western, Maxine's steer placed fourth and was sold for 13 cents a pound.

The 1940 Winter Calf Show was an all Hereford show of 12 steers, eight taken to the National Western Stock Show. In 1942 no Winter Calf Show was held but six Routt County 4-H members took steers to the National Western Stock Show: Alice and Frances Peavy from Steamboat Springs, Floyd and Lawrence Phillips from Yampa, and Gladys Martin from Hayden.

Excitement surrounded the 1947 Winter Calf Show when the Steamboat Springs VFW Post organized it as an annual event. Sixteen steers paraded down Lincoln Avenue to a special arena built between Routt County National Bank and the Safeway on 8th and Lincoln. Judge Bill Ross, from Elk River, picked a steer owned by Robert Nefzger as Grand Champion and Floyd Phillips of Yampa had the first place feeder calf. But the Winter Calf Show never recaptured the spark and imagination which fired its early years and it was dropped soon thereafter.

L IVESTOCK JUDGING has been an integral part of 4-H since it was introduced to 4-H Dairy Club members in the summer of 1929. Evangeline Simmons (Utterback) returned to Routt County after college at Colorado A & M and conducted several summer livestock judging sessions with Elk River clubs. Then, in July 1931, Ferry Carpenter organized the Dawson Ranch Livestock Show and Judging Contest. This became a premier event for the cattle industry in Northwest Colorado for years to come. Teams from Grand, Moffat, Rio Blanco and Routt counties vied for a large silver cup.

Although the first Routt County Judging Team—Avis Dixon, Lawrence and Vaughn Powell—came in second in the 1931 contest, it paved the way for continuing excellence in 4-H judging programs. The following year's team—Arlene Elgin, Buford Hufstettler and Barry Greenwood—claimed Routt County's first judging championship and the silver trophy.

New scales, 1983

Livestock judging continued through the 1930s's, held at the Dawson Ranch Contest and occasionally at the Fair and at contests at the Middle Park Fair in Kremmling. In 1935 a Routt County team—Maxine Trull, Alice Peavy and Bud Rider— came in second at Kremmling. A 1938 judging team—James Kauffman, Gilbert Martin and Bud Rider—won contests at the Routt County Fair and at Gunnison. The Gunnison competition, one of the oldest continuing contests in the state, attracts many Routt County teams but this is the only time they won it.

The 1950s were major years for livestock judging competition. That year more than 60 4-H members turned out for the county judging contest, won by Sally Green and Jim Dorr. Between 1957 and 1962 the contest was open to members from Moffat, Grand and Rio Blanco Counties and Routt County sent livestock and dairy judging teams to the State 4-H Conference in Ft.Collins. Judging teams were also active competitors at Gunnison and at the State 4-H Conference in the early 1970s, when Sam Haslem spearheaded the program, and Barbara Brenner, David Kuntz, J. May, Doug Monger, and Bernadeen, Noreen and Valeen Jacobs were active. The 1972 team won a contest at Fairplay.

Bill Gay began coaching livestock judging teams in 1986 and within two years built a program with 20 enthusiastic participants who began to dominate judging competition on the Western Slope. Junior and senior teams were competing in the Front Range Judging Contest in Adams County and consistently took first or second in the Rio Blanco Judging Contest; senior teams continued going to the state contest in Ft.Collins. In 1988 Brad Carnahan was Colorado's fifth place swine judge.

Expert coaching paid off in 1990 when a senior team—Chip Herold, Travis Hampton, Rod and Tonya Wille—did what no other Western Slope livestock judging team had ever done: won the Front Range Judging Contest and went on to win contests in Moffat and Rio Blanco Counties and in Montrose. In state competition they finished ninth in a field of 23 teams and the junior team—Amy Apple, Jeffie Duncan, Cody and Jed May— swept competition.

Livestock judging teams continued to be top contenders and in 1991 the senior team won at Rio Blanco County and placed fifth in Douglas County; the junior team won at Rio Blanco and Garfield Counties.

EQUESTRIAN EVENTS have grown from 40 horses in the 1970s to more than 80 in the 1990s. Olive Morton, who became Superintendent in 1988, Bill Gay and Mary Kihlstrom have been announcers of the Fair's successful events.

Speed events—Barrel Racing, Pole Bending and Goat Tying— were added to the Fair's 4-H Horse Show in 1994. The following year roping projects began in Steamboat Springs and Hayden, and Break Away Roping, the first rodeo-type event since the Junior Rodeo was cancelled in 1956, began at the Fair. Jesse Franz won the first contest.

Another unusual horse program, pioneered in Routt County in 1987, was Horse Vaulting, performing gymnastic maneuvers on a horse trotting in a circle. Joan Pascetti and Kathy Hockin supervise the project in which Aileen Hockin starred at state and national contests in 1989 and 1990, attaining one of the highest ratings in the sport.

An emphasis on level testing—for beginners, intermediates and advanced riders—began in 1986 in order to get more riders tested and assigned competition levels. Within a year Sunny Booco, Molly Forsyth, Rebecca Weaver and Tina Williams became advanced riders and by 1987 Rebecca became Routt County's first "level four" advanced rider.

Today's advanced Western riders are Sherrie McNeal, Casey Sopcowicz and Shawneen Guire who was the second Routt County 4-H member to attain "level four" in Western Riding; when she reaches it in English riding in 1996, she will be one of the few 4-H members in Colorado certified in both Western and English riding.

A Horse Council was formed in 1944 to develop and coordinate horse projects under the direction of Alicia Samuelson, its first leader. The Horse Council has established several training clinics and supervises the Northwest Colorado Horse Show and the Autumn Classic Junior Horse Show. It also sponsored two trail rides to raise funds for the Muscular Dystrophy Foundation.

SHOOTING SPORTS, started in 1984 by Bruce Sigler of Yampa, were immediately popular. Bob McKune and Jim Stanko started the program in Steamboat Springs in 1985 and Tim Frentress and Gene Boatman began it in 1986 in Hayden. Through the years as many as 54 4-H members have been involved, learning shooting techniques and safety skills in archery, shotgun, trap, .22 target rifle, .22 hunt rifle, and air rifle categories.

The highlight of each year is competition at State Fair, usually attended by 25 members of junior and senior teams. Routt County teams dominated contests during the late 1980s and early 1990s. In 1985 team members won 79 ribbons, seven team first place awards and the Overall Best Trophy.

Outstanding shooters included:

From South Routt: Brad and Tad Carnahan, Chip Herold, Travis and Wes Milway, Philip Manzanares, Mark and Paul Ritkowski, and Steve and Pete Sigler

From Steamboat Springs: Scott Engler, Travis Etzler, Dan and Daryl Kemry, Daniel Lockhart, Rusty McKune, David More, Pat Stanko, Nick Vineyard and Debra Wagner

From Hayden: Alex Epp, Tim and Nathan Frentress, Jacques Denker, Shawn and Jay Dee Hockaday and Travis Nash

By 1993 team members began shooting in National Rifle Association Sectional Meets at the Cherry Creek Gun Club in Aurora. They also participated in a Prone Tournament in Grand Junction. In 1995 a Junior Air Rifle Team—Ebin Abshire, Casey Estes, Tyler Knott and Walker Montgomery—came in second in the NRA Western Sectionals. Darwin Wille in 1993 and Paul Jazwick in 1994 also took home regional honors, placing first in the American Legion Western District Air Rifle Tournament. In 1995 Daniel Lockhart took second in both the American Legion and National Guard Western District Air Rifle Tournaments.

Shooting sports continue to produce contestants and trophies although the archery program has been discontinued. Teams competing at the State Fair consistently bring home individual and team awards in shotgun, .22 target rifle, and air rifle.

1981

EXHIBIT DAY, the annual judging of 4-H projects, began because the Routt County Fair was held in September after the State Fair. Since project champions were eligible for the State Fair, Exhibit Day was held in either July or August. Project Champions were identified, and delegates to Camp Tobin and the State Fair designated.

The first Exhibit Day was held in October 1929, the "final" event of the 4-H year. Forty-three members from Clubs in Yampa, lower Oak Creek, Elk River, Foidel Canyon and Hayden met in Steamboat Springs to show their projects and turn in Record Books.

The first Exhibit Day to forward exhibits to the State Fair was in July 1930 and, despite rain, more than 100 members and parents attended. Mary Wixson remembers riding the train into Steamboat Springs from Hayden for Exhibit Day in 1935. It was held at the Cabin Hotel, "the finest hotel in Northwest Colorado," a 100-room centrally heated building which occupied the site of the Bud Werner Memorial Library until it burned in 1939. "It was the most fun we ever had," says Mary who still grins when she recalls a whole day off, swimming, shopping, seeing the style show and watching the judges.

Betty Lyons (Craig) judging cookies, 1989

During the years the Fair was held in August, Exhibit Day became part of the Fair. However, when the Fair was moved back to August in 1992, Exhibit Day fell on the opening day of the State Fair so it was rescheduled for a few days prior to the Routt County Fair as a kick-off event. While this arrangment permits Routt County 4-H members to participate in the State Fair, it deprives area residents from seeing the prize-winning exhibits until after they return from Pueblo.

FASHION REVUE, sometimes called a Style or Dress Revue, has been part of Exhibit Day most years. It was first staged in 1935, when Lola Robinson won. In 1938 the Dress Revue was part of Exhibit Day held in Steamboat Springs' Cabin Hotel just months before it burned down. Eileen Hitchens (clothing), Maxine Maters (food) and Mary Jean King (dress revue) took championships.

Participation peaked in 1941 when there were 79 participants and after the war, in the 1950s when the Dress Revue was renamed the Style Revue, it further increased in popularity and competitive intensity. Helen Sherrod created a dynasty, which lasted into the 1970s, working with girls from all parts of the county. Not only did they win in the 4-H divisions, but they were also consistent winners in statewide contests: Colorado Woolgrowers' Make It With Wool, the Colorado State Grange's Make It With Cotton, and the Colorado Cowbelles' Clever with Leather.

Three boys joined 70 girls in modeling garments in 1957. *The Steamboat Pilot* reported that "Donald and Ronald Boettler and Bernard Knott manfully displayed bold pattern aprons in front of the judges." By 1962 there were 93 girls in the Style Revue and Mary Ann Duckels, of Steamboat Springs, went on

to win the State Revue and represented Colorado in the National 4-H Fashion Revue in Chicago where she placed third.

During the early 1970s, Style Revue was renamed Fashion Review and became a separate event, held in June until 1986. Boys returned to the contest during the 1980s, when they also entered winner's circles in home economic projects. David Long became the first boy to win Grand Champion in Clothing Construction in 1980; Jerry Whaley was Junior Reserve Grand Champion in 1988 and 1989; and Danny May was Intermediate Champion in 1994.

Teffanie Traux, Jennie Panepinto, Tonya Willie and Julie Redmond in the 1985 Fashion Revue.

DEMONSTRATION DAY is set aside for 4-H members to demonstrate a project, a requirement for participants in 4-H clubs. Through the years there have been County and/or District Demonstration Days and Demonstration Contests at either the State 4-H Conference or at the State Fair. The County Demonstration Day has been held as part of Exhibit Day, as a Fair event, or as a special event. Since the 1980s the top individual and top team are eligible to go to a state contest held at the State Fair. The event dates from the mid-1930s when 4-H members in clothing and food projects were required to give demonstrations, and was first won by Marguerite Gwillim and Marlene Hinkle (sewing) and Iva Spencer (foods).

HOME ECONOMICS GRAND CHAMPIONS

Year	Foods	Clothing	Fashion Revue
1929		Hazel Long (1st Year)	
		Avis Diton (2nd Year)	
1930	Violet Muirhead	Jean Conner	
1931	Laverne Orr	Jean Conner (Overall)	
		Helen Kelton (1st Year)	
1932	Doraphine Laughlin	Florence Allen/Loraine Brockman	
1933		No Fair	
1934	Bessie Jo Hanks	Mary Heintz	
1935	Madeline Bradburn	Sara Clark/Lola Robinson	Lola Robinson
1936	Maxine Trull	Kathrine Hudspeth/Marretta Hinkle	Sara Clark
1937			
1938	Maxine Matters	Eileen Hitchens	Mary Jean King
1939			
1940	Enid Reynolds	Ramone Kayser	Ina May Perry
1941	Edith Reynolds	Kathrine Hudspeth	Katherine Hudspeth
1942	Donna Williamson	Annabell Jones	No Dress Review
1943		Marian Light	Marian Light
1944	Arabell Jones	Marian Morris	Shirley Arnold
1945	Verna Decker	Neva May Peters	Donna Williamson
1946	Neva May Peters	Harriet Kemry	Jeanne Poole
1947	Patsy Smith	Joyce Bakke	Iva Decker
1948	Betty Lou Whitlock	Patricia Wheeler	Patsy Wheeler
1949	Joanna Ray	Patsy Strutzel	Leroyce Mosher
1950	Patsy Strutsel	Darlene Truax	Darlene Truax
1951		Darlene Truax	Darlene Truax
1952	Wilma Harms	Mona Starbuck	Lenore Ekstrom
1953	Bonnie Smith	Mona Starbuck	Mona Starbuck*
1954	Mary Jane Harmon	Mary Jane Harmon	Lenore Ekstrom
1955	Eugenie Dorr	Mary Jane Harmon	Phyllis Bird/Kathleen Klumker*
1956	Jackie Sherrod	Janice Gumprecht	Joann Montgomery
1957	Sarron Williams	Joann Montgomery	Jackie Sherrod
1958	Sandra Decker	Jackie Sherrod	Jackie Sherrod
1959	Mary Ann Duckles	Larue Mosher	Larue Mosher/Carol Cullen
1960	Donna Carver	Phyllis Workman	Carol Younger
1961	Marilyn Baird	Linda Norris	Linda Norris
1962	Marilyn Baird	Mary Ann Duckles	Mary Ann Duckles
1963	Beverly Williams	Arloa Knott	Suzanne Hamil
1964	Sherry Murphy	Linda Robinson	Marie Sandelin
1965	Jackie Crawford	Marie Sandelin	Marie Sandelin
1966	Mary Beth Flanders	Marsha Stees	Marsha Stees
1967	Deanna Wood	Sherry Murphy	Ethel Halpenny
1968	Nancy Dowling	Gail Rossi	Ethel Halpenny
1969	Ruth Ann Mosher	Gail Rossi	Deanna Wood
1970			
1971	Terri Haslem	Valerie Gocken	Sandy Green
1972	Cindy Brunner	Barbara Brenner	Mavis Stees
1973	Cindy Brunner	Sherry Nay	Cindy Brunner/Barbara Brenner*
1974	Kathy Baldwin	Valeen Jacobs	Valeen Jacobs
1975	Bambi Lombardi	Valeen Jacobs	Valeen Jacobs
1976	Cathy Miller	Terry Nay	Kelli Root/Terry Nay*
1977	Mary Beth Brenner	Doris Hawk	Doris Hawk
1978	Laura Stetson	Bernadeen Jacobs	Bernadeen Jacobs/Laura Stetson
1979	Mary Ann Rossi	Kayron Baalhorn	Sherry Nelson /Donna Monger
1980	Michelle Harding	David Long	Cheryl Hoaglund/Lori Hayes
1981	Keith Villa	Mary Ann Rossi	Sherry Nelson/Mary Ann Rossi
1982	Ty Zabel	Julie Redmond	Ceena Truax/Edwina Peterson
1983	Julie Redmond	Rita Cooper	
1984	Audra Wagner	Barbara Sandefur	Barbara Sandefur/Julie Redmond
1985	Nina Cloven	Shelly Hicks	Teffanie Truax/Julie Redmond
1986	Tonya Willie	Julie Redmond	Julie Redmond/Audra Wagner
1987	Grant Smith	Julie Redmond	Tonya Wille/Jennie Panepinto
1988	Amy Cupp	Julie Redmond	Julie Redmond/Jennie Panepinto
1989	Abby Herfurtner	Krista Monger	Krista Monger/Tonya Wille
1990	Sajon Covillo	Heather Carrell	Tonya Wille/Jessica Hinde
1991	Tammy Ray	Jessica Hinde	Jessica Hinde/Naomi Gloria
1992	Kate Perry	Jessica Hinde	Jessica Hinde/Brandi May
1993	Carrie deGanahl	Jessica Hinde	Jessica Hinde/Brandi May
1994	Carrie de Ganahl	Brandi May	Brandi May/Trish Warner
1995	Danielle Wagner	Dawn Underwood	Dawn Underwood /Sophie Holly

* To State Fair

A CHIEVEMENT DAY, the annual recognition and awards program for 4-H members and leaders, has its origins in a gathering of parents and members of the Clark 4-H clubs in November 1930. The program included, songs, humorous sketches and a review of accomplishments. The idea caught on and in 1931 several clubs held achievement programs for their members and in 1932 the home economics clubs celebrated Achievement Day with the Home Demonstration Clubs.

The first countywide Achievement Day was held in May 1936 when 73 members from 14 clubs received awards. The first club to receive awards for 100% completion were Hayden's Happy Hours Helpers, Milner's Happy Hours Sewers and Phippsburg's Stitch and Chatter Sewing Club.

Achievement Day moved to November in 1949 and is still held at that time. Members from 19 clubs attended, and the first Outstanding Club Award was presented to Arlene Truax's sewing club, which won the most ribbons and collected two first place and four second place awards in clothing projects at the State Fair. Walt Weber preserved the entire program on a state-of-the-art "recording device" so clubs could play it at their meetings.

Nita Herold, 1982

Early Achievement Days were usually marked by a dinner and speech by an agricultural college specialist, the county commissioners or local notables, however, in the 1950s the format began to include fewer speakers and more awards. The 1953 Achievement Day was marked by two new awards. Boys Market established a $20 cash award for the 4-H club holding the most progressive activities. First won by the Busy Fingers 4-H Club, it was given annually until the early 1970s. *The Steamboat Pilot,* which sponsored the other new award until 1989, recognized the year's outstanding reporter. It was first won by Carol Pieper and Beverly Kier.

Achievement Day in 1954 was one of the largest ever, attended by 350 members and parents. The Steamboat Springs Chamber of Commerce launched their Special Achievement Award in 1955. First winners of the Achievement Award were Kathleen Klumker and Joann Montgomery. Three more businesses started sponsoring awards given until the early 1970s: a Ralston-Purina Trophy for each fat animal champion at the Fair, a J. C. Penny Award for the Clothing Construction Champion, and the Dorothy Shop for the Style Revue Champion.

An unusual award highlighted the 1959 Achievement Day, when Louis Coghill presented Rita Moore a breeding ewe for her outstanding sheep breeding project. Coghill continued the practice for several years until he moved his ranching operation out of the county but Rita's daughter, Nita Herold, remembered the gesture in 1986 by presenting Julie Whittingham with a breeding ewe for her Best First Year Sheep Breeding Project.

Through the years several awards have become prestigious. The oldest of these is an annual award started by the Routt County Stock Growers Association in the late l940s for the Overall Livestock Project. Willie and Shirley Stender and Aaron Huffstettler took most of them during the 1950s. Early in 1960, when changed to honor excellence in an Overall Beef Project, Bill Gay garnered most. Emphasis again shifted in the 1970s when the Routt County Cattlemen started giving the award for the Best Overall Beef Record Book and established a traveling trophy which remained with a three-time winner. David Kuntz promptly won it the first three times.

New hay pen, 1983

Awards for showmanship in all species were also started. The first Sheep Showmanship Award was presented in 1962 by Dan and Doris Knott, who continue the tradition.

During the 1960s various Steamboat Springs restaurants, most frequently the El Rancho, began catering the Achievement Day dinner at the Steamboat Springs Community Center, (later the Good News Building), which burned in 1993. In the 1970s the program was held either at the Steamboat Springs High School or Steamboat Springs Junior High School and by 1986 increased attendance transformed it into a potluck at the Exhibit Hall, a continuing tradition. The number of awards presented at Achievement Day and the popularity of the event has, since 1993, drawn as many as 500 4-H and FFA leaders, parents and members to the dinner.

BEYOND OUR BORDERS: STATE AND REGIONAL EVENTS

District and State events open opportunities for leaders and members to expand their horizons. Routt County 4-Hers have been involved in these activities since they began in the 1930s.

STATE 4-H CONFERENCE, frequently called June Conference, is a three-day series of workshops and contests for leaders and 4-H members at Colorado State University in Ft.Collins. Routt County has been participating since 1953 when Douglas Ross and LeRoyce Mosher attended. During the 1950s and 1960s events revolved around contests such as livestock, dairy and home economics judging. While judging contests continue, once popular talent contests, involving one-act plays and square dancing, have been replaced by workshops for delegates.

State officers, elected from county delegations at this conference have included Routt County 4-H members and leaders:

Members
Patsy Smith, Toponas, State 4-H Secretary, 1951
Kenneth Monger, 1969
Marsha Gray, 1972
Audra Wagner, 1988
Krista Monger, 1991
Adonna Daughenbaugh, 1992
Lori Jazwick, 1993

Leaders
Evelyn Monger, Northwest Colorado Representative, 1969
Rita Herold, District President, 1987-1990; State 4-H Leader Chairman, 1993-1994; Advisor, 1995
Mary Kay Monger, District President, 1990-1993

STATE FAIR AND CAMP TOBIN have attracted Routt County 4-H members, leaders and parents since 1930.

State Fair exhibitors must be County Fair champions except in the Livestock Division where entries are open to any 4-H or FFA member. Traditionally the County Extension Agent delivers and picks up Routt County's exhibits and 4-H members do not accompany their projects to Pueblo. The majority of Routt County exhibitors earn blue ribbons, although since Laverne Orr of Yampa captured the title in foods with a plate of gingerbread and oatmeal cookies in 1932, many have captured Grand Championships and Unit Championships.

Problems presented by hauling livestock to Pueblo and dates, which frequently conflict with the Routt County Fair, have limited local participation in livestock divisions. Mary Peavy took the first steer to the State Fair in 1938 and placed fifth. Not until 1987, 49 years later, did a Routt County steer owned by Darcy Camilletti place among the top entries. During the mid-1990s the Booco sisters—Jody, Jessie and Jaimie—have placed in the top ranks with both steers and swine.

Since Mary Khilstrom began taking horse performance teams to the State Fair in the 1980s, Routt County 4-Hers have been top competitors. Lane Kihlstrom has the distinction of earning Reserve Champion Horse Showman in 1978.

Camp Tobin is the area set aside for 4-H exhibits, a dining hall, and dormitories at the Colorado State Fairgrounds in Pueblo. It is the hub of 4-H activities during the State Fair: Fashion Revue, Demonstration and Cooking Contests, Talent Shows, the 4-H Dog Show and State 4-H Officers meetings. Until World War II interrupted activities, 4-H members attending the camp had to be delegates selected by their counties who, in addition to seeing the Fair, participated in a program of 4-H activities. Routt County selected its delegates at Exhibit Day based upon the quality of projects and records.

The first Routt County Delegate was Enid Etzler in 1930 and the first delegation, selected in 1931, consisted of Bufford Huffstettler of Yampa, Bob Heller of Hayden, and Bud Rider and Doris Scott of Clark. Beginning in 1935 the county Dress Revue winner was also a delegate to the camp.

Delegates were selected in several ways during the 1950s and 1960s but the prime criteria remained a top quality project and exceptional records. Today there are no official delegates to Camp Tobin. It is basically a dormitory and dining hall for 4-H members, leaders and parents attending the State Fair. County 4-Hers can earn a berth at the Fair by working as clerks and guides.

Rita Herold was 14, the youngest age allowed, when she attended Camp Tobin in the 1950s. She remembers:

"Camp Tobin wasn't a camp in the traditional sense. It was the official designation for the program and facilities for Colorado 4-H members at the Colorado State Fair. The most infamous part of the camp were the old Army barracks-style dormitories, one for girls and another for boys. Each county was entitled to send two representatives, district demonstration winners and exhibitors in the Junior Livestock Show. I remember the intense heat, living on lemonade and ice cream because it was too hot to eat, and learning nonsense songs. The Style Review winners were professional, and the tour of the CF&I Steel foundry fascinating, and the carnival fun. My favorite was going to the sheep and cattle shows."

WESTERN REGION 4-H ROUND-UP is a gathering of winners of select 4-H projects at contests in many other Western states and Canada. It began in the early 1940s and is held during the National Western Stock Show in Denver in January. Routt County 4-H members who have attended are:

1940 Keith Yount (potatoes)
1946 Margaret Canaday (fleece)
1976 Steve Portouw (electric)
1980 Jim Redmond (sheep breeding) and Kirk Zabel (leathercraft)
1983 John Redmond (sheep breeding)
1984 Nita Herold and Raylene Vetter (demonstration)
1989 Jay Whaley (beef breeding)
1996 Andy Kurtz (leathercraft)

THE NORTHWEST COLORADO LIVESTOCK EXPO began in Grand Junction in 1967 as a training clinic for 4-H project participants. It is a two-day workshop on grooming and showmanship techniques, in market and breeding classes open to 4-Hers from the seven counties comprising Northwest Colorado. It is the only event of this kind and is held in each of the participating counties on a rotating basis. Unlike a fair, members can bring only one animal to Expo.

Awards and scholarships are awarded for points earned for knowledge about a project, record books, attendance, showmanship and class placings. Prizes include full tuition at Northeastern Junior College, scholarships at Colorado State University, Colorado Mountain College and Colorado Northwestern Community College, and savings bonds.

Depending upon the location, between 12 and 25 Routt County 4-Hers attend Expo, where they are consistently among the top competitors. David Kuntz was Routt County's first Overall Winner followed by Roxanne James, Adonna Daughenbaugh, Janet Baker and Jeffie Duncan. Janet Baker, Jeffie Duncan and Tonya Wille have earned scholarships to Northeastern Junior College.

THE INTERSTATE EXCHANGE PRO-GRAM permits Routt County 4-H families to share their homes, activities, lifestyle and interests with members from other parts of the country. The first interstate exchange occurred in 1983 when 4-Hers from Galveston visited Routt County. Since then Routt County 4-H members have visited or welcomed members from Texas, Tennessee, Delaware, New York, Louisiana, Illinois, Florida and California. Although a summer program, Routt County hosted Florida over the 1986 and 1995 Christmas vacations in order to permit members to experience snow; five hours after leaving 86 degree Florida weather a group from Sarasota arrived at Hayden where it was 22 below zero in 1986.

Holly May, 1983

ROUTT COUNTY DELEGATES TO THE INTERNATIONAL 4-H YOUTH EXCHANGE (IFYE)

This is a six-month exchange program for college-age 4-H members who tour Colorado sharing their experiences upon return.

1957 Wanda Gumprecht (Japan)
1970 Bill Gay (Philippines)
1992 Nita Herold (Norway)

ROUTT COUNTY DELEGATES TO 4-H NATIONAL CONGRESS

National trips and scholarships rewarded outstanding National Report Forms, judged at local, state and national levels. State winners received a trip to 4-H Congress held in Chicago. The first national winner was Kenneth Monger in 1969. John Redmond set national records for 4-H in 1984 when his National Report Form was first in the state in Achievement, first in Agriculture and first in Ag Careers; and he won Overall Best National Report Form and a $750 Santa Fe Railroad Scholarship. National Report Forms were dropped in favor of a resume in 1994 and discontinued in favor of regional conferences in 1995.

1962 Mary Ann Duckels	1982 Mary Ann Rossi
1969 Kenneth Monger	1983 Jim Redmond
1972 Marsha Gray	1983 Jody Kayser
1973 David Kuntz	1984 John Redmond
1974 Larry Portouw	1986 Nita Herold
1976 Steve Portouw	1988 Audra Wagner
1979 Donna Monger	1990 Krista Monger

ROUTT COUNTY DELEGATES TO WASHINGTON FOCUS

Called the Citizenship Short Course when started in the early 1960s, this is a national program which permits delegates from each county to spend a week in a Washington, D.C. dormitory while studying government. Not until 1971 did delegates from Routt County began attending every year; since 1979 the county has sent two delegates. Records do not indicate whether local members attended in 1964 or 1965, or whether participants in citizenship workshops at the Colorado 4-H Conference attended between 1966 and 1971.

1963 Sharon Scott, 4-H Council President	1983 Deborah Link and Lane Kihlstrom
1966 Cheryl Signs	1984 John Redmond and Ty Zabel
1969 Kenneth Monger	1985 Tracie Goulet and Philip Rossi
1972 Richard Haslem	1986 Darcy Camilletti and Nita Herold
1973 Barbara Brenner	1987 Julie Redmond and Kip Kihlstrom
1974 Cathy Rickerby	1988 Audra Wagner and Joli Porter
1975 Deanna Kuntz	1989 Kaylynn Rossi and Tonya Wille
1976 Vicki Morton	1990 Rachel Smith and Shannon Yeager
1977 Betty Jean Rickerby	1991 Adonna Daughenbaugh and Krista Monger
1978 Donna Monger	1992 Lori Jazwick and Jeannie Zimmerman
1979 Laura Stetson and David Ethridge	1993 Jessica Hinde and Brandi May
1980 Cheryl Hoaglund and Luke Tellier	1994 Shawneen Guire and Crystal Muhme
1981 Jody Kayser and Kirk Zabel	1995 Alex Epp and Mark Monger
1982 Mary Ann Rossi and Jim Redmond	1996 Jeff Clyncke and Laurel Selbe

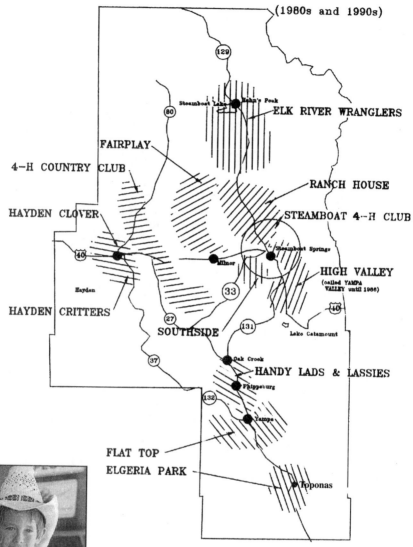

(1980s and 1990s)

ELK RIVER WRANGLERS

FAIRPLAY

4-H COUNTRY CLUB

RANCH HOUSE

HAYDEN CLOVER

STEAMBOAT 4-H CLUB

HIGH VALLEY
(called YAMPA VALLEY until 1966)

HAYDEN CRITTERS

SOUTHSIDE

HANDY LADS & LASSIES

FLAT TOP
ELGERIA PARK

COUNTYWIDE: The Routt County 4-H Junior Rifle Club with coaches in South Routt, West Routt and the Steamboat Springs area.

Routt County 4-H Clubs

Following is a complete list of 4-H Clubs chartered through the state or recorded at the Routt County Extension Office. It does not include clubs which existed for less than a year.

From the 1920s
Elk River Dairy Calf Club
Fairplay Baby Beef Club (1)
Foidle Canyon Morning Star Club
Hayden Dairy Calf Club
Stitch & Chatter Sewing Club
Stitch & Time Sewing Club
Sunshine Makers Dairy Calf Club
Yampa Dairy Calf Club

From the 1930s
Bake & Chatter Club
Busy Stitchers Club
Clark Busy Fingers Club
Deep Creek Blue Ribbon Beef Club
Forestry Club
Happy Go Lucky Bakers Club
Happy Hour Sewers Club
Hayden Happy Hour Helpers Club
Hayden Krispy Krust Kookers Club
Mesa Maids Club
Milner Clothing Club
Middle Trout Creek Club
Sidney Valley Baby Beef Club
Steamboat Sewing Club
Yampa Busy Bees Club
Yampa Baby Beef Club
Yampa Pig Club

From the 1940s
Busy Thimbles Club
Can If You Can Can Club
Cook Easy Club
Deep Creek Livestock Club
Dinah's In the Kitchen Club
Early Birds Sewing Club
Fashionable 4-H Club
Hilton Gulch Willing Workers Club
Kapable Kitchen Kooks Club
Keep Em Sewing Club
Mothers Helpers 4-H Club
Pin and Needle 4-H Club
Real McCoy 4-H Club
Saddle Mountain 4-H Livestock Club
Saddle Mountain Cooking and Sewing Club
Sew and Sew 4-H Club
The Be Busy Club
The Go Getters
The Kitchenettes
The Lucky Four
The Tinkling Spoons
Tidy Twelve 4-H Club
Two In One 4-H Club
Yellow Jacket Sewing Club
Young Homemakers Club

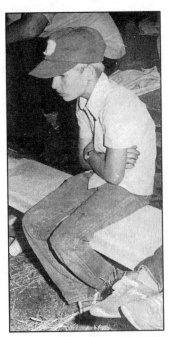

1978

During World War II

(Some new and others which changed their names to patriotic themes)

American Helpers
All Out For Victory 4-H Club
Patriotic Bakers
Steamboat Defense Club
Uncle Sam's Sewers
Victory Canners
Victory Gardeners
Victory Sewers
Victory Sewing Sisters

From the 1950s

Aunt Jemima 4-H Club
Bear River Riders Club
Busy Bakers Club
Busy Kitchen Queens
Buttons & Bows
Cinderella 4-H Club
C & S (Cooking and Sewing) Club
Early Bird Sewing Club
East Routt Soil Conservation Club
Egeria Park Livestock Club (2)
Elk River Livestock Club
Flat Top 4-H Club (3)
Golden Crust 4-H Cooking Club
Green Ridge Ag and Livestock Club
Handy Lads and Lassies (3)
Happy Go Lucky 4-H Cooking Club
Hayden Clover Club (3)
Hayden Livestock Club
Jolly Girl Sewers
Kitchen Kuties
Little Toilers
Luck Diamond Livestock 4-H Club
Merry Mixers 4-H Club
Merry Kind and Willing Club
Mix and Whip Club
Muffin Misses
Mt. Harris Garden Club
Oak Creek Busy Beavers
Ranch House 4-H Club (3)
Rip N Stitch It Club
Round Mountain Livestock Club
Sidney Livestock Club
Spool Mates
So and Sew 4-H Club
Tell Tailors Club
Yampa Valley 4-H Club (4)
4-H Chuck Wagon Rangers

From the 1960s

Eager Beavers Club
Kaua 4-H Horse Club
Knit & Sew Club
Measure For Pleasure Club
Pins and Needles Club
Rowels and Reins Club

Sew and Dough Club
Spoon and Needles Club
Stitch It N Fix It Club
The Golden Thimbles
White Cloud Club

From the 1970s

Arena Cleaners (5)
Fish Creek 4-H Club
Las Vaqueras 4-H Club (6)
Pinnacle Peak 4-H Club
Routt County Dog Care & Training Club
Steamboat City Slickers Club
Steamboat Guys and Gals (7)
The Egg Beaters
The Stitchers
Wheeling Homesteaders
4-H Country Club (3)

From the 1980s

Flying Images 4-H Vaulting Club
Hayden Critter Club (3)
High Valley 4-H Club (3)
Pine Valley Club (8)
Oak Creek Leather 4-Hers
Oak Creek High Mountaineers
Routt County 4-H/Junior Rifle Club (3)
Southside 4-H Club (9)
Steamboat Rabbit & Cavy Club (10)

From the 1990s

Elk River Wranglers, 1991
Fairplay 4-H Club, 1929
Flat Top 4-H Club, 1958
4-H Country Club, 1974
Handy Lads & Lassies, 1954
Hayden Critter Club, 1989
Hayden Clover Club, 1958
High Valley 4-H Club, 1986
Pine Valley Club (11)
Ranch House Club, 1956
Rowels and Reins, 1968-1990
Routt County 4-H/Junior Rifle Club, 1986
Routt County 4-H/K-9ers Dog Club, 1995
Southside 4-H Club, 1984-1996
Steamboat 4-H Club, 1995
Trailblazers 4-H Club, 1993-1995
Young Riders 4-H Club, 1992-1994

FOOTNOTES

(1) Oldest existing club, now called the Fairplay Club
(2) Became the Egeria Park 4-H Club until 1987
(3) Still active
(4) Existed until 1988 (4) Existed until 1990
(5) Changed to Young Riders in 1992
(6) Changed to Steamboat Equestrians in 1980)
(7) Began as Griping Grannies Club
(8) Inactive as of 1993
(9) Inactive as of 1996
10) Also called Raisin Makers
(11) Inactive as of 1993

ROUTT COUNTY 4-H LEADERS

Although every attempt has been made to include leaders who have been involved with the program for ten or more years, or who have distinguished themselves during their service to 4-H, faulty records and memories assure that it is not complete.

From the 1920s
Howard Bailey, Hayden
Leo and Sadie Coyner, Clark
Nellie Fahrion, Deer Park
Katherine Gourley, Foidle Canyon
Percy Hitchens, Fairplay
C.E. Margerum, Yampa
Glen Root, Clark

From the 1930s
Alma Baer, Steamboat Springs
Vauna Hill Clark, Steamboat Springs
Winifred Hitchens, Milner
Ruby Peters, Phippsburg
George Phillips, Yampa
Margaret Sampson, Hayden
Anna Van Cleave, Steamboat Springs

From the 1940s and 50s
Loy Audrey, Phippsburg
Bonnie Dobbs, Steamboat Springs
Beulah Entsminger, Mt. Harris
Audrey Hitchens, Milner
Elsa Jones, Yampa
Antoinette Kasper, Oak Creek
Catherine Montgomery, Yampa
Gladys and Francis Moore, Yampa
Evelyn Semotan, Deep Creek
Arlene Truax, Steamboat Springs
Ed Trull, Saddle Mountain

From the late 1950s to 1965
Mable Beasley, Toponas (10 years in 1955)
Winnie Carroll, Hayden (10 years in 1959)
Bob Gay, Sidney and Yampa Valley
Otto Gumprecht Sr., Toponas
Ila Grace Harms, Steamboat Springs (5 years in 1954)
Carl Herold Sr., Yampa Valley (5 years in 1959)
Ben Hibbert, Yampa Valley
Pat Holderness, Hayden
Art and Florence Hudspeth, Sidney and Yampa Valley
Ramona Kirby, Toponas
Georgia Klumker, Toponas (10 years in 1958, 20 years in 1968)
Ina Muntzert, Toponas (5 years in 1959)
Helen Moore, Hayden (5 years in 1954)
Jo Ray, Yampa/Toponas
Bonnie Simonton, Hayden (5 years in 1956)
William Stender, Elk River (10 years in 1954)
Willie Stender, Elk River (5 years in 1959)
Hazel Wheeler, Elk River (5 years in 1955)

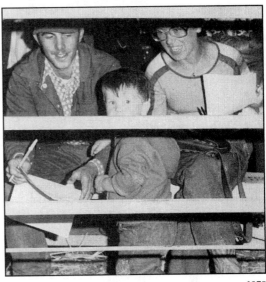

1978

ROUTT COUNTY 4-H LEADERS RECOGNIZED AT ACHIEVEMENT DAY 1975-1995

45 Years
Helen Sherrod, 1996

30 Years
Mary Kihlstrom, 1996
Penny Shupp, 1995
Doloris Solace, 1988

25 Years
Lydia Hockaday, 1996
Cynthia May, 1994
Joe and Virginia Rossi, 1988
Bonita Steele, 1979

20 years
Marsha Daughenbaugh, 1994
Harold Brenner, 1984
Carl and Rita Herold, 1996
Kay Kayser, 1981
Georgia Klumker, 1967
Mary Kay Monger, 1995
Mary Stees, 1978
Hattie Yeager, 1995
Joe and Betsy Zimmerman, 1994

15 Years
Barbara Ficke, 1988
Ramona Kirby, 1970
Linda Long, 1982
Betty Rae Jones, 1978
Evelyn Monger, 1974
Jack and Wanda Redmond, 1988 Lily Shupp, 1970
Shannon Sparkman, 1995
Jack Sprengle, 1985
Connie Wagner, 1993

10 Years
Yvonne Baker, 1991
Ilda Booco, 1976
Janet Camilletti, 1986
E. Jean Cooper, 1981
Chris deGanahl, 1993
Helen Duncan, 1967 .
Kathy Duncan, 1995
Kris Estridge, 1993
Jim Ficke, 1984
Tim Frentress Sr., 1995
Kathy Hockin, 1991
Ben Hibbert, 1967
Bill Gay, 1995
Rita George, 1982
Norton Jacobs, 1979
Renae May, 1988
Bob McKune, 1995
Ellie Meyer, 1991
Al Miller, 1982
Larry Monger, 1988
Pat Sandefur, 1982
Bruce Sigler, 1995
Ruth Smith, 1981
Eileen Stetson, 1979
Frank Stetson, 1980
Karyl Webb, 1983
Charlotte Whaley, 1993
Patsy Wilhelm, 1980
Pete Wille, 1990
Shirley Zabel, 1984

AWARDING PINS, to recognize tenure is a tradition dating from 1940 when Achievement Day was changed from spring to winter and Ferry Carpenter was the dinner speaker. Seventy-five members received one-year pins and special recognition for outstanding projects was awarded Warren Annand, Glen Barber, Kay Barns, Willard Gneiser, Buster Hitchens, Billy Marshall, Alice, Frances and Mary Peavy, Ina Mae Perry, Marvin Scott, Charles Ward, Jack Williams and Keith Yount.

In 1945 Bronze pins were given to members who had been in 4-H less than five years and silver pins to those with five or more years. That was the year that Skeeter Werner, later an Olympic skier and successful New York model, received a bronze pin and an award for champion of the third year sewers, and the prestigious Douglas McArthur Victory Garden Award went to Lincoln Hudley of Mt.Harris. Routt County National Bank, now Norwest Banks, continues to donate the pins as they have since the early 1960s.

It was not until the 1970s that some leaders had served a quarter century. The first three 25-year leaders recognized were Helen Sherrod (1975), Mary Stees (1978) and Bonita Steele (1979). Virginia Rossi, Outstanding County Leader in 1986, was the first Routt County leader to receive state recognition, a 1988 award designated her one of the top six leaders in Colorado.

OUTSTANDING LEADERS/JUNIOR LEADERS/CLUBS

Recipients of recognition from the state:
1986 Virginia Rossi
1992 Marsha Daughenbaugh
1993 Rita Herold
1995 Mary Kay Monger

	Leaders	Junior Leaders	Clubs
1929	C.E. Margerum		
1951			Elk River Livestock Club
1953			Busy Fingers Club
1954			Busy Fingers Club
1955			Busy Bee Club
1956			Merry Mixers Club
1958			C & S Club
1959			Rip N Stitch It
1964	Ramona Kirby		Busy Fingers Club
1966			Hayden Clover Club
1967	Georgia Klumker	Marsha Stees	Hayden Clover Club
1968	Mrs. Don Hoelzen	Jan Crawford	Busy Fingers Club
1969	Ben Hibbert		Stitch & Fix Club
1970	Ramona Kirby	Marsha Gray	Yampa Valley Club
1972	Mrs Kelly Klumker	David Kuntz	Hayden Clover Club
1973	Evelyn Monger	Barbara Brenner	Yampa Valley Club
1974		Cathy Rickerby	Wheelin Homesteaders
1975		Cathy Rickerby	4-H Country Club
1976	Kay Kayser		Yampa Valley Club
1977	Harold Brenner	Donna Monger	Hayden Clover Club
1978	Mary Stees	Donna Monger	Fairplay Club
1979		Laura Stetson	Fairplay Club
1980		Kirk Zabel	Yampa Valley Club
1981		Cheryl Hoaglund	Yampa Valley Club
1982		Philip Rossi	Flat Top Club
1983		Jennifer Harding	Fairplay Club
1984	Virginia Rossi	Ty Zabel	Flat Top Club
1985	Helen Sherrod	Ty Zabel	Flat Top Club
	Jack Sprengle		
1986	Cynthia May	Rebecca Northrup	Fairplay Club
1987	Lydia Hockaday	Rebecca Northrup	Fairplay Club
1988	Rita Herold	Audra Wagner	Fairplay Club
1989	Susan Smith	Tonya Wille	High Valley Club
1990	Marsha Daughenbaugh	Jay Whaley	4-H Country Club
	Mary Kay Monger		
1991	Charlotte Whaley	Debra Wagner	Fairplay Club
1992	Joe Zimmerman	Shawneen Guire	Fairplay Club
1993	Alicia Samuelson	Shawneen Guire	High Valley Club
1994	Jan Rossi	Shawneen Guire	Handy Lads and Lassies
1995	Don Babcock	Shawneen Guire	Fairplay Club
	Darlene Babcock		

LAMB MARINADE

A keepsake recipe from the Maneotis Family, the perfect marinade for any Maneotis lamb you purchase at the Junior Livestock Sale.

1 stick butter
1/4 lemon juice
1/2 cup Worchestershire

Salt, pepper and garlic salt to taste. Melt butter. Add lemon juice, Worchestershire and seasonings. Heat thoroughly and brush on chops, ribs or kabobs before grilling.

CHOCOLATE CHIFFON CAKE

From Evelyn Monger who has taken five blue ribbons with this recipe. Evelyn, an Iowa farm girl who moved to an Elk River Ranch 50 years ago, says she thinks judges just like chocolate.

1/2 cup cocoa
3/4 cup water
7 egg yolks, beaten
1 3/4 cups flour
1 3/4 cups sugar

1 tablespoon salt
1 1/2 teaspoon soda
1/2 cup salad oil
1 teaspoon vanilla
1/2 teaspoon cream of tartar

Boil cocoa and water and cool. Add to egg yolks, flour, sugar, salt, soda, salad oil and vanilla and beat 4 minutes. Beat egg whites with cream of tartar until very stiff peaks form. Fold egg whites into egg yolk mixture and pour into ungreased 10-inch tube pan. Bake at 325 degrees for 55 minutes, then 350 degrees for 10 minutes. Invert pan to cool.

ZUCCHINI JAM

From Lydia Hockaday, long-time resident and Fair exhibitor

6 cups zucchini, peeled, shredded and drained
6 cups sugar
1/2 cup lemon juice
6 ounces crushed pineapple, with juice
2 small packages apricot jello

Cook zucchini 6 minutes on medium heat; begin timing when it's bubbling. Add remaining ingredients. Cook six more minutes. Remove from heat and add 2 small packages of apricot jello. Stir until dissolved. Pour ito hot jars and seal with hot water bath, 5 minutes. Makes 5 pints.

Perspective

ENID ETZLER:
First Local Youngster To Go To the State Fair
From *The Steamboat Pilot*, September 26, 1930

Camp Tobin was the home for us 4-H girls and boys while at the fair. There were two big dormitories, one for the girls and one for the boys, and a big eating house. The picture shows were given in the boy's dormitory...There were all sorts of freaks at this carnival, such as a cow with six legs, goose with a scoop bill, cow with a camel back... I saw Holsteins that looked as large as buffaloes to me and they wore lots of blue ribbons. I saw pugnosed hogs, six kinds of sheep, three kinds of turkeys, three kinds of ducks, two kinds of geese and all kinds of chickens, bantams on up. Herefords and Shorthorns were so fine they looked like pictures to me...A motto in the picture show at Camp Tobin said that defeat was not surrender.

Enid Etzler, daughter of Robert Etzler, was 12 years old and a member of the Fairplay 4-H Club when she wrote this account.

1988

AS MUCH FUN AS YOU CAN STAND
From Jamie Denker

To me 4-H is when hard work leads to fun...It could be sewing that same stitch 50 times until you're happy with it or cooking those cookies so many times you've memorized the recipe...You don't give up if your pig is a little overweight or if your dog decides that he would rather be doing anything else than listening to you. You work with that dog until he listens; you adjust the pig's food...Then along comes Fair (where) everybody has all the fun they can stand.

Jamie Denker, a 14 year old eighth grader, has been in Hayden Critter 4-H Club dog, pig, horse and vet science programs since she was nine years old. She is the eldest of four children and a member of the school band.

THE DAY I SHOW THE GRAND CHAMPION STEER
From Ty Louthan

(Photo: Jill Montieth)

I have a dream. I will have a steer and name him Big Muscle. He likes me and I like him. I raise him up to show at the Fair. He has muscle and he looks good. I spiffy him up. I wash him real good. I comb all the sawdust out of his hair. I give him a little drink.

We show in the middle of the day. I tie him up to the rail and talk to him for a while. This is how I say it: "We got to win so don't be wild out there. Just stand still even though it's hot and you like warm better than hot. You're a good old steer."

By the time I finish talking to him it is 11:30, an hour passed just sitting there alone, him and me. I untie him and put him back in the blocking chute. Then I get the sawdust out and comb his hair up again. I check my watch and it is on the dot 11:49. I say, "I'll be right back Big Muscle. I have to change my clothes." I change my clothes in a heartbeat. I pee real fast. I am back so quick Big Muscle is amazed. He looks at me as if to say, "We're handsome and we're going to win."

I look at my watch again and it says 11:55. My heart is racing just as fast as Big Muscle's. I look at my watch again and it says 11:59. I hear the judge say "You have five minutes to get ready." I give Big Muscle a little drink. Tyler Knott looks over at me with a look that says he is determined to win. I'm not sure. I'm thinking my steer has a little more muscle and his has a little more fat.

The judge starts calling names: Jeffie Duncan, Nick Camilletti, Wes Milway, Jamie Booco, Ty Camilletti, Tyler Knott, and finally me. My heart is whipping out of my skin.

I am the first one into the ring and the judge looks like he's going to loose his glasses when he sees Big Muscle. I know right off the bat it's me or Tyler Knott. The judge looks us all over before he says, "I'll put Nick Camilletti in second and Ty Camilletti in first because he's more muscled up. I'll put Tyler Knott in Reserve Grand Champion because he has more finish. And now I'll pick the Grand Champion." He puts down the mike and comes over and slaps Big Muscle on the butt. Big Muscle doesn't budge because, remember, I told him not to mess around out there.

Ty Louthan, 11, has been a member of the Hayden Critter Club for three years and has taken ribbons in leathercraft, swine and shooting sports.

Rod Wille and his Grand Champion Rambouillet Ram, 400 pounds of ill temper during the 1991 show, where he also took Reserve Champion in Market Lamb. The following year, Rod exhibited both Grand Champion and Reserve Champion Market Lambs.

FAMILY FOOTSTEPS IN THE FLAT TOPS

From Tyler Knott

4-H has been a tradition in my family for many years. My grandfather was in 4-H when he was growing up in Yampa. My dad, aunt and cousins were also active in 4-H, therefore, it was natural for me to become involved.

4-H has helped me learn more about myself and my abilities. Working with animals teaches me skills that I may use later on in life as a rancher. I have also learned that record keeping and being responsible for myself and my actions are important in order to succeed in life.

Not only does 4-H help individuals learn more about themselves, it teaches them how to work and get along with others. It is also a great way to meet other youth from around the state and country. By joining a club, I have learned leadership skills and the importance of helping in our community.

4-H has become a very important part of my life. It's like one big extended family!

Tyler Knott, 12, has been a member of the Flat Top 4-H Club since 1992, when he was in third grade in the Sorocco Schools and exhibited the Grand Champion pig.

THE VIEW FROM HIGH VALLEY

From Rod Wille

I joined the Routt County 4-H program at the age of ten because my parents talked me into it. I took part in several projects: breeding and market sheep, livestock judging, exchange trips and leathercraft. It wasn't until years later that I realized what a major influence 4-H has had in shaping my life.

Leathercraft was the only project I had in my first year. My father was the leader and I spent one whole summer on my display, which received Reserve Grand Champion, and gave me the confidence to enroll in leather projects for the next eight years. When my grandfather gave me two bum lambs, my heart became set on taking sheep to the Fair.

I entered Rambouillets in the breeding sheep show for nine years. That was the beginning of a rigorous work ethic, which was tested by raising Suffolk and Hampshire breeds for market sheep. Every summer I would get the sheep ready to show and every year I had the same goal: to win Grand Champion. Only the last year did I succeed.

I joined the livestock judging team, learning how to identify quality animals, how to defend my decisions and how to speak with confidence and proper grammar. I traveled to New York and Louisiana, meeting people from different backgrounds and comparing our similarities and differences.

I currently share the responsibility of life on a family ranch, which is both fun and an important source of income. I got into the sheep business primarily because of my involvement in my 4-H breeding sheep project. Growing up with sheep was fun, interesting and challenging; now it is a way of life. Although agriculture is a tough way to make a living, 4-H gave me the confidence to face the future.

Rod Wille, a member of High Valley 4-H Club for 11 of his 22 years, is thinking about continuing education which will equip him to become an Extension Agent.

MAKING THE MOTTO COME ALIVE
From Virginia Rossi

We were introduced to 4-H work by neighboring parents and children who gave life to the 4-H motto and were really growing with the 4-H experience.

When a friend encouraged our oldest son, Steve, to show a heifer calf at the Fair as a junior exhibitor, we were sold on the idea and 4-H immediately became our "thing." Steve, his brother Paul and sisters Judy and Gail became charter members of the club we formed in 1962. Cheryl Rossi, a cousin, was the junior leader. Today that club is run by another cousin, Jan Rossi.

Our club was named for the Flat Top Mountains that form a beautiful background for the area. Through the years membership grew to as many as 35 and involved several Junior and Project Leaders. Because parents were also leaders, they were enthusiastic participants. At one time or another members have been enrolled in every project offered by the state and when the girls wanted to know about hair and skin care, they found a leader and piloted the program in Colorado.

One Christmas season members drew names of seniors at the Routt Memorial Hospital's Extended Care Center and delivered gifts. The program was so successful that other South Routt clubs joined the next year. Additional community service projects, most still in place, have involved getting the building ready for the museum in Yampa, making valentines, Halloween Jack O Lanterns and May Day baskets for all the seniors residing in South Routt.

It is true that 4-H programs give individuals the chance to "learn by doing," affording the satisfaction of completion and competition. Our club earned trips to Washington, D.C., Chicago, Missouri, Denver and the State Fair in Pueblo. It was active in the Exchange Program. Many graduating seniors were awarded scholarships based on their 4-H achievements. One of our most rewarding experiences was seeing a shy first- year member, who would hardly say "here" at roll call, begin entering discussions and making motions at meetings.

The opportunity for growth and accomplishment 4-H affords young people has not changed through the years. The excitement, drama, and sometimes trauma, of getting ready for the Fair will also never change. Those memories will always bring a smile. When you count all the young people, nearly one hundred, who have been involved in the Flat Top Club and multiply it by all the clubs in Routt County, it makes us proud to be a part of 4-H, helping kids make the best better.

142

JOE AND VIRGINIA ROSSI founded the Flat Top 4-H Club 32 years ago but Virginia quit wearing her club T-shirt the day she looked in the mirror and decided it was accurate but inappropriate to walk around with a sign saying "Flat Top" on her chest. All nine of their children were active 4-Hers, receiving 10 and 11 year pins, and three of their older grandchildren were 4-H Club members.

The Rossi's Hart Mountain Ranch is a 2,000-acre spread at the base of Heart Mountain, seven miles outside of Phippsburg on County Road #15. Heart Mountain takes its name from a unique heart-shaped shale slide where Rossi kids and cousins still wear out the seats of their jeans sliding down the shale face. It became Hart Ranch when the eldest Rossi son, Steve, misspelled the word heart while making the sign for the ranch as a teenager.

The Rossis still feed their 350 mother cows with a team and backup their coal furnace with two wood-burning stoves. Their vacations continue to involve taking a load of cows to Brush or Fort Collins and Virginia has no plans to purchase a breadmaking machine. She says her mother was right in claiming, "A good loaf of bread is like a kid. It's better if spanked."

Virginia and Joe Rossi (Photo: Rossi family)

The Rossi home is sunny and spacious and filled with big oak tables which invite you to share their hospitality. One wall displays children's graduation pictures and cap tassels. Another is covered with 4-H ribbons and plaques. There are championships in clothing, foods, wildlife, forestry and poultry. There's a picture of Philip, who still has a few Black Baldy cows from his FFA Heifer Project, with his 1984 Grand Champion Steer at age 17. It hangs next to the emerald and brass clovers Virginia received for outstanding service during 28 years as a 4-H leader.

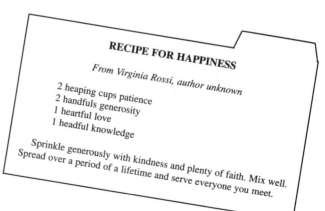

RECIPE FOR HAPPINESS

From Virginia Rossi, author unknown

2 heaping cups patience
2 handfuls generosity
1 heartful love
1 headful knowledge

Sprinkle generously with kindness and plenty of faith. Mix well. Spread over a period of a lifetime and serve everyone you meet.

143

PECAN DELIGHTS

From Yampa's Susie Crowner who earned a blue ribbon for these cookies at her first Fair in 1982

2 cups sugar
2 cups cream
1 cup butter, melted
1 cup white Kayro syrup

1 teaspoon vanilla
1 1/2 sacks pecan halves
1 large package chocolate chips

Mix 1 cup cream, sugar, butter and syrup in a 6-quart saucepan and bring to boil over a high heat. Add remaining cup of cream and bring back to a boil, stirring occassionally. Cook to a soft ball stage in cold water, 226 degrees on a candy thermometer. Remove from heat and stir in vanilla. Pour out onto well-buttered jelly roll pan that has the bottom thoroughly covered with pecan halves. Cool. Frost with chocolate chips which have been melted over hot water. Cut into squares.

SUGAR COOKIES

From Marge Markle, long-time proprietor and baker at a Hayden cafe. Marge has been entering the Fair since she was an elementary school student at the Pagoda School and exhibited an embroidered hankie.

2/3 cup shortening
3/4 cup sugar
1/2 teaspoons grated orange peel
1/2 teaspoon vanilla
1 egg

4 teaspoons milk
2 cups sifted flour
1 1/2 teaspoons baking powder
1/2 teaspoon salt

Cream shortening, sugar, orange peel and vanilla. Add egg, beat until light and fluffy. Add milk. Blend sifted dry ingredients into creamed mixture. Divide dough in half. Chill 1 hour. Roll to 1/8 inch on lightly floured surface and cut with round cookie cutter. Bake on cookie sheet at 375 degrees about 8 minutes. Cool slightly and remove from pan. Cool on rack. Decorate. They may be sprinkled with white or colored sugar prior to baking.

4-H RECIPE

From the 1976 Fair Book
By Kelly Scott, Eagle County

4 cups energy
2 cups faith
1 cup hope
1 cup patience
2 teaspoons good luck

Mix well with a dash of humor. Add one tablespoon kindness. Blend all of the above ingredients with Extension Agents, Leaders, Parents, Superintendents and Judges. Slowly add showmanship classes, dress reviews, dances and one large concession stand. Mix in food exhibits, leathercraft, photography and veterinary science. Work in more projects with junior leaders. Add State Conference, Camp Tobin, Girls Resource Symposium, Conservation Workshops and Citizenship Short Course. Blend well with other 4-Hers. Simmer for 10 years of enjoyment and excitement. Serves purposeful youth.

The Town of Hayden and the Hiway Bar

The Town
From Pat Holderness

Hayden was laid out by William Walker along the path his cows followed to their pasture south of town. Characteristics of the population, like the community, have been slow to change. When the Moffat Road went bankrupt, clawing its way over the Continental Divide, Hayden lost the opportunity to become "Queen City" of the Yampa Valley.

It was to have been the half-way headquarters for the highest standard gauge railroad in the world between Salt Lake and Denver until it came to an abrupt halt 17 miles west of Hayden in 1913. Today Hayden is attracting young home-owners, who enjoy the small town lifestyle. Hayden has always been a sleepy little community which does not get too excited over growth projections or go out looking for change. It retains its heritage as a center for ranching and farming and is meeting a new role as a "bedroom community" for Steamboat Springs, 25 miles east.

In the 70s a large number of residents worked on building power plants at Hayden and Craig; today more work at the Yampa Valley Regional Airport, the mines and in resort services at Steamboat Springs. Although there are fewer ranchers and farmers, the atmosphere remains rural and "laid back." Life revolves around kids and family, school and 4-H activities. And you can still snowmobile in the streets.

The third post office in Northwest Colorado opened on November 15, 1875 in Hayden. Until then mail had been delivered to Hayden's Camp on Bear River during the US Geological Survey in 1873 and 1874, and the town took its name from the director of that survey, Dr. F. V. Hayden.

Cavalry Major James B. Thompson, Colonel Porter M. Smart and sons Gordon and Albert built cabins in the summer of 1876. They also built a log cabin, with a dirt floor and roof, to serve as the Routt County Courthouse between the first commissioner's meeting on May 25, 1877 and May 1, 1879 when records were moved unceremoniously in pack saddles to Hahns Peak. Major Thompson and family left before the Ute uprising in 1879, but Gordon and Albert Smart and family lived through the incident.

After the Utes were removed to Utah in 1880, Samuel B. Reid moved his family from Snake River to a ranch on Dry Creek in what became the Town of Hayden. William R. Walker arrived from Georgia in 1881, followed by relatives from Georgia and North Carolina. Surveyor Ezekiel Shelton, who came to assess coal deposits in the Yampa Valley for Denver businessmen, liked what he saw and moved to land near Hayden with his son, B.T., in the spring of 1882.

On July 3, 1883 Dave Taylor, his brother Dan, Archie McLachan and Captain Lucian H. Ralston camped at the Shelton cabin with two Negro families, the Buckners and Davises, where they were joined later that same day by the Ranney brothers and Al Ryan. Hayden then consisted of three ranches: Shelton's; Reid's, housing a little store and post office; and Walker's, serving as a dance hall and saloon for the "glorious" Fourth of July celebration which included horse races and a box social.

When the Hayden School District was created with 28 pupils in 1882, it was the second district in Northwest Colorado; the first was at Slater on the Little Snake River. A small cabin on the Reid Ranch served as the first school. School was held on different ranches until a log schoolhouse was built in 1889.

A Sunday School was organized in 1885 by the Reid, Peck, Walker and Shelton families, and four years later at a town meeting it was decided that a Congregational Church would best serve the community. Meetings were held in the log schoolhouse until the present church was erected in 1903.

Editor George Smith described the town in the *Routt County Republican*: "By

1899 Hayden looked like a long settled eastery community and many of the ranch houses are imposing structures which would grace a city. A large two-story public school was being built and Odd Fellows and Woodmen of the World Lodge established. The business houses are two general merchandise stores, two saloons, a drug store, planing mill, shoe shop, blacksmith shop, livery stable and hotel."

Hayden was incorporated on March 13, 1906. A plat for the first addition of West Hayden Townsite added more than 100 acres to the area which was incorporated in 1908 by the Cary Brothers and James H. Peabody in anticipation that the railroad would build shops and roundhouses in Hayden. Although property sold high during this "boom," the West Hayden Townsite remained largely agricultural.

Hayden's main street in 1913 shows the town well in the middle of Walker (now Walnut) Street.

(Photo: Elizabeth Roller)

In 1910 the Hayden Volunteer Fire Department, forerunner of the West Routt Fire Protection District, was organized. A franchise for a water system, wooden lines from the Yampa River into town, some of which remained in use for more than 50 years, was installed. Norris W. Brock received a franchise to supply gas and electricity to the town and three street lights were installed to the delight of drunken cowboys, who repeatedly shot them out. Electricity was available during daylight hours only on Tuesdays, so housewives could do their ironing, and was shut off promptly at 10 pm every night.

Many houses in the area were built with concrete blocks from the Hayden Concrete Company, a partnership involving Brock, Ed Miles, James Wadge, David Flitner, and Peter and his son Melvin Hoffstetter; the name was changed to the Hayden Concrete, Gas and Electric Company when a boiler, engine and generator were installed in 1910. During World War I the Hoffstetters began producing Flavo Flour in a mill, which later burned. The business was purchased by Colorado Utilities in 1928.

Six school districts consolidated with the Hayden District in 1919 when bonds were issued for construction of the Hayden Union High School. The beautiful buff-brick building, large gymnasium, swimming pool, labs, library and manual training and domestic science rooms were hailed as one of the most modern facilities in the state. Youngsters from the model mining town of Mt. Harris, the largest town in Routt County in 1920, were bussed seven miles west to high school where the mix of teens from ranches and mines produced unbeatable athletic teams. A new elementary school was built on the site in 1948 which was turned into offices and a middle school after the Hayden Valley Elementary School was built on Breeze Basin Boulevard in 1979. The Hayden Union High School building was replaced in 1972, and the physical education facility completed in 1984.

Ferry Carpenter was as instrumental in developing the school system as he was in building the Solandt Memorial Hospital, opened on March 16, 1923. Because it was a product of the Depression, many volunteer hours and subscription dollars were contributed to honor a beloved physician who died on a call in 1916. For many years the hospital was supported by a Grand Charity Ball which drew patrons, as the hospital did patients, from every corner of Northwestern Colorado and Southern Wyoming. The building continues to house clinics for doctors, dentists and public health nurses.

During the 60s the water and sewer treatment systems were installed; gas lines and parks built; streets paved and the Depot transformed into a museum. The first town planner was hired in 1962 and the Yampa Valley Airport at Hayden opened in 1966 in anticipation of growth caused by the proposed power plant seven miles east of town. Colorado Ute launched construction of two coal-fired electric units in 1960; they were fired in 1965 and 1977, doubling the town's population between 1970 and 1977.

During the "energy boom" in the 70s and 80s, wheat land southwest of Hayden was annexed to form Golden Meadows, a housing suburb for employees of strip mines feeding coal to the Hayden plant and another under construction in Craig. By the 1990s Cyprus Yampa Valley Coal Corporation, the largest strip mine supplying Public Service Company of Denver opened the longest underground longwall mine in the world. Additional land was annexed on Hospital Hill, several trailer parks built, and water and sewer lines were laid to the Yampa Valley Regional Airport two miles Southeast of town.

The Hiway Bar is the oldest business in Hayden, the town gathering place, a social component of the community. The land was originally a part of a homestead belonging to William Walker. It was acquired in 1897 by Jim Norvell to house his mercantile, Yampa Valley Bank and liquor store until he "got religion" in 1900. Legend holds that when Norvell became "the cowboy preacher", he rolled the barrels out the door, opened their spigots, and let the booze run into the streets to the dismay of his customers.

In 1933 Norvell leased the building to Sam Lighthizer who converted it into a bar and cafe. The backbar, made in Germany and used in Leadville, was installed after Prohibition was lifted. Other owners have included Don Bierig (1951-56), Chet Clow (1956-72), Alma Hurst and/or Chris Ensworth (1973-81), James Camilletti (1984-89) and Fawna and Bill Odon (1990-present).

(Photo: Pat Holdernses)

One For The Road

From Chris Ensworth

The Hiway Bar is where the crowd migrates when the rodeo performance ends. Every booth will be packed at least two bodies beyond capacity, and people will be standing four deep at the bar trying to get a cold brew to cut the dust. Late comers will be greeted with raucous laughter, cigarette smoke, the smell of stale beer and the blare of the juke box. It's a chance to catch up on the news and reflect on changing times with friends and neighbors and also an opportunity to continue the chatter, whoop and holler.

Action at the Hiway Bar during Fair week mirrors the activity at the Fair as it mirrors the seasons. People drop in during the week on treks to the Fairgrounds to deliver animals and exhibits. There will be rushes before and after the livestock sale, parade and rodeo and before the dance. And late at night there will be scouting parties to the barbecue, to insure pranksters have not moved the coals in an effort to hide the beef.

The Hiway Bar, like Shorty's Cafe, the churches and the women at the library are part of the community's Internet in real space. It is where the metal of newcomers is tested, initially with a heavy dose of pranks—a peek at "rattle snake eggs," a good blow on a handmade goose call which blankets the hooter's face with baby powder. It is the place where every joke, good, bad or indifferent lives forever. The Hiway Bar is where every segment of the community rubs elbows and mixes drinks in close quarters. The pecking order is sorted; disputes are resolved or a gentlemen's agreement to disagree is hammered out.

When ruffled feathers cannot be smoothed with words and laughter, issues are sometimes settled with the exchange of blows, usually from fists and feet. In keeping with the not-so-changing times, armaments have been introduced to the fray: pool cues, pool balls, ash trays, glasses, beer mugs, bar stools, knives, sometimes a gun, and on at least one occasion a machete. Anything that can be

148

grabbed, pitched, pulled loose or swung is fair. The only house rule is, "Don't break what you can't afford."

The bar, along with its western counterparts, shares the aliases of Gin Mill, Watering Hole and Bucket of Blood. It is a place to sort out society's changing mores, so there have been sortings between cowboys and sheepmen; cowboys and sheepmen vs. the coal miners; cowboys, sheepmen and coal miners vs. construction workers; cowboys, sheepmen, coal miners and construction workers vs. hippies; cowboys, sheepmen, coal miners, construction workers and hippies vs. tree huggers. There have been times in the not so distant past when you could measure how much business the bar had endured by the blood on the sidewalk in the morning. But as one 6'4", 250 lb, hard-as-a-rail coal miner explained, "It's just for fun."

The Hiway Bar is a place to test your skills and abilities against your neighbor's. So on the spur of the moment, and with a few side bets put down, you can observe traditional arm and leg wrestling or a spontaneous foot race down main street, determine who has the fastest ATV in a race around the block or see whose snowmobile can jump the farthest across US 40.

The billboard, which greeted visitors from the west for 20 years, fell victim to highway widening and Lady Bird Johnson's Beautification Program. It was painted in the late 1960s by Curtis Zabel, who was raised east of Hayden and raised Herefords and Longhorns in the Lower Elk River Community before winning international recognition for his bronze sculpture. The sign was commissioned by the Hayden Lions Club and salvaged pieces have been mounted on a barn at the junction of the Williams Fork and Dunkley Pass Roads. Shirley Zabel, who was born in Maybell was a Fairplay 4-H Club Leader in cooking, sewing and sheep for ten years. Her mother was a Moffat County leader for 25 years, her sons long-time members because "It's the best experience you can give a child."

It is a place to bring friends, your dog, your horse, your motorcycle. It is a place which reflects the styles of the times, so it has seen poker games, slot machines, a streaker or two as well as a male stripper. It is a place to polish your belt buckle with your love of the moment or a lifetime.

The Hiway Bar is where you keep in touch with the foibles of your neighbors: who shot the dog duck hunting; who buried his new truck crossing the Yampa River; who is doing whom, in or out of marriage. It is where you sell raffle tickets for the American Legion or pass the hat when someone has been injured, taken ill or lost everything in a fire. It is a place to exchange political commentary on the state of the nation, practice up on a few words for the town board, county commissioners and road crews.

The Hiway Bar is just like any other local watering hole. It is a place to be neighbors. It shows the wear and tear of time and the people who have shared it, which is why winds from the west have given the building a decided list to the east.

Chris Ensworth owned the Hiway Bar from 1974-1981, after she left the novitiate and taught physical education in the Hayden Schools and before she became news director for the *Northwest Colorado Daily Press* and KRAI and publisher of *The Free Weekly* in Glenwood Springs.

After the Rodeo

Visit

THE HIGHWAY
BAR & CAFE

Hayden, Colo.

For Warm Beer . . .
For Cold, Greasy Food . . .
For Sneering Service . . .

JACK'S POPULAR BAR
AND CAFE

Craig   Colorado

Jane Lockhart says she banked at the Popular Bar in Craig because that's where Grandpa Edmundsom hung out and he was always good for a $5 bill during Fair.

Turning Frontier Into Homeland

Our Fair is special because we still have so many people who are rooted here. Like so many other mothers, 4-H leaders and volunteers, I do a lot of thinking about the rituals, traditions and legends surrounding the Routt County Fair. Although you can see it all in an hour, it's a much more complex experience and has a profound impact on individuals, families and community.

Looking Into the Past and Future
From Linda Long

One of the problems with the world today is that people don't know who they are or where they came from. There is no family unit. Some kids today don't know who their fathers are or never have the opportunity to learn where their roots are planted from their grandparents. You have to know where you came from in order to know where you are going.

I know where I came from. I look at my grandchildren and know where they came from. I have a sense of pride in my family. I can feel the warmth, depth and security of family all around me, something that can never be taken away.

The Routt County Fair unites generations. I was introduced to the Fair by my grandparents and enjoy sharing the Fair with my children and grandchildren. The Fair is much the same. It was something the family did together. We worked together for months preparing the best steer or hog, or raising the best potatoes, or finding Grandma's special recipe for Blue Ribbon Cookies, or watching Mom spend months on that warm quilt. The whole family was involved in the work, excitement and anticipation.

The Fair has always been a big community picnic, a time for family and neighbors to take off from work to watch, listen, learn, relax and visit. At a time when today's fast pace leaves no time for the good old barn dance and pie social, the Fair continues to pull families together to play. Not that the Fair isn't work; it's the climax of a year's efforts.

Linda Long, Reserve Grand Champion Open Class (leaf lettuce) with her five-year-old grandaughter Courtney, Reserve Grand Champion Junior Class (kale) in 1991.

The Fair is also about striving to be your best. It brings out the best in people. It is an attitude which carries through life. Not everyone can win a Grand Championship ribbon, but we can all be blue ribbon winners. Having that "can do" attitude" makes you a winner, not just at the county fair but throughout life.

I'm still the new kid on the block, but striving to meet the standards of the Grand Champions who preceded me has helped me develop skills, build good work habits and take pride in my work. You don't know which item you are going to take to the fair so you strive to do your best with them all.

Although some of winning is luck, a lot of it is learning the art of displaying the "finished" product. I am a detail person. It's the attention given to small details, going that extra mile, that is a trademark of a Grand Champion. Maybe that's why I enjoy being a county fair judge. It forces me to stay ahead of what's happening in the field. Sometimes it's hard to decide whether to recognize the quality of an exhibit, or to reward the hardships overcome and the learning required to produce it.

What I enjoy most is sharing and teaching but, when all is said and done, I'm still the student. I have never judged a fair that didn't teach me more than I taught. Sharing is a great feeling. Fair gives me the opportunity to explore my own strengths, make new friends, and hopefully, make a positive difference in other lives.

THE CORNER CLOSE TO HEAVEN

By ARTHUR CHAPMAN, author of
"Out Where the West Begins," etc.

(Written for the Routt County Fair Association.)

There's a corner, close to Heaven,
    Where the clouds and mountains meet,
Where there's trout in every streamlet
    And the fields are full of wheat;
Where there's cattle on the hillsides
    And there's coal beneath the plain,
And the hot springs rest the weary
    And relieve the suff'rer's pain.

Here the home folks fit the picture—
    Once you meet 'em they're your friends;
Here life's really worth the living,
    So you feel when each day ends;
Here are trails where trouble ceases,
    Here's a new land, full of zest,
In our corner, close to Heaven,
    Where the streams flow to the West.

Come to the Fair and you will surely realize then that
Life is Worth Living

Visitors who come to Northwestern Colorado never fail to spread among their friends at home glowing descriptions of the attractions of the country, its healing waters, scenic attractions, life giving climate, good roads, hunting and fishing, as well as the abundant resources in the way of natural wealth, oil, coal, mineral and the fertility of the soil. This long neglected section of Colorado is about to become an object lesson in expansion and development such as has rarely been seen in recent years.

From the 1926 Premium List and Classification Book

152

Family♥A♥Fair

BIRDIE PERRY DECKER made quilts for each of her 18 grandchildren, 44 great grandchildren and 9 great-great-grandchildren. During her 90 years, Birdie Decker embroidered a lot of pillowcases, tablecloths and intricate wall hangings, and crocheted a lot of afghans and bedspreads. Her daughters, Verna Whaley of Phippsburg and Iva Laman of McCoy, say her quilts were exhibited at many a Fair.

Ivan Decker was one of the few cowboys to ride General Pershing to a finish. (Photo: Margaret Hogue)

Ivan Decker (1898-1985) came into South Routt County when he was six, and Bertha (1903-1993) when she was eight. They homesteaded 360 acres east of Toponas in 1928, hauled timber from the saw mill to pay for the logs in their cabin, raised cattle, grain and lettuce, spinach and potatoes.

Ivan wore a buffalo robe while delivering mail with a team for 38 years. He loved the rodeo—riding broncs, roping calves and serving as a pickup man—and in 1910 was first to ride General Pershing. Birdie made her daughters' dresses from flour sacks, served angel food cake with whipped cream and jello, and quilted.

Marie says she is particularly proud of this quilt because the quilting, like each ribbon, stands for a lot of work. (Photo: Jill Montieth)

MARIE HOLDERNESS may hold the record for spawning the most exhibitors in the Routt County Fair. Marie is 87, the mother of 4, grandmother of 11 and "Granmarie" to 20 great-grandchildren. In 1996 her clan took 42 ribbons, including rosettes in Livestock Showmanship, Wearable Art and Decorate Your Duds. She counts because "It thrills me to death to see these grandkids carrying on a great tradition."

Marie was the centerpiece of a parade float in 1995 when the theme was Love-A-Fair. While she sat in a rocking chair knitting, her offspring—Montieths, Medvesks and Camillettis of all ages—surrounded her on a flatbed watering flowers, making bread and doing "ranch things." The legendary quilt made from her Fair ribbons hung over an antique trunk. Her daughter Carolyn Montieth, who choreographed the children and their costumes, was kneading out whole wheat dough. A two-year-old great-granddaughter who was supposed to be churning butter, fell asleep in her chair.

Like so many of the old pros, Marie still relishes reading the judge's comments when she retrieves her quilts and needlework. And she loves to reminisce: "The Routt County Fair was always a big event. It was more than a fair. It was a fall celebration after shipping the cattle and getting in the harvest. It indicated the season was over. Everyone entered the celebration from exhibits to the rodeo. Shorty's Cafe always buzzed with excitement."

153

Marie's parents, Shorty and Stella Huguenin, presided over Shorty's Cafe from 1919 until 1945, boarding teachers, railroadmen and dozens of ranch youngsters who lived too far from town to attend school. Marie was the younger of two girls born on an Elkhead Homestead and, with local farmer Fred Holderness, raised a family of four. Dorothy (Dotty), married Lawrence Decker of Hayden, is a pharmacist in Colorado Springs; Gerry who married Milner rancher Errold Hitchens; Ward who married Saundra Updike of Craig, is a professor of civil engineering at the University of Southern Colorado; and Carolyn married Jim Montieth, of Mt. Harris, and lives in Shorty's remodeled home.

Runs In The Family

Jocko Camilletti (top), past president of the Routt County Fair Board, took the Grand Championship in 1971 and 1972 followed by his sons Todd (center), Grand Champion in 1988 and 1989, and Ty (bottom), Reserve Grand Champion in 1991.

154

Centennial Farms

Three Routt County ranches are recognized as Colorado Centennial Farms. Farms and ranches owned and operated by the same family for at least 100 years are eligible for the award which is sponsored by the Colorado Historical Society, the Colorado Department of Agriculture and the Colorado State Fair. Eligible properties must be 160 acres or, if less, have gross yearly sales of at least $1,000. Recipients are honored at the Colorado State Fair in Pueblo. The National Trust for Historic Preservation also recognizes properties where historic structures, at least 50 years old, are maintained.

THE GREEN RANCH

Leon H. Green left his family's homestead near Sterling, Colorado and was working in Four Mile Canyon near Boulder in 1894 when he lost his left eye in a blasting accident. He soon recovered from the wounds, and in the fall of the same year, married Mary Emily Darling Thorpe. The newlyweds came to Routt County to homestead in a covered wagon pulled by a team of horses with a milk cow and a team of mules tied to the back. Thus began the Green Ranch, now over a century old, which Leon recorded with the name "Crags Ranch" in 1912.

Brand for Leon H., Jerry L. and Judy Green.

Located in the Williams Fork Valley, the Greens raised oats, wheat, barley and hay, as well as cattle and other livestock. They had one son, William, born in 1897, who worked alongside his dad in maintaining the ranch. Bill went to rural schools in the area, and was sent to school in Illinois for a while, living with his Aunt Kit.

Brand for William S. and Elizabeth Green.

But young Bill Green loved the ranch in Routt County, and after he married Elizabeth "Babe" Dorey, they remained there the rest of their lives, raising three children—Leon, Raymond and Virginia—and expanding the ranch operation to include registered Quarter Horses as well as cattle. Bill served as county road boss on the Williams Fork in the 20s and 30s, maintaining roads with an eight-horse-powered road grader. He also served four terms as a Routt County Commissioner (1949-56 and 1961-68) and was always very involved with the Routt County Fair.

Brand for Leon S. and Mabel Green.

Leon Green, who grew up on the ranch and remained there his entire life, married Mabel Yoast in 1937, and the couple had two children: Jerry and Sally. The children attended one- room schools at Dunstan and Beardsley and went to high school in Hayden. Jerry graduated from Colorado State University where he met his wife, Judy Herskind of Strasburg, Colorado.

They competed in college rodeo finals while attending CSU. Jerry and Judy both taught school in Grover, Colorado before returning to the family homestead on the Williams Fork where they continue to raise hay and commercial and registered Angus cattle.

HITCHENS OVERLOOK RANCH

The Hitchens Ranch on Highway 40, just east of Milner, is the oldest continuously owned ranch in Routt County. James Hitchens first settled the land in 1884, when he filed water rights, although he did not gain patent to the property until 1886. The landscape was ideally suited to James, who migrated

to the United States from his native England with two brothers, William and Joseph.

As a youngster, James had worked with the rest of his family in coal mines in England and was used to hard labor. Colorado first attracted the Hitchens men because of its extensive mining—quartz, coal, silver and gold—but the beauty of the land and lifestyle lured them all into becoming ranchers on the Western Slope.

(Photo: Diane Hitchens Holly)

Today the house and lands comprising the Overlook Ranch are operated by Diane Hitchens Holly, James' great-granddaughter and her husband, Arny Holly. They are joined by a fifth generation, the Holly's sons Cody and Travis and daughter Sophie.

Throughout the many decades of Hitchens history, family members always have been resourceful about diversifying their operations to meet current economic challenges, which have been many. Innovation began with James Hitchens, who tapped the natural reservoir, Lake Windemere, brought water around the mountain via a series of trenches and created a pond near his two-room log house; then dug trenches above the lake in order to resupply the water.

Brand for Albert and Errold Hitchens

James ran the post office called Pool, Colorado and supplied freighters attracted by his wife Emma's good cooking.

The Hitchens had nine children and the youngest of these, Albert, was born in their sod-roofed log house in 1892. Albert recalled in an interview published before his death in 1985, how he moved the house his father had built in Milner after retirement in 1918. The house was moved from Milner to the ranch in 1929. "I had 26 head of horses on it and I had it on four bobsleds. You had to jack the house up and pull the sled under it. It took them eight hours to move the house up here," he continued, "Well it sat for about a year before we did anything about it. It took a week to set it. They dug out the basement after they

4-H

Brand for Diane and Arny Holly

set the house."

Albert and his wife Winnifred, a school teacher known to recite Shakespeare while running the workhorses, raised cattle as well as grain and used the newly arrived railroad to ship to market. Albert had attended barber school and was widely known for his hair-trimming abilities as well as his love of music and dancing. The couple's youngest son, Errold, took over ranching operations in 1960.

Errold married Gerry Holderness and continued to cultivate hay, barley, oats and wheat on the property. Errold also worked at the Seneca Mine near Hayden. To supplement low prices for both grain and cattle, Errold and Gerry both worked at the ski mountain in the winter and became active in the Steamboat Springs Winter Sports Club. The couple had two children, Dean and Diane. Today the Overlook Ranch is farmed and attracts visitors for cattle drives, horseback rides and pheasant hunting.

THE SUMMER RANCH

The Summer Ranch, seven miles south of Steamboat Springs, was settled by John Summer Sr., a native of Austria who came to Georgetown in the early 1870s. In 1889 Summer took over a Routt County homestead claim which was being relinquished by a Frenchman and moved his wife and 12 children to lands between Steamboat Springs and Oak Creek, soon to become known as Sidney.

In September of their first season, Summer's 13-year old son Louis recalled in a 1950 interview, a raging fire almost wiped them out: "As the flames swept east, they were fanned by a west wind. Deer and antelope were running ahead of the flames. Grouse and sage hens were flying toward the river bottoms," Fireguards were being plowed by the new homesteaders in the tinder-dry oak hills, the frantic horses being held down by the weight of the plows. In one cabin a young homesteader's wife was about to give birth; terrified neighbors moved her bed to the front yard, bringing out tubs of water to fight back the flames, Louis recalled.

Brand for Vernon and Evelyn and Vernon and Edyth Summer

Fortunately the combined efforts of the homesteaders were successful and the fire was brought under control, but Louis never forgot it. The fire had many good effects, he recalled later. Dead timber furnished firewood and dry logs and poles for building materials, and the thinned thickets made it easier to hunt wild game they depended on for food.

Louis Summer and his wife took over working the family ranch in 1927 and, when John died in 1936, bought the property. Louis' son, Vernon, born in 1917, still works the ranch. Three generations of Summers have been resourceful and resilient to changing economic conditions, raising hay and other crops as well as livestock. Although Sidney no longer exists, it was once a thriving little corner on the Routt County map. "It was never a town," Vernon recalls, "It was just a stopping place." A blacksmith shop, general store and school were serviced for many years by the Moffat Line which stopped at the tiny depot.

Vernon married Edyth, a former Hallmark Card Company illustrator, 19 years after they met at a Farmers' Union dance in 1943. They lived in his grandfather's house until 1962 when they built a new house on the site. Both were active on the Tread of Pioneers Museum Board and Vernon was a Routt County Planning Commission member (1970-1980), National Farm Organization Charter member (1968), and long-time member of the Farmer's Union and Routt County Cattlemen's Association.

Vernon is renowned for his love of local history and his remarkable memory for dates and details. He began skiing on four-foot pine skis with toe straps at the age of four, became a competitive cross-country skier in 1937, and joined the National Ski Patrol in 1961. He attended the Sidney School where he and Oliver Bartholomew constituted the entire eighth grade graduating class in 1930, and commuted to school in Steamboat Springs by horseback, team, and the Craig train which cost 50 cents a day.

ROUTT COUNTY

A FEW pointed paragraphs taken from the Prosperity Edition of Northwestern Colorado tell of some of the wonders of this rich, healthful county.

THERE are more favorable opportunities that can be taken advantage of by settlers in Northwestern Colorado than in any other section of the West. In mining, coal, oil, agriculture, stock raising and many other pursuits there are abundant opportunities for accumulating a competence.

IF considered only as an investment there is nothing more attractive than Northwestern Colorado land at present prices, for improved and irrigated acres can be purchased for less than the government charges for water under some of its reclamation projects. Unimproved, unirrigated land is worth from $10 to $40 per acre; the best improved irrigated and productive land from $25 to $100 per acre. It is the best and safest investment to be found in the entire country.

IN Norwestern Colorado is found every variety of soil and climate necessary for the production of hay, grain, vegetables and fruit.

THE livestock industry will always be a paramount industry thruout the region, fundamental factors make it so.. The livestock industry has been in a bad way for some time, few stockmen have been making any money on their herds. At the same time the great hay business which has been built up thruout the years is about done. With the automobile and truck displacing the carriage and wagon, it is hard to conceive of any come-back in the hay business. There is constant strife for allotments on the range, and at the same time thousands of hay meadows are blooming with hay that cannot be sold. It does appear that the livestock practices of former days are due for the discard and that new methods must prevail.

IN Northwestern Colorado there are many splendid openings for investment in agriculture, coal, oil, timber, mineral and other safe profit-earning property. With the development now in progress prices will double in a few years.

DAIRYING has a great future in the Bear River valley, and the day is not far in the future when development in that respect will be far in advance of its present stage. The great dairy districts of the country are those which have "grown into the busness." It requires dairy temperament in the individual, dairy mindedness, together with suitable cows, suitable feed, adequate market organization and outlet. All these can be developed only thru conscientious, intelligent effort. The league is constantly at work along this line. Progress cannot be observed from week to week, but five years will show a big difference and the solid establishment of a great flourishing dairy industry in the tunnel district.

THE development of the head lettuce industry, particularly around Yampa and Granby, is a marvel in agricultural growth. In a few years these high alttiude districts have become known in every part of the country for the excellence of their product.

From the 1924 Premium Book and Classification List

The year before the Moffat Tunnel opened, "releasing the untold wealth of Routt County to the markets of the world," the Fair Book boasted that the yield of grains and grasses, without irrigation, is heavier here than in any other county in Colorado.

Agriculture in Routt County

Wide fertile valleys, climate, rainfall and winter runoff make the Yampa Valley one of the most productive in the state. Abundant pastures and rich mesas enhance the growth of livestock, grains and produce. This diversity has permitted pioneers who were not afraid to dream, work, and adapt to change to prosper. It has been cruel to wheeler-dealers, speculators and those who would transform the valley into where they came from.

The Routt County Fair showcases the area's agriculture. It has always been the place where the wisdom of experience and the challenge of new techniques were developed and exchanged, where the old-timer, the youngster and the newly-arrived are educated. The Fair is Routt County's "melting pot."

THE CATTLE INDUSTRY

Cattle are the mainstay of the area's agricultural economy. The industry dates from the early 1870s when Texas Longhorns were driven to summer pastures along the Yampa and Little Snake Rivers. Because Colorado had not yet become a state, lands currently comprising Routt and Moffat Counties were open range for large herds. Early cattlemen, like George Baggs and Ora Haley, headquartered large ranches in the Browns Park area and ranged cattle from the Wyoming and Utah lines to the Continental Divide and White River.

Although "wanna-bes" attempted to establish small deeded and fenced ranches in the late 1870s and early 1880s, the range belonged, by right of use, to the big outfits like the Two Bar, Ell Seven, the Sevens, and the Keystone and Leavenworth Cattle Companies. The 1890s produced an abundance of prominent personalities who made small fortunes in open range grazing. Jim Norvell and Jerry McWilliams bought and sold large herds and ranches; the J.B. Dawson family and the Cary Brothers assembled holdings sprawling over ten and twenty thousands of acres.

Because year-round open range grazing was a risky business, most outfits "shoved up" to high mountain meadows in the spring and in winter "shoved down" to lower desert country in Brown's Park and south and west of Craig. When winters were easy and prices were up, cattle barons made money hand over fist; when the winters were harsh or summer drought hit or prices plummeted, they went broke in droves.

Changes at the turn of the century put an end to open range grazing. In 1905 the National Forest System was established, followed by cattle allotments in 1906. Homestead Acts in 1902 and 1916 opened free grazing land for modest 640-acre spreads for stock raising. These small homesteads brought other changes: haying became important, because smaller herds could be maintained all winter on the homestead. Smaller herds, in turn, required breeds which could more rapidly gain weight during summer grazing in order to be ready for a fall market.

The answer proved to be pure-bred English-type breeds. The first of these were Shorthorns, brought in during the late 1880s and early 1890s. By the turn of the century, the Cary Brothers, Evan Marr, Sam Adair, Terry Miller, Scotty Annand and Carl Pritchett were among the top Shorthorn breeders.

The Grand Champion Steer at the 1906 National Western Stock Show came from the Cary Shorthorn Herd. The Maxwell- Miller Shorthorn Herd, run on the Lower Elk River between 1912 and 1922, was one of the most famous in the United States. Their cattle were shown at Denver's National Western Stock Show and the Chicago International Livestock Exposition. Henry Martin and Bill Sherrod ran the last pure-bred Shorthorn herds in Routt County.

Hereford and Hereford-cross cattle became Routt County's dominant breed. George Trull brought the first Herefords into Routt County around 1895, quickly followed by Perry Clark, Coke Roberds and Si Dawson, Ferry Carpenter and Jack White. In 1925 Carpenter bought out the operation he and White had started in 1909 and the Carpenter Herd remains the oldest continuing Hereford Herd in Routt County. Although most of the herd was dispersed in a sale shortly after his death in 1980, Carpenter's daughter Rosamond retained a few and remained in the cattle business until the ranch was sold to The Nature Conservatory in 1994.

Although the Dawson Ranch claimed to be the fifth largest cattle operation in the United States in the 1920s, other large turn of the century cattle ranches were developed by J.C.Temple and Jim Whetstone of Hayden; Pat Cullen and Jack Ellis of Steamboat Springs; and the Perrys, Birds, Roups and Laughlins of Yampa and Toponas.

By the 1950s Routt County boasted several nationally known purebred Hereford operations run by Francis Miller, Bill Ross, Ivan Decker, Jack Reagor, Pine Grove Ranch of Steamboat (Nefzgers), The Big Horn Cattle Co. of Hayden, R.E. Jones, Marshall Peavy, Quentin and Evelyn Semotan, J.F. Stetson, Kenneth Whiteman, Eddie and Wad Hinman, George Kemry, William Stender, Lyle Barber and Henry Robinson. These ranches laid the foundation for a large and prosperous cattle industry in Routt County. Angus Cattle, slower to gain in popularity, were bred in the late 1940s. Best known of the three outfits on the Elk River was J.E. Barbey's Angustorra Ranch.

Exotic cattle, breeds which trace their origin to Europe, did not attract attention until the early 1960s when several ranches tried raising and crossing Simmental and Charolais. By the late 1970s Limousin and Limousin crosses were popular, and in the 1980s and 1990s Gelbvieh, Salers and crosses of these breeds could be found on many ranches.

Although several Routt County ranches still have registered pure-bred herds, the majority run cross-breeds. The main market for pure-bred breeders lies in selling bulls, which can be bred to cows of a different breed, in an effort to ease calving and promote profitability.

160

THE SHEEP INDUSTRY

Much to the displeasure of cattlemen, sheep outfits in Wyoming and Utah saw Routt County's high country as an attractive summer range. By the early 1890s several attempts were made to bring sheep into the Little Snake River Valley and Big Red Park. This caused Routt County cattlemen to form several cattle associations and set up deadlines patrolled by line riders on the Wyoming and Utah borders.

When Routt County cattlemen sent riders to turn back sheep which had crossed these lines, the "sheep wars" began. The first confrontations did not amount to much because every time the sheepmen got word that the cattlemen were coming, they retreated into Wyoming, abandoning or losing considerable numbers of sheep. It is reported that in one case the cattlemen used whiskey and saloon girls from Brooklyn to distract sheepherders while they stampeded their animals back into Wyoming.

Newspaper reports claim "the greatest sheep stampede" occurred in 1903 when the Cow Creek Sheep Company tried to summer sheep near Hahns Peak and more than 300 riders, representing outfits from Yampa to Browns Park, met at Steamboat Springs to ride north. Within hours after they swept into the unsuspecting camp, sheep and sheepherders had scattered and retreated into Wyoming.

The deadlock was broken in 1907 when the Forest Service set up a permit system on the Routt National Forest, allowing cattle to graze the lower mountain areas and sheep to roam the high meadows along the Continental Divide. In 1908 Wyoming sheepmen were issued a permit for 10,000 sheep. The following fall, 8,901 ewes were trailed to Steamboat Springs, without opposition, and shipped out on the railroad. The drive opened the floodgates. By 1911 over 70,000 head of sheep grazed the Park Range, a number which peaked at 143,274 in 1931. During the early years more than 80% came from Wyoming outfits; by 1927, 50% were from Colorado flocks.

With the advent of sheep on the Routt National Forest came two new drive trails: the "High Trail" which ran along the Continental Divide from the Wyoming border to Rabbit Ears Pass; and the "Lamb Trail" from Hinman and Elk Parks into the Steamboat Springs Stockyards.

The threat from Utah sheep, bloodier and more involved with political maneuvering, did not materialize until 1911. In the first of these conflicts, an attack on the George Woolley Ranch south of Craig that year, 110 sheep were killed. One herder was killed and sheep were clubbed to death in raids on several Utah bands between 1920 and 1923.

The real threat came in the form of two stock drive trails from the Stock Yards in Yampa and Craig to the White River National Forest. They were designated by the Forest Service and allowed sheep to be shipped by rail to Yampa or Craig and then trailed to the National Forest. This prompted the "Colorado-Utah Sheep War" in April 1920. Ferry Carpenter, the cattlemen's attorney, negotiated a peaceful settlement.

The solution: As sheep were driven from Craig to the White River National Forest, they traveled through Rio Blanco County on a section of county road. Ferry Carpenter persuaded the Rio Blanco County Commissioners to abandon the road; the road reverted to private property and the sheep were trespassing and could not continue to the forest; their only recourse was to return to Craig where they were shipped back to Utah. Carpenter then went to Washington and persuaded the Interior Department to abandon the Stock Drives.

During the 40s and 50s small farm flocks, 200 to 500 ewes, became popular and several large cattle ranches began to raise flocks of sheep.

Isadore Bolton is a classic example of how the ability to work hard, change and diversify brought success to many Routt County farms and ranches. Isadore walked into the Elk Head Country in a cutaway coat and brown derby hat in 1913 without a cent in his pocket. He filed on a homestead and worked on hay crews for $1 a day until he could buy a team of mules; then he worked on the railroad until he could buy cattle. When he lost money on the cattle, he borrowed money to buy 1,000 ewes and made enough money wintering and lambing them out to pay off the loan and show a profit.

Bolton built the sheep flock owned by the Davis Family, proprietors of Hugus Company Stores, into a very profitable venture and joined them in a partnership to run both sheep and cattle. When cattle prices dropped or they lost money, sheep were profitable. At the time of his death in 1952 he was worth over $2 million. He was also a staunch supporter of the Fair and contributed cash prizes for winners of the 4-H Winter Beef Show in Steamboat Springs during the 1930s.

Margaret Brown, known as "the shepherdess of the Elk River Valley," is another legend of the industry. Widowed in 1918, shortly after arriving in Routt County, she was faced with having to run a cattle ranch or leave. Not wanting to leave, she sold her cattle, bought sheep and became one of Colorado's few women sheep operators. Starting with 300 ewes, she built a very successful operation and paid off the ranch and additional land.

Among the largest local sheep producers during the 50s and 60s were Louis Cogshill and Andrew McDermott of Steamboat Springs, and Andy Maneotis of Oak Creek. John Peroulis and John Papoulas of Moffat County ran large flocks in the Hayden area and the Chew Family of Jensen, Utah brought sheep and cattle from Utah to ranches in the Clark area during the summer.

Sheep are classified as wool or meat breeds. Wool breeds are usually white-faced, the type of most large range flocks. Meat breeds are black-faced, the type of smaller farm flocks and 4-H and FFA youth flocks. Although sheep breeds, like cattle, are crossed for various reasons, they are of the white- or black-faced variety.

Routt County has always had numerous small farm flocks run by families who also ran cattle or raised grain. These operators, staunch Fair supporters with 4-H and FFA children showing in wool and fat lamb classes, included: Leonard Ekstrom, Leonard Flanders, Chuck Fulton, Ben Hibbert, Chuck Hogue, Bob Kagie, Dan Knott, Vic Morton, Francis Moore, Wes Signs, William Stender, Dave Trogler, Russell Whitmer, R.B.Winter and Gilbert Yoast.

Several pure-bred flocks, started as 4-H projects in the 1980s and 1990s, achieved recognitions for the quality of lambs they produced. Noted Suffolk flocks were raised by the Redmonds (Jim, John and Julie) of Yampa, the Carnahans (Tad and Brad) of Oak Creek, Janet Baker and Darrell Hoaglund of Steamboat Springs, and the Turons of Hayden.

The Willie Rambouillett Flock received the most recognition during the 1990s. Although begun as a 4-H project for Rod and Tonya Wille, their parents, Pete and Charnelle, soon became involved and today the Rambouillett Flock is nationally recognized with both ewes and rams consistently among the top in classes at the National Western Stock Show. Rod continues to breed a Suffolk and Suffolk cross flock for 4-H sales with lambs which place in the top of showing and carcass classes.

162

Ferry Carpenter's Highland-Hereford steers broke to yoke in the summer of 1950. (Photo: Hayden Heritage Center)

TRANSPORTATION

Transportation has always played a major role in Routt County's agriculture. Northwest Colorado is isolated by the Park and Gore Ranges, difficult to cross by both road and rail, even without the aggravation of winter snow. Large cattle drives were the only way to get to railheads and access eastern markets.

Two cattle trails were established in the early 1880s: The Muddy Trail followed the Yampa River before it turned north out of western Moffat County to the Union Pacific Railroad in Southern Wyoming; the Wolcott Trail began south of Hayden, crossed Twentymile Park to Toponas and ran south to meet the Denver and Rio Grand Railroad at Wolcott.

When the Denver Salt Lake and Pacific finally broke through Gore Canyon and moved into Egeria Park, Toponas and Yampa became railheads. Steamboat Springs became the major cattle shipping point when the railroad arrived in 1909 and was soon recognized as the "Cowiest Town in the USA." Cattle driven down the Beef Trail, from California Park and Elk River, converged with cattle coming off high summer pastures on the Park Range, meadows south of town and the Twentymile Park area.

In 1951 cattlemen ordered record numbers of cars to ship to Denver Stockyards; only 25 years later, in 1976, the last cattle car left Steamboat Springs. This "Super Train" was organized by Chuck deGanahl of Yampa and County Agent Sam Haslem, and carried 1,719 head of cattle in special cars for the trip to the Omaha Nebraska Stockyards and market. Cattle from Hayden and Steamboat Springs were loaded in the morning and South Routt ranchers trailed cattle into Yampa and loaded in the afternoon. The following year several South Routt ranchers shipped cattle from Yampa, the last rail shipment of livestock in Routt County.

Although the railroad opened doors to the county's other vast agricultural resources, isolation and hard times tempered the ranchers' tolerance of homesteaders. Not until coal mines began opening in the early 1900s did significant numbers of settlers come into Northwest Colorado. Finding land available, many miners took to farming and ranching while the railroad, struggling with the financial burden of keeping lines over Rollins Pass open in the winter, attempted to turn new families into new customers.

FARMING

The Homestead Act of 1916 opened land and opportunity, and towns along the railroad line joined in campaigns to promote the wonders of Northwest Colorado. New settlers were quickly attracted to the upper Elk River, Deep Creek and Long Gulch areas north and south of Hayden and the Great Divide country in Moffat County. Before the turn of the century the pioneers were primarily stock men; these homesteaders were interested in rich, fertile soil and immediately began plowing in order to plant grain.

"Man on Binder" by A.G. Wallihan (Photo: Hayden Heritage Center)

Their timing was excellent. Virgin soil, coupled with a wartime-high demand for cereal grains, assured a good living. The 1924 Fair Book boasted that Routt County was one of the leading producers of non-irrigated grains. It led Colorado counties in producing winter wheat (averaging just over 30 bushels per acre) and spring wheat (averaging over 23 bushels per acre); other record-producing gains were oats (52 bushels per acre) and barley (36 bushels per acre). With wheat bringing around $1 a bushel and oats and barley selling at just under $1, grain farmers could make between $30 and $50 per acre.

This vast supply of grain created a demand for grain elevators. Yampa Valley Milling and Elevator Company opened in Steamboat Springs, producing Best Flour and Joe Dandy Breakfast Food; Hayden Milling and Power Company began milling Flavo Foods, advertised as "different and better." By the mid 1960s farmers in both towns organized co-ops which became strong supporters of the Fair, 4-H and FFA youth programs. The Steamboat Elevator closed in the early 1980s, the Hayden Elevator in the early 1990s.

Threshing grain became a fall ritual for farmers. The first threshing machine in Routt County was delivered to the Ute Indians on the White River Reservation in 1879. But the Utes, not overly excited about becoming farmers, displayed their displeasure by massacring Indian Agent Nathan Meeker, attacking the Army relief troops under Major Thornburg, and burning the threshing machine.

Abram Fiske, who settled on what is now the Carpenter Ranch in 1880, is credited with planting some of the first wheat and alfalfa in Routt County. In order to thresh the wheat, he and his son Charlie went to the Thornburg Battle site to recover the cylinder, bull wheel and tumbling rod from the burned thresher in 1884. That fall the Fiskes rigged the cylinder between two tree stumps and fed it by hand until, the next season, they built a threshing machine out of the original parts and opened the first threshing service in the valley.

They threshed grain in Dunkley Park and down Williams Fork until shortly after the turn of the century when the machine was sold to William Yoast who, with his son Marion, continued to use it into the 1920s. Marion finally pulled the machine to the Hayden Fairgrounds, where it was restored by volunteers and VoAg classes. In the early 1980s it was moved to the Hayden Heritage Center where it remains on display.

Operating a thresher required a steam tractor not every farmer could afford, so large farms would thresh for neighbors. This provided employment for young men and seasonal workers who could tolerate hard work and long hours in return for great home cooked meals, a good bed and an occasional dance at the local country school or Grange Hall.

164

Haying, like threshing, became a summer ritual. Hay was put up for local winter feed and, because of its quality, was in demand for sale outside of the county. The skeletal remains of several types of stackers, still standing in meadows throughout the Yampa and Elk River Valleys, are the Beaver Tail Slide, Mormon, Overshot and the Basket Swing. Hay was also baled during the 1930s and 1940s but, because balers were not very mobile, they were set up after the hay had been stacked. Hay was fed into the baler, pulled out and stacked. Most baled hay was shipped to eastern markets on the railroad.

Construction of huge hay and livestock barns, many built between 1900 and the early 1930s, was another by-product of farming. Many still stand as land marks. They usually had large hay lofts for storage and a rail and hay hook system to get the hay into them; some used rail and hook systems to clean manure in stall areas, others were renowned for good barn dances.

PRODUCE

The railroad opened Denver produce markets to profitable new county industries. The most lucrative was the strawberry industry which flourished from the early 1900s until around about 1920. A strawberry developed by L.R.Remington fueled this boom. Old-timers claim the berries were too big to fit into a water glasses. They ripened in the fall, just in time to fill a void in the Denver market. Although they were grown along the Elk River, around Hayden area and on the mesa south of Steamboat Springs, major production took place in a small valley north of Steamboat Springs called Sheddeger's Park. After local papers advertised profits of over $500 an acre, land jumped from $150 to over $1,500 and the area was renamed Strawberry Park.

The demise of the strawberry industry began with hard, early frosts in 1915 and 1916 and culminated in the country's entry in World War I which eliminated both demand and labor to work the fields. By the end of the war Denver markets had found new suppliers. But Daisy Leonard Anderson and her brother, Ernest Graham, continued to raise and sell strawberries, garden produce and small animals until the mid-1960s. Produce from their gardens was hard to beat at the County Fair.

Routt County's first cash crop was head lettuce. The first plot was planted in 1921 on the Wheeler Brothers place near Yampa by Frank and John Kenly and Fred Halstead. They shipped three car loads and reported a profit of just over $3,000. Finding that lettuce could be grown on small 5-20- acre plots, at profits exceeding $100 per acre, generated immediate interest. The three cars shipped in 1921 soared to 113 in 1923; the next year Yampa shipped 192, Oak Creek 21, Toponas 16, Steamboat Springs 11 and Milner 1. The Yampa Valley Head Lettuce Association, formed in 1923, included large growers: C.E.Crowner, Dr. J.H.Cole, Lon Dixon, E.H.Godfrey, Ray Kaufman and Ed Rich. By the 1940s members of the Association had nearly 3,000 acres in lettuce production.

World War II marked the decline of the lettuce industry. The labor force evaporated and, by the time the war ended, refrigerated trucks and chain stores stole the Denver market. Several large producers continued raising vegetables to the early 1950s. Floyd Stewart and Howard Warner had nearly 200 acres on the Elk River in head lettuce, spinach, peas and cauliflower. They shipped 90 cars of produce in 1945 but, after shipping the last car load from the Elk River Valley, sold out in 1947.

Two major South Routt producers did not sell out until the mid-1950s: Jack Holden and C.E.Crowner & Sons. Jack, who developed over 500 acres of lettuce and spinach in Egeria Park, was instrumental in building Stillwater Reservoir for irrigation and at one time employed 175 people. C.E.Crowner converted his ranch to hay and cattle and, by the late 1980s began installing new irrigation systems which permitted them to develop a quality hay and alfalfa operation.

In addition to head lettuce and spinach, the Routt County produce industry recorded over 500 acres in peas during the late 1930s and into the 1940s. Cabbage, cauliflower, celery, carrots, turnips, rutabagas and artichokes were raised between Oak Creek and Yampa; cantaloupe and watermelon were grown in the "banana belt" around McCoy.

During the 1920s and 1930s fruit production was also tried in the Hayden area. The 1928 Fair Book reported that "Routt County's days as a mecca for fruit peddlers from the Grand Valley are near an end. Each year more people are setting out cherry, apple and pear trees that will in a short time supply the needs of the County." Crabapples were promoted, certain varieties bearing fruit five out of six years, but most became backyard ornamentals and there is no record of any serious fruit production in the county. Sugar beet production was promoted during the 1920s and 1930s, primarily by the Moffat Tunnel League and the railroad which wanted the business of shipping them to processing plants on the eastern slope. Although County Agents Percy Ingram, Floyd Moon and Edison Barr planted test plots and fields throughout the county, there is no record of any real production. Otto Gumprecht had the last test field in 1957.

Potatoes proved a popular cash crop among farmers and small land holders who claimed a good field could produce up to 90 bushels an acre. Potatoes also could be stored in cellars dug in the sides of hills where frost and cold ground preserved them for sale throughout the winter. Because they did not have to be shipped immediately following harvest, growers could wait for the highest price.

County Agent Floyd Moon started and aggressively pushed the first certified seed potato program in the 1930s. His efforts helped to make Routt County a major source of certified seed potatoes and opened a new market. The Yampa Potato, developed as result, was a high altitude potato which produced well and, for a few years, was more popular among local growers than standard Pontiac Red or Russet-Burbank varieties. Potatoes grew well in almost every section of Routt County. Sidney became a major shipping point for potatoes because it was easily accessible to farmers on the Mesa and Twentymile Park without requiring travel into Steamboat Springs. To make storage and shipping easier a large potato cellar was built at Sidney; Mystic and the lower Elk River area also had quite a few fields and a cellar. Production also flourished around Hayden and Oak Creek, particularly during the Depression, because it was a cash crop as well as a staple food for impoverished farm and ranch families.

World War II crippled the industry and only a few producers remained by the early 1950s. Three of them were: Louis and Gudio Rossi of Oak Creek, J.B.Terhune of Yampa and Lloyd Williams of Steamboat Springs. Seed potatoes from the Louis Rossi Ranch placed extremely well in various shows and his son, Dean, won the Junior Seed Potato Contest at the National Western Seed Potato Show in 1957. Lloyd Williams was the most persistent of the seed potato growers, continuing to develop different varieties of potatoes into the early 1960s. The last certified seed potato effort in Routt County took place in the early 1970s when County Agent Sam Haslem conducted a Colorado State University test plot on Deep Creek.

Rich soil, coupled with the quality of area grains and hay, periodically prompts interest in production of certified seeds for grain and grass. But because certification depends upon the interests of the County Agents, the industry has not been pursued consistently. During the 1930s Floyd Moon was the first to actively promote certified seed in potatoes as well as wheat, barley, oats and alfalfa. The most recent test plots were run on dryland grasses by Sam Haslem in the mid-1980s, and on alfalfa by C.J.Mucklow in the early 1990s. Wheat test plots, established by Haslem and Dan Sullivan in 1982, are still being maintained by Mucklow and Jim Stanko who expanded them to include varieties of barley in the 1990s. Although these plots led to development of a spring wheat suitable to Routt County and Cory Guire named it "Yampa" in a contest, certification was never finalized. Forrest Frentress of Hayden, who raised Manchar Brome Grass seed in the 1980s, was the last certified seed producer in the valley.

THE DAIRY INDUSTRY

Early advertisements promised dairy farming would be the "star" of Routt County agriculture. They boasted that rich grasses and favorable climate assured production of superior cream, butter and cheese. The Moffat Tunnel League and the railroad, the industry's heaviest boosters, launched a Dairy Calf Program for area children in 1923.

The Dairy industry was attractive because it did not require as much land to run a small herd of dairy cows as it did a herd of beef cattle; the "cream check" provided regular and steady income; and what did not sell could feed the family or the hogs and chickens. The 1924 Fair book included compelling figures: A rancher owning 50 beef cows could expect an average of 40 calves to sell at $30 each for an annual income of $1,200; 50 dairy cows would each produce $100 worth of milk in addition to a calf to sell for an annual income of $5,000.

Despite the numbers, dairy farms were slow to appear. Almost every farm and ranch began running some dairy cows and, by the early 1940s, milk production supported creameries in Hayden and Steamboat Springs and healthy rail shipments of cream to Denver. The primary chore for every farm and ranch child raised in the 1930s and 1940s was morning and evening milking.

Substantial dairy herds and milking barns, equipped with state-of-the-art milking machines, appeared after World War II. One of the first major dairy herds was established by Irvin Soash in the Mystic area, and John Sinden developed a large dairy just east of Steamboat Springs. Other herds were started by Orval Bedell, Don Blake, Don Clark, Chuck Fulton, Carroll Harvey, Wayne Light, Don Lufkin, M.E. Selbe, Allen Muirhead, Lester Thropp, Hollis Tufly and Russell Whitmer.

The 1956 Extension Service Annual Report listed 30 dairy farms in Routt County which, with all the ranches and farms supporting a few milk cows, kept the valley's three creameries busy. These were: The Hayden Valley Dairy owned by Ray and Mary Yoast; Moffat County Creamery in Craig owned by Chuck Crosthwaite; and Selch Dairy, owned by Charles Selch in Steamboat Springs which, according to the newspaper, processed more than 400 gallons of milk a day.

Late in the 1950s new government regulations and cheap milk from chain grocery stores put an end to the dairy business. The Selch Dairy closed its doors in the early 1960s and now one has to look long and hard to find a ranch or farm family milking a cow. There are, however, still a few dairy calves shown at the

County Fair by 4-H and FFA members. In 1993, the Estes Family of Yampa showed Ayrshire cows, the first time the breed had been seen at Fair since the 1930s.

POULTRY AND SWINE

L ong cold winters have hindered development of large poultry and swine operations but, like dairy cattle, almost every ranch or farm raised chickens to supplement income and family groceries.

Chickens have always been popular in Routt County. Selling eggs to local stores and townspeople is still a source of income that pays winter bills for many ranch and farm families. Because eggs are not easily hatched in Routt County, most chickens were ordered from east slope hatcheries. One of the joys of April and May was to go to the post office to listen to the pleasant chirping from boxes of baby chicks. Today they are imported by feed stores and kept in large heated stock tanks until sold.

The only serious poultry operation in Routt County was run by the Alumbaugh Family of Milner. Their poultry farm, located on the site of the present trailer court, housed 50,000 birds and in 1955 butchered 23,000 fryers and 9,000 turkeys in their modern processing plant. Federal regulations and competition from chain grocery stores curtailed operations and the Alumbaugh Farm closed in the early 1960s. Today only a few farms and ranches raise chickens, ducks and geese, and turkeys are almost always 4-H projects.

Swine operations have also been cyclical in Routt County. Between the late 1920s and the Depression, several large hog operations thrived and in 1932 the railroad reported shipping several car loads of hogs. Many ranchers and farmers raised four or five sows and as many as 30 weaner pigs for supplemental income or family dinners. Fairly sizeable hog operations were run by Henry Appel of Twentymile Park and Ortle Ralston on Southside in the 1930s and M.E. Selbe of Steamboat Springs and Herb Summer of Hayden in the 1940s. George Temple of Hayden currently maintains the only real swine operation in the county.

Most hog operations are 4-H and FFA projects. During the 1950s and early 1960s as many a five members would show between eight and ten hogs; one year in the late 1960s only one hog was shown at Fair and, after heated bidding with Keith Studer, Bill Sherrod bought him. By the 1980s 4-H swine projects gained in popularity and by 1995 more than 150 were being raised.

As a result of these projects, several 4-H families have started small swine breeding operations to supply the 4-H demand. Robin Lighthizer and Mike Williams of Hayden, and David Long of Oak Creek have developed good programs which make quality hogs available to the 4-H and FFA. Brad and Tad Carnahan of Oak Creek, Jeffie Duncan of Steamboat Springs and Dusty Whaley of Phippsburg used their 4-H swine projects to breed and sell pigs to other 4-H members.

Hogue Ranch
(Photo: Sureva Towler)

Farm and Ranch Organizations

The same independence and individuality that are the hallmark of the nation's farmers and ranchers have been a liability when it comes to negotiating prices and marketing products. Many organizations have been formed to tackle this problem and those described here have made major contributions to the Routt County Fair and other countywide youth programs.

ROUTT COUNTY CATTLEMENS ASSOCIATION

Cattle associations formed, before the turn of the century, in order to meet the threat of sheep invasions or to protect large outfits from rustlers. Almost every region in the county had some form of association and, as the Forest Service began allotting and enforcing grazing permits, others were created by permitees to address issues concerning their allotments.

The Depression prompted a brief period of inactivity. Four cattle associations served Routt County from the 1930s into the 1950s: The Routt County Stock Growers Association, backbone of the industry until the 1960s; the Routt County Pure-Bred Cattlemen's Association which represented these breeders during the 1940s and early 1950s; the Bear River Stockgrowers Association representing South Routt Ranchers during the 1940s and 1950s; and the Steamboat Stock Growers Association, short-lived in the early 1950s.

Si Lockhart was instrumental in merging these groups to form the Routt County Livestock Growers Association. It was incorporated as The Routt County Cattlemens Association in 1960 and elected to the National Cowboy Hall of Fame in Oklahoma City in 1966. Created to promote and protect the interests of the livestock industry, particularly cattle, the organization has hosted tours which resulted in contracts from Midwest feedlots, sponsored a feeder calf and yearling sale at the Steamboat Springs feed barn (late 1950s and early 1960s), and taken strong positions on measures impacting rustling and branding.

Routt County has hosted four state association meetings, first in the late 1940s, then in 1973, 1983 and 1993. Art Hudspeth is the only Routt County cattleman to have served as state president although many have contributed as district representatives and committee chairs. The board of directors meets quarterly and holds two general meetings a year, one of which is a June barbecue which rotates between Steamboat Springs, Hayden and Yampa. For many years their annual membership dinner-dance was a major social event.

ROUTT COUNTY CATTLEWOMEN

Organized and in 1975, cattlewomen affiliated with the American National Cowbells, now the American National CattleWomen, in order to promote professionalism and become effective spokeswomen for the beef industry. The organization has always developed and supported resources for women, educators, consumers and legislators. Napkins with local brands are a major fundraising tool.

Since 1994 the Routt County CattleWomen have sponsored the Fair's Ranch Woman Contest which showcases the energy, skills, sense of humor and wardrobe every conscientious ranch woman must possess. The contest is a timed performance of select ranch chores: driving a fence post, starting a tractor, hanging out wash, diapering the baby, eartagging a cardboard box, vaccinating

a cantaloupe. The Sunday morning crowd-pleaser is an old fashioned laugh-in, perhaps because it does not stray too far from reality. According to Lynne Sherrod, most contestants are not ranch wives "because they do this stuff every day and are ready for a break by Fair-time."

Krista Monger, Ranch Woman Contest 1995 winner, dresses for calving. (Photo: Lynne Sherrod.)

"*It's always amazing to watch the CattleWomen. They drop their exhibits at the hall. Check their kids and animals. Put in time at whatever booth they are sponsoring. Attend whatever event their child is in while assuring the next one is ready to go. And because, more often than not she's a 4-H leader, make the rounds of other club members' projects while entertaining bored babies. Good natured competition, satisfaction in a year's work, and the uniqueness of a place out of time. The sense of community inspired by the Fair cannot be duplicated, anywhere.*"

– Lynne Sherrod, long-time member
of the Routt County CattleWomen

SPICY PORTUGUESE STEAK KABOBS

From the Routt County CattleWomen who served 1,600 samples to shoppers in Steamboat Springs grocery stores after it won the 1995 National Beef Cookoff.

	Seasoning:
1 1/2 pounds top sirloin steak, cut into 1 1/4" cubes	2 tablespoons chopped fresh cilantro
1 large red bell pepper, cut into 1" pieces	2 tablespoons olive oil
Salt	1 tablespoon cayenne pepper sauce or 2 tablespoons hot pepper sauce
	1 clove garlic, crushed
	1/4 teaspoon red pepper, crushed (optional)

Combine seasonings and toss to coat cubes. Alternately thread beef and bell pepper on six 10" metal skewers. Place kabobs over medium ash-covered coals. Grill uncovered 8-11 minutes for medium rare, turning occasionally.

170

ROUTT-MOFFAT COUNTY WOOLGROWERS ASSOCIATION

Unlike cattlemen, sheepmen have been represented by the same organization since sometime around 1910 when, like the cattlemen, they organized to address issues impacting grazing on National Forest and BLM lands. Concerns about predator control bonded the group, which taxes members to finance programs and legislation addressing the issue.

In the early 1930s, The Woolgrowers Association organized the Craig Ram Sale, one of the oldest continuing sales of purebred sheep on the Western Slope.

1982

Today the sale is handled by the Moffat County Woolgrowers. In 1966, the same year Chuck Hogue became president, the Routt County Woolgrowers formed their own group. The split reflected the focus of Moffat County: large owners on large spreads, and Routt County: smaller owners of farm flocks many of whom also ran cattle. Predator control remained a joint function until 1972 when each county formed predator control committees.

By 1968 the Routt County Woolgrowers had created a Wool Pool, which attracts national recognition and bidders because of the quality and cleanliness of its fleeces. Fifteen years later Routt County sent more fleeces to the National Western Stock Show than any other county in the country.

County Commissioner Doc Utterback spearheaded extension of a county loan which funded the organization until it could organize a system to assess and collect taxes. Although the idea of setting standards and providing a large volume of wool for a better price is not new, the pool was one of the first to use a contract to secure compliance among members who all participate in shipping in June. For the past several years the pool has attracted the country's top prices for wool.

In addition to their annual meeting, woolgrowers hold an annual picnic at a members' ranch where liquid refreshment is supplied by the pool's high bidder.

WOOLGROWERS AUXILIARY

During the 1950s and 1960s The Auxiliary sponsored a local Make It With Wool Contest in which several 4-H girls won state and national honors. To finance their activities the auxiliary sold pillows, pelts and dusters and, when disbanded, donated its assets to help purchase a CAT scanner for the Routt Memorial Hospital.

"Government statistics show that Routt County has a greater yield per acre of winter wheat, spring wheat, oats, barley, rye and hay, without irrigation, than any other county in Colorado. This is due to the richness of the soil and the abundance of precipitation."

– From the 1926 County Fair Premium and Classification Book

171

LAMB GYRO MEATLOAF WITH PARTY POTATOES

From Jeanne Maneotis, daughter-in-law of Andy and Mary Maneotis. Andy came into the country from Greece at age 13 and was instrumental in building the woolgrowing industry here.

Meatloaf:

1 pound ground lamb	1 tablespoons minced dry onion
1 pound ground pork	2 tablespoons oregano
2 eggs	1 teaspoon each: garlic salt, pepper, salt
2 teaspoons minced dry garlic	1/2 cup seasoned bread crumbs

Mix and bake all ingredients in a large loaf pan in a 350 degree oven for 60-70 minutes. Drain fat and serve hot.

Party potatoes:

5 pounds potatoes	1 stick butter
8 ounces cream cheese	Small carton half-and-half cream

Boil potatoes and drain. Add cream cheese, butter and cream. Whip. Season to taste with garlic, salt, onion salt, and dry chives. Top with shredded cheese and melt in oven.

A 1995 survey of 13 Routt County ranches, running 200-500 mother cows, indicated that local cattlemen operate efficiently. These statistics, based upon data gathered during the preceding two years by Colorado State University Extension Director C.J.Mucklow, represent averages:

- 93.2% of the cows in Routt County become pregnant after breeding compared to 93.1% nationwide.

- 90.9% of Routt County cows have calves compared to 89.3% nationwide.

- 6.4% of the calves died compared to 4.3% nationwide.

- 84.7% of the cows weaned calves compared to 85% nationwide.

- Average weaning weight averaged 513.6 pounds for steers and 503.9 pounds for heifers, together 517.6, compared to 537 and 503, together 520, nationwide.

- Average pounds gained for all calves, including those lost, was 432 pounds compared to 441 nationally.

172

ROUTT COUNTY WHEAT GROWERS

Although the county elects officers and holds an annual meeting conducted by the U.S. Department of Agriculture Farm Service Agency, formerly the ASCS, and the Extension Office, the organization operates as an auxiliary of the Colorado Wheat Growers Association. It supports wheat and small grain test plots and weed control programs and contributes to a statewide award for the Grand Champion 4-H Bread Project.

THE FARMERS UNION

The Farmers Union, active in Routt County in the 1940s and 1950s, is the oldest farm organization in the county. It sends youngsters to an annual camp near Divide and continues to sponsor the 4-H Overall Outstanding Record Book Award.

THE FARM BUREAU

The Farm Bureau has supported 4-H programs and the Fair since the late 1960s. For many years they underwrote the sale price of low-bid animals at the Junior Livestock Sale. They sponsored the Fair's Catch-A-Calf Contest and converted it into beef and sheep breeding projects for 4-H and FFA members. They have also sponsored various awards for 4-H Achievement Day. The Routt County 4-H Council paid tribute to the Farm Bureau's years of support in 1995.

THE NATIONAL FARM ORGANIZATION

The National Farm Organization (NFO), strongly supported by farmers and ranchers in the 1970s, is dedicated to improving prices and marketing agricultural products. Although it had a substantial membership and sponsored awards for 4-H Achievement Day, membership began dwindling in the early 1980s.

"The emphasis on agriculture is the most important lesson of the Fair: how to make a living off the land."
– Marsha Daughenbaugh
4-H Leader, 1983

Wagon mines were selling coal for $1.50 per ton in 1924. The Babson Mine, or Dry Creek Mine, had an order for four cars of coal when it was taken over by Business Manager H.B. "Johnny" Pleasant, Mine Boss Jack Mills and Babson, represented by attorney Ferry Carpenter. The Routt County Republican said Henry B. Babson, who came from Illinois and owned land around Pilot Knob and Dry Creek, "is a millionaire and owns more coal land in this country by far than any other man. Babson with his money and connections will do something worthwhile in this county in the way of coal production when we get good transportation." (Photo: Hayden Heritage Center)

The dragline at Twentymile Coal's strip mine is affectionately called "Effie." The three at Trapper are named in honor of three ladies: The Queen Ann (Bassett), Molly Brown and Baby Doe. (Photo: Cyprus Amax Minerals Co.)

Coal Production (In tons)	
1919	254,162
1920	966,912
1930	837,801
1940	913,942
1950	832,928
1960	446,445
1970	1,990,535
1980	7,220,154
1990	4,414,772

In longwall production, a continuous miner creates underground entryways. Along the entryways, a shearer moves back and forth across the face of the coal bed, extracting up to 3,000 tons of coal an hour. (Photo: Cyprus Amax Minerals Co.)

From pick and shovel to high tech

*Influenced by technology, market demands, and social conditions, mining has undergone many changes. At the turn of the century, settlers used picks and shovels to dig "Routt County Gold" out of **one-man mines** on hillsides. They heated their homes with coal, and sold it to their neighbors, who hauled it in horse-drawn wagons. These mines were called **wagon mines** even after pickup trucks replaced wagons. No mines today are strictly wagon mines, although some operations accommodate local customers needing a truck load for home heating.*

In the early 1900s, with the arrival of the railroad, coal production by companies who hired workers from around the world increased. The miners and their families shopped at company stores and lived in mining camps — such as White City, Pinnacle, and Haybro near Oak Creek, and Mount Harris and Bear River west of Steamboat Springs.

When hand drills and blasting powder began to supplement picks and shovels, miners were able to dig bigger and deeper holes. Continuous miners, still in use today, are huge, electrically-powered rotors that break up the coal underground. The coal is then transported out of the tunnels on conveyors.

*After blasting powder was outlawed in Colorado in 1943, surface mining, or **strip mining**, proved more profitable than tunnel mining. Surface miners remove the overburden of soil and rocks with a dragline and haul coal out by trucks. The dragline, the size of two football fields, consists of an enormous bucket, plus housing for the cables and controls.*

*During the 1950s, and until the 1990s, surface mining was the favored method. As recently as 1983, area planners assessing coal reserves considered only surface production. However, in the 1990s **longwall technology** rejuvenated underground mining. Today both surface and underground mines are operating.*

Coal mining is a highly-regulated industry. Permitting plans, reclamation procedures, and safety standards are carefully and frequently monitored.

One-man mines heated homesteads throughout the county. Kasper Weberkirch, pictured here in 1918, ran this one at the junction of Coyote Creek and Fish Creek with a cart pulled by a mule or donkey. This is one of the small South Routt mines which caught fire and continues to burn. (Photo: Hayden Heritage Center)

From the Oak Creek Times, June 30, 1912

176

History Of Mining

ver since gold was discovered at Hahns Peak in 1866, miners have carved their niche in the valleys and hillsides of Northwest Colorado. Although the disappointing deposits at Hahns Peak dampened the fevered excitement of "gold in them thar hills," the area's "black gold" has boosted — and battered — prospectors, investors, communities, and politicians ever since.

Surviving economic roller coasters and technological changes, mining remains a key industry in the area. At the beginning of 1996, three surface mines and one underground mine were operating in Routt and Moffat counties, including Cyprus Twentymile, the largest active coal mine in the state. In 1995, approximately 800 miners produced almost 15 million tons of coal in these two counties, 59% of the state's total coal production.

The source of black gold is the Yampa Coalfield, which sprawls across Northwest Colorado and parts of Utah and Wyoming. Its formation began 65 million years ago when volcanos, earthquakes, and convulsions created the Rocky Mountains. Time, heat and pressure transformed swamps into beds and seams of low sulphur, low ash, and high BTU coal — which meet today's environmental standards.

The early years

In the 1880s, homesteaders and pioneers in Routt County tapped into the fertile coal beds, creating one-man mines as a source of heat for their homes. At one time as many as 70 family mines met the demands of developing communities.

Inside the Babson Mine, 1920s. (Photo: Jennie Dinwiddie collection at Hayden Heritage Center)

The "Moffat Road," which reached South Routt in 1908, created markets beyond the valley's settlements. Soon, four mines opened along the railroad tracks — the Yampa Valley, Routt County Fuel, Juniper, and Oak Hills. The latter, at the site of what is now Phippsburg, was a company town started by David Moffat. Once the site of the railroad's roundhouse, Phippsburg is still a railroad switching station for coal trains. Many of its older homes are remodeled mine shacks and box car houses.

In 1914 the Hayden brothers closed the Juniper and opened the Haybro Mine, which at that time was Routt County's only shaft mine. A small town grew up around this mine, but today only one building remains. Now a single-family home on County Road 131, it was the former post office, pay office, and doctor's office.

As the railroad extended, in 1913 and 1914, mines opened west of Steamboat Springs, in the Bear River Canyon and Mount Harris. In 1915, Victor American consolidated the Yampa Valley and Routt County Fuel mines. Victor American also owned the Wadge Mine at Mount Harris.

In the 1920s Elmer Margerum, Brazilia Hastings and George Gwynn opened separate wagon mines near Seven Points, west of Oak Creek. Margerum's mine was a one-man operation and never amounted to much. Hastings operated a hardscrabble family mine, using oak brush for mine ties. Joined by several Nebraska men, Gwynn built a road, gravity tram and mining camp, and was the first in Routt County to truck to the railroad for shipping. The Depression defeated all three operations.

The New Deal gave impetus to small, wagon mines. George Steele opened the Apex mine on upper Trout Creek in the early 1930s. He and his four sons, Ben, Ray, Carl, and Vick came to Routt County from coal mines in Oklahoma in the late 1920s. All worked at Haybro except Carl who, in 1928, got a job working a team of horses at Keystone. At this time, they were opening the mine and building the tipple to load coal onto the trains. In the early years, much of the coal was traded or bartered, and it was hard to get cash enough to buy blasting powder. When George Steele retired in 1942, Carl and Vick operated the Apex through the war until 1945.

Angelo Bosha bought Apex in 1945 and sold it to Gene and Leo Sullivan in 1963. In the meantime, Carl Steele had returned to Keystone, and worked there until it closed in 1958. He then leased Keystone and formed the Routt Mining Corp., with his sons, Duane and Gordon. They operated Keystone as a wagon mine until 1965. Keystone is a unique case of a mine starting as a tipple and ending as a wagon mine. In 1965 the Steele brothers purchased Apex from the Sullivans, and operated it until 1976. In that year, the Routt Mining Corp. and Apex were sold to Sunland Mining, which closed the mine in the mid-1980s.

Although it produced high quality coal, the Apex had only a four foot seam, and everyone working in it was bent over. During World War II, it exploded killing Joe Glass. (The state outlawed black powder in Colorado mines in 1943. It was at the Apex that Ethel Steele, Duane's mother, became the first woman in the state to hold a shotfirer's license.

COLORFUL COMMUNITIES

The story of mining is a story of communities. Growth in the fledgling industry resulted in close-knit groups of workers and their families. Workers from competing mines rubbed elbows at nearby bars and dance halls. Hauling rugged sleds behind four- and six-horse teams, they frequently broke trail through snow-covered winter roads, hauled fuel to town, and carried supplies to remote ranches. In the coal camps near Oak Creek and Mount Harris, they lived at the mercy of the mining companies, which owned their houses, stores, and souls, and paid in company "script."

Mount Harris, founded by the Colorado-Utah Coal Company in 1914, quickly became the largest community owned by a coal company. Two years later, the Victor American Fuel Company opened a second mine in the area on the James Wadge homestead. The third and smallest mine, the Pinnacle-Kemmer Company (P-K), imported 150 men from Wyoming to work its mine east of the Wadge. The P-K mine, which was never very successful, closed in 1940.

Mount Harris housed many miners who worked to pay mortgages on their ranches and farmlands. The company town was orginally called Harris, but the post office changed it to Mount Harris, so that it wouldn't be confused with another town named Harris.

The town became the hub for three mining camps and for local farmers and ranchers who sold beef, chicken and eggs door-to-door, and traded at the company store. By 1920, Mount Harris was the largest community in the county with 1,295 residents — 46 more than Steamboat Springs.

Bear River, established when the mine was opened in 1915 by John Connell and P.M. Peltier, was near the middle of the Bear River Canyon, east of Mount Harris. Between 1935 and 1940, Bear River boasted 150 families, a general store, post office, school, boarding house and hotel. Bear River closed in the early 1940s, and almost 40 years later, in 1979, the Sun Coal Co., a subsidiary of A.T. Massey Coal Co. out of Richmond, Virgina, opened a surface mine. Its office and tipple were at the old Bear River townsite. The mine supplied coal to Central Illinois Power in Peoria. It employed 43 workers at the height of its short life. Plummeting prices and conflict with its construction contractor caused Sun mine to close in 1981.

The tipple and crushing facilities are gone, but a few maintenance buildings and dwellings remain visible from Highway 40 — reminders of an earlier time.

Oak Creek, one of Colorado's most unique communities, is foremost a byproduct of coal. The beginnings of the town date to the 1890s, when the Schusters, serving as dummy entrymen for David Moffat, filed on coal outcroppings which later became the Moffat mine. The B. G. Schuster Ranch, at the head of Oak Creek Canyon, served as a company town for the Moffat mine. Then, in 1907 three businessmen from the Cripple Creek area — Sam Bell, John Sharpe and D.C. Williams — bought the Schuster ranch in order to lay out a townsite. In December 1907, the town was incorporated and the following year the railroad arrived.

The longwall at Twentymile Coal. (Photo: Cyprus Amax Minerals Co.)

Oak Creek grew rapidly with coal mining immigrants, railroaders, and seasonal workers who tilled nearby produce fields. When it made a bid for the county seat in 1912, Oak Creek was a self-contained boom town, with general stores, lumber yard, restaurants, saloons, pool halls, drugstore, churches, and hotels.

The town was a melting pot of workers from all over the world – Japanese, Turks, Italians, Indians, Poles, and Czechs. Some fled tyranny in their own countries, or came in search of "the good life." Their various backgrounds and lifestyles contrasted sharply to the Victorian morality of early homesteaders. Oak Creek's reputation as a "wide open town" became South Routt's legacy. A live-and-let-live attitude encouraged bootlegging, gambling and prostitution. "Mayor" Andy Black, who moved to Oak Creek from Steamboat Springs' "red light district," ran the town for 30 years.

In the 1960s "hippies" adopted the community, turning Bessie Dallas' Colorado Bar into their gathering place. Many of these so-called flower children stayed on and raised their children in South Routt. Today, a "hands-off" attitude still characterizes the southern part of the county.

The story of mines is also a story of conflict. During the early 1900s, mining was embroiled in serious labor upheavals and volatile politics.

By 1912 the Socialist Party ticket elected every candidate in Oak Creek, defeating the Taxpayers' Party and controlling Oak Creek during the 1912-1913 strike. When the Socialist Mayor refused to resign under pressure from mine owners, businessmen, and Sheriff Amos H. Chivington, they were denied the right to field a ticket in 1914. As a result, they simply reorganized as the Independent Party and, with Progressive Party support, swept the field. "Labor wars" intensified in 1913 and 1914, when Mount Harris miners joined the union efforts. Serious labor conflicts continued until New Deal reforms.

Three major explosions brought further turmoil to the mining towns: five died at the Moffat in 1921, 34 were killed at the Wadge Tunnel in Mount Harris in 1942; and one at the Apex in 1943.

After World War II (with the introduction of electricity and natural gas for home heating, and diesel power for trains), the traditional demand for coal came to an abrupt halt. Mining camps at Keystone, Haybro, Victor, Moffat, and Mount Harris turned into ghost towns. The economies of Oak Creek and Phippsburg nearly collapsed.

Edna Mine

Mining of the black gold didn't vanish entirely, however. Production methods switched from underground mining to more economical strip, or surface, mining. In 1945, Smith and Swenson (S & S) Coal Company opened the Edna mine, in the canyon just north of Oak Creek. Pittsburg & Midway purchased it in 1961, along with the Osage mine at McGregor which had opened four years after the Edna. P & M sold both properties to Gulf Oil Corporation in 1963. The Edna mine, which operated continuously for half a century, was the oldest, largest, and highest (8,200 ft. elev.) strip mine in Colorado when it closed at the end of 1995.

Cyprus Empire Mine

Also, in 1995 the Cyprus Empire mine, eight miles south of Craig on Highway 13, became idle. Re-start depends on many factors, such as market demand and coal prices. At its peak in the late 1980s, the Empire mine produced 2.2 million tons annually.

The mine was started in the early 70s by the Salingo brothers as a continuous operation and expanded into longwall production. In the mid-70s, the mine was sold to Ziegler Coal Co., who operated it for a year or two, before selling to Houston Oil and Natural Gas. In March 1980, Amoco purchased it and named it Empire Energy Corp. In June 1985, Amoco spun off its coal operations to Cyprus Minerals Co., and the corporate name changed from Empire Energy Corp. to Cyprus Empire Corp. In November 1994 Cyprus Minerals and Amax Coal Co. merged, but the mine is still known as Cyprus Empire.

Twentymile Mine

Twenty miles from where skiers hit the slopes 3,000 feet above the streets of Steamboat Springs, Twentymile coal miners hit the slopes 1,100 feet below the ground.

Located southwest of Steamboat Springs, the site has been producing since 1962, when Energy Fuels Corporation began surface mining operations — known as the Energy mine, or Foidal Creek mine. In 1983, Twentymile Coal Company began development of an underground mine.

The tipple at Twentymile Coal. (Photo: Cyprus Amax Minerals Co.)

The mine employs more than 330 people, and produces about six million tons annually. This is 77 percent of all coal mined in Routt County and a fifth of the coal produced in the state, making it the largest active coal mine in Colorado, and what is believed to be the longest longwall operation in the world.

A good nickname for Twentymile mine would be "record-breaker." In September 1994, its miners broke the world record for clean coal produced from a single longwall mining operation in a single month — 534,557 tons. Then they broke their own record in October 1994 — 548,575 tons. In December 1995, Twentymile re-established its world record with 689,759 clean coal tons.

In the spring of 1996, the mine doubled its length to 22,000 feet — more than three miles. Its entryways are 20 feet wide and 9 feet high, and the shearer moves back and forth across the face of the longwall at a rate of up to 84 feet per minute, extracting up to 3,000 tons of coal an hour.

Like most mines, Twentymile has a family tree with many branches. Harrison Eiteljorg started it in 1962, and it operated as Energy Coal Co. for several years. Bob Adams of Energy Fuels Corp., purchased it in the early 70s, and sold to Getty Oil in 1981. After a year or so, Getty sold it, and in 1985 Cyprus Amax Minerals Co. took ownership, and started underground coal production. Cyprus, headquartered in Englewood, Colorado, owns 24 underground and surface coal mines in the U.S. and Australia.

The end of the tunnel is not in sight at Twentymile. The remaining known reserves at the mine will provide 89.6 million people their energy needs for one year. Or, put another way, every person currently living in Steamboat Springs would have 15,000 years of electrical energy from Twentymile's coal reserves.

Seneca Mine

Uncovering the Wadge and Wolf Creek coal seams, the Seneca mines have produced coal continuously since 1964. The surface mines supply the Hayden electrical generation station. Started by Seneca Coals Ltd., the operation is now owned by the Peabody Coal Co.

The Seneca story is one of expansion and change. In 1968, the dragline was moved five miles, across the Yampa River to the Seneca II mine, southeast of Hayden off Twentymile Road. Then in 1975, Seneca added another dragline to produce coal for Hayden Station Unit 2. In 1990, they moved one of the draglines to Seneca II-W and began production there near Hayden Gulch Road (County Road 53).

Now under construction is the Yoast mine, scheduled to open later in 1996. The Yoast is named after Leonard Yoast, a rancher who formerly owned the property.

Seneca operates 24 hours a day, employing about 100 people, and producing approximately 1.5 million tons of coal annually. It has reserves of 15 million tons.

The mine boasts 529 days without a lost-time injury, and a previous record of a million accident-free hours. It has won several national awards for safety, and state awards for its reclamation and environmental efforts. Reclamation specialists return the land to the approximate original contours, redistribute 12 inches of topsoil and use native species for revegetation. Each year Seneca crews seed more than 50 acres of mined land to provide habitat for mule deer, elk, grouse, marmots, bluebirds, eagles, and numerous other wildlife. Also, livestock graze selected areas in managed pastures.

Trapper Mine

Trapper mine is a surface coal mine located six miles southwest of Craig. With an annual production of 2 million tons, it is the third largest producing coal mine in the state. The mine employs 150 people.

The name "Trapper" reflects local history — fur trapping was an important livelihood in the area in earlier times. The mine's logo depicts a fur trapper, and its pits are named for oldtime firearms — Ashmore, Browning, Colt, Derringer, Engield, Flintlock, Gatlin, and Hawken.

Opened in 1977, Trapper's original owner, Utah International, contracted with Colorado Ute, the owner and builder of the Craig Generating Station, to supply coal through the year 2014. In 1983, the mine was sold to the new owners of the Craig Station. They are: Tri State Generation, Thornton, Colorado; Salt River Power District, Phoenix; Platte River Power, Ft. Collins; and PacificCorp., Salt Lake City.

In 1994, Trapper received the *Sentinels of Safety* award, given annually by the Mine Safety and Health Administration to the safest coal mine in the United States. They have also received the Department of Interior's prestigious *Excellence in Surface Coal Mining Reclamation Award*. In 1995, the Colorado Association of Commerce named Trapper the *Colorado Company of the Year* in the Energy and Natural Resources Division.

Colowyo Mine

The Colowyo mine was opened in 1977. At its surface mine on Highway 13 between Craig and Meeker, the mine employs about 300 workers, who produce just under 6 million tons of coal annually. The coal is shipped to points in Utah, Texas, Colorado, Kansas, and Illinois. Colowyo Coal Company L.P. is an affiliate of Kennecott Energy, headquartered in Gillette, Wyoming. Known for its high safety standards, Colowyo boasts that its employees worked more than one million hours in 1995 without a lost-time accident.

The Quarter Horse in Routt County

Horses played an important part in the development and homesteading of Routt County at the turn of the century. This small area amassed more foundation Quarter Horse breeders than any other area of the country and became known as the "cradle of the Quarter Horse breed."

The qualities of the horse, particularly its ability to follow the zigzag path of a cow, made it an ideal animal for ranch life. The Quarter Horse is fast and named for its ability to race at great speed for a short distance. Its showcase is the quarter mile. Speed, combined with balance and agility make it the perfect horse for roping and working cattle.

Si Dawson and Coke Roberds, were responsible for putting Routt County on the map. They owned and bred such stallion greats as Old Fred, Peter McCue, Buddy Nile, Champagne and Ute Chief. Western Horseman described Si as "a free spirit; life was an adventure to him. He kept a herd of buffalo on his Hayden ranch and crossed them with cattle to get what he called Cattalo."

Coke moved to Colorado in 1908 from Oklahoma for health reasons. He immediately partnered up with his old high school friend, Si Dawson. In Oklahoma he had nine Steel Dust mares acquired from a Texas horseman. He bred them to his prize stallion, a pinto Palomino named Primero. When he moved to Colorado it was also necessary to move his horses, not an easy task in those days. His only choice was to send them by rail. On the way to Colorado, the train crashed near Wolcott badly injuring Primero, and the stallion had to be destroyed.

Old Fred
By Robert S. Temple

Coke Roberds
(Photo: American Quarter Horse Association)

He was right of the lead team,
Settin' the pace on hill or stream.
He was workin' on the Wolcott stage,
He would be written on history's page.
A Palomino he was, head held high,
Slight dish of face, bright of eye.
One of the Greats it has been said,
Father of Quarter Horses, he was Old Fred.

A master breeder of horses saw him there,
A little thin and coarse of hair,
Underfed and never groomed,
But for the master's eye, he would a' been doomed.
His quality shown like a star at night,
With him, the future of Quarter Horses was bright.
With Steel Dust mares by him bred,
Came great colts, sired by Old Fred.

He had lots of spirit and never tired,
Working hard as by the Angels inspired.
This trait of his always bred true,
All of his offspring had that fire too.
He was one of the foundation sires,
That would great horse breeders inspire.
His spirit lives on, although he's dead,
Father of Quarter Horses, he was Old Fred.

(From History of Hayden & West Routt County 1976-1989, Hayden Heritage Center, 1990)

By all accounts, the two friends liked nothing better than horses. Horse talk. Horse trading. And, of course, horseback riding. Si's daughter, Delphine, once wrote "If a PhD in Horsemanship and Love of Fine Horses as well as Memory of Breeding were given, Papa would have won Magna Cum Laude."

At the time, people were breeding driving and riding horses and horses for the cavalry. Si and Coke wanted to improve their looks, temperament and abilities, so they bred for the qualities that emerged as the American Quarter Horse: heavy muscles, sturdy, with a good head and straight legs.

Si and Coke, who were always looking at horses, soon became interested in a foal from a stallion called Peter McCue. Dawson went to Cheyenne, Oklahoma where, upon finding Peter McCue for sale, he bought him for $5,000. The horse was shipped to Colorado by train and, as the story goes, was greeted by four feet of snow on the ground. In order to reach the ranch, Roberds is credited with jury-rigging a stall on top of a wagon by replacing the wagon wheels with sled runners and hitching his best team to the contraption.

Peter McQue
(Photo: American
Quarter Horse
Association)

Peter McCue, foaled in 1895, was a magnificent animal. The famous American Quarter Horse foundation stallion stood sixteen hands and weighed 1,430 pounds. And he was fast. He was once clocked at running a quarter mile in 21 seconds, a major record for the time.

Coke needed to replace Primero with another stallion. On a trip to Wolcott with his wife Beulah he found Old Fred pulling a freight wagon. Coke bargained with the owner and bought the stallion for $300.

Coke had a lively sense of humor. He told anyone who would listen that his horses never bucked. One day, according to an account in Western Horseman, Coke and Jack Blasingame were herding horses down to water at the river. When they got into deep water, Blasingame swung his boots and spurs up to stay dry and, in the process, nicked the gelding causing the horse to go wild. He bucked so high and so hard that the saddle blanket came out from under the saddle and Blasingame had to hang on to the horn for dear life. When the horse settled down, Blasingame said to Coke, "This here horse damn near bucked." "Yes, Jack, he came close," Roberds replied.

The name of that horse was Mose. He was good looking although tenderfooted and Coke eventually let Jack, who married Alice Peavy, have him. Although Roberds never intended to become a horse breeder, he was successful at it. According to Western Horseman, he sold $100,000 worth of horses between 1920-1952.

Many modern breeders can trace their finest Quarter Horses back to Routt County and to the joint breeding efforts of these two best friends with "an eye for horses." Coke and Si are both included in the American Quarter Horse Association Hall of Fame in Amarillo, Texas. Both are honored at the Hayden Heritage Center as founders of the American Quarter Horse breed.

Marshall Peavy

Marshall Peavy was born in 1898 and ranched near Clark for more than 30 years. He started out as a cattleman and, although he continued to raise cattle, he and his wife Mavis quickly acquired a reputation as breeders of "VZ" Quarter Horses. Marshall was unique among breeders in that he was concerned with all aspects of breeding. Not only did he select the sires and the dams but he raised the colts, took the time to break and train them, and then rode them in races and horse shows.

According to Bill Gay, Marshall was "the most colorful of the early breeders." He was fiercely competitive and rode his own horses in the arena whether racing, cutting or roping. And he liked to laugh. There is a story about the day Marshall got stopped for speeding. He appeared at the courthouse and was fined $5.00. On the way out he gave the clerk a ten dollar bill. Thinking he'd made a mistake, the clerk tried to give him back $5.00. Marshall looked at him and said, "I'll be going the same speed out of town, so just keep it."

Marshall got his start in 1916. He bought his first stallion, Bob H, from Coke Roberds when it was a four-year-old. From Coke, he also acquired some Primero mares. Two years later he bought Mary McCue and Queenie at Si Dawson's dispersion sale.

Mary McCue became a top brood mare, producing Ding Bob, perhaps Marshall's favorite stallion. Queenie produced the mare which bred to Sheik produced Monte, the gelding Marshall was riding when he died. Monte was a fine horse and excelled in everything he did from cutting to roping. At the first American Quarter Horse show in Tucson in 1941, Monte won ribbons in every working class he entered.

In 1928, Marshall bought a three-year old stallion from Coke Roberds named Blue Eye. Evelyn Peavy Semotan named him Sheik and, because he was so gentle, rode him bareback to pick up the mail. Sheik replaced Bob H as Marshall's principal stallion. Sheik was a result of Peter McCue and Coke's buggy mare, Old Pet. Marshall kept Sheik for five years and then sold him to a man in Texas where he started a new branch of the Quarter Horse family.

His next stallion was Ding Bob. Ding Bob produced Denver's first Palomino show champion stallion, Saladin. Saladin was out of Evelyn's mare, Fleet, and she enjoyed the fact that Marshall "drooled" every time he saw him. Saladin produced Gold Heels, the first American Quarter Horse Association Grand Champion stallion of the National Stock Show in 1944. Evelyn, Marshall's widowed sister-in-law, finally gave Saladin to Marshall who later gave Ding Bob to Evelyn. Saladin was also responsible for Irish Molly, Mary K and Melody, mares that raced well and then produced well for Quentin and Evelyn Semotan.

Marshall and Quentin Semotan helped found the Rocky Mountain Quarter Horse Association. Around 1938, Marshall was hired by the American Quarter Horse Association to inspect local Quarter Horses for confirmation, quality and bloodlines and to get them registered. It is interesting to note that of over three million Quarter Horses registered today, the Semotan, Peavy and Gay's all had Quarter Horses registered in the first 6,000. Clearly they laid the foundation for establishing the breed.

Marshall's last stallion was Gold Heels. At Denver's first Quarter Horse Show, Gold Heels took the Grand Championship and won the Rocky Mountain Quarter Horse Association's first derby in 1943. Gold Heels was known as the sire of Quarter Horses and Palominos. Marshall's daughter, Mary Stees, carried on the line after her father's death.

In 1944, at the age of 45, Marshall died tragically when Monte stepped in a prairie dog hole and stumbled; Marshall, who rode a short stirrup, was attempting to catch a calf and was thrown.

Evelyn and Quentin Evelyn Semotan

Quentin Semotan's father Joseph was a horseman and homesteader. He established a homestead on Day Creek in 1886. Quentin, born in 1910, inherited his father's love of horses and his gift for handling them. He added to his natural abilities by breaking horses for Marshall Peavy.

In 1936 he met his match in Evelyn Peavy, who had been married to Marshall Peavy's brother Laurance, a fine horsewoman who also shared his passion for breeding horses. The attraction was instant and they soon married. Evelyn had a deep respect for Quentin's abilities. In an article in Western Horseman, she was quoted as saying, "Quentin's ability with horses is well known in Routt County. He always had a good saddle horse and he broke horses with a gentle hand. He really can ride, he is a sight on a horse."

Evelyn bred Ding Bob to Fleet, producing ten colts which formed the basis of the Semotan herd. Quentin purchased Star Duster as a colt in 1945. He had taken his cattle to the stock show and sold them. While Evelyn was off somewhere else, he took the money and bought what became his champion stallion. Evelyn returned and found him standing by the stall, as happy as could be. Although she probably had other plans for the money, it proved to be a good decision.

Using Star Duster on his Ding Bob and Roberds-bred mares, Quentin developed a strain well known to horse breeders across the country. Star Duster was a great champion, earning top place in 46 out of 47 showings. He was one of only two horses to beat Poco Bueno, and he won the Champion of Champions in 1946 at Fort Worth against 16 grand champions, including Poco Bueno. From him Semotan produced Barbara Star, out of a Ding Bob mare, who was Honor Roll Halter Horse of the Year in 1956.

Evelyn Peavy Semotan had a way with people as well as horses. She was especially close to Roberds and was the only person he allowed to bring a mare to his stallion Buddy Nile. Mary Nile was the result, out of Evelyn's mare, Fleet.

Quentin firmly believed in the future of the Quarter Horse and to that end he spent a lot of time and money traveling to fledgling AQHA meetings to judge and assist other breeders.

He had a way of finding a "nick," making a good match between a dam and a sire. Both Semotans excelled at finding that "nick" and had the high selling entry in the National Quarter Horse Sale on several occasions in the 1950s.

Word of their magnificent Quarter Horses spread throughout the country and fellow horse lovers traveled a far way to see their legendary animals. The ranch, located on Elk River, became a destination for both tourists and breeders. According to an article written by her granddaughter in *The Steamboat Pilot,* "Evelyn greeted each guest with fresh baked goods and a personal tour of the horses."

Evelyn was also an accomplished horse historian. She painstakingly collected some of the early pedigrees of the Coke Roberds horses and shared them with the AQHA. Without her, the AQHA wouldn't have known the origins of many of the foundation horses because Roberds never wrote anything down and failed to see the need for a registry. When Quentin dispersed in 1965, he sold his last two mares: the daughter of Mary Nile to Bill Gay, and the daughter of Laura's Panzorita to Vern Waggoner.

Bob and Bill Gay

Bob Gay was another early breeder of Quarter Horses. He started breeding them for ranch work and colt roping. Lassie Gay, a beautiful liver chestnut, won second place at the first Quarter Horse show in Hayden. Bob bred Lassie Gay to Upset L, a Star Duster colt owned by Leonard Lighthizer. The result was Cracker Gay, who Bob's son, Bill used for roping and showed at halter in Hayden. The horse was Reserve Champion Halter Gelding several years in a row. Bill Gay continues to breed the Roberds-Semotan line of horses on the Gay Ranch in Pleasant Valley.

The Stetsons, Dan Casement and Leonard Lighthizer

Frank and Lucienne Stetson's specialty was breeding horses for use on working ranches. Poco Bimbo, a dark blood bay was one of their most beautiful and well known horses, who topped the National Western Stock Show Sale in 1958. He was a son of Poco Bueno, sired by King P-2-3-4, the industry's most famous father-son team.

Dan Casement set standards for style, type and design of horses. Casement ranched on the Elk River in the 40s, bred a horse named Red Dog and became president of the American Quarter Horse Association. He was an advocate of "Bull Dog" type horses—exemplified by Red Dog, King P-2-3-4 and Poco Bueno—as opposed to Quarter Horse breeders who leaned toward a more Thoroughbred-type horse.

Leonard Lighthizer was known as "the guy with the eye for great breeding horses." Bob Gay's Lassie Gay was bred to Spanish Cash, owned by Leonard Lighthizer, and produced an excellent halter horse, Spanish Cashier. He also bought Upset L, out of Star Duster who, with Spanish Cash, contributed significantly to the continuation of quality Quarter Horses in Routt County.

Guide To Major References

S

T

V

W

Y